When
Mothers
Work

When Mothers Work

LOVING OUR CHILDREN WITHOUT SACRIFICING OUR SELVES

JOAN K. PETERS

PERSEUS BOOKS
Reading, Massachusetts

Library of Congress Catalog Card Number: 98-86287

ISBN 0-7382-0028-x

Perseus Books is a member of the Perseus Books Group

Text design by Helene Wald Berinsky
Set in 11-point Bauer Bodoni by Pagesetters, Inc., Brattleboro, Vermont

1 2 3 4 5 6 7 8 9-DOH-0201009998
First printing, August 1997
First paperback printing, July 1998

Find us on the World Wide Web at
http://www.aw.com/gb/

For Peter,
Who rose to the challenge

And Lily,
Whose love amplifies our own

CONTENTS

ACKNOWLEDGMENTS

Most books are a collective effort to some extent. This one, because it explores living family life in a new way, is more collective than most. At one point, I envisioned a book jacket covered with the photos of all the people whose words, wisdom, and experience broadened my vision and gave life to theory. First among them, perhaps in the upper right hand corner, would be my agent, Susan Ginsburg, a consummate professional and a mother of four who also found time to nurture this book from its wobbly beginnings to its maturity. I am ever more grateful for her emotional and intellectual intelligence.

For upholding the dying art of editing, eternal gratitude to my marvelous editor Liz Maguire. Not only did she turn this book's structure rightside up, but she brought out its very best with her keen attention to textual detail and an unwavering sense of the important points. And to marketing director Elizabeth Carduff, whose support and deep-felt response to this book has turned business into pure pleasure. I have a special place, too, for my publicist, Sandi Mendelson, whose reputation, ideas, and enthusiasm launched me into this post-production stage with lovely new wings. And to Tiffany Cobb, the book production coordinator, whose startling efficiency saved the book and its lightning production schedule from many a mishap.

The other photos on this fantasy book cover are of the people who allowed me to draw portraits of their lives. Not only did they all help me to articulate the most difficult parenting issues of our time, but they taught me better ways to overcome them. Their generosity with time, thoughtful discussion, and personal narratives still move me. For their eloquence and self-scrutiny, heartfelt thanks to Gioconda Belli, Neil Brown and Amsale Aberra, Angela and Matt Soper, Jennifer Prost and Michael Laser, Lochlin and Sandy Reidy, Kathy Meetz, James Richardson, Kierra Foster-Ba, Eugenia Wiltshire, and to those who asked for anonymity. Others, like Dave and Debbie Casson, Susan Geffin, and Mark and Tracy Waite, who spoke with me on particular aspects of parenting, made important contributions and indelible impressions on me.

My own reflections were immeasurably deepened by the insights of the experts I quote throughout this book. My greatest thanks to Charles and Diane Gottlieb—friends of a lifetime; innovative, empathic, and grounded thinkers. Not only did they spend two days doing little else besides answering my incessant questions, but they also responded to the many new questions that arose as I wrestled the manuscript into its final form.

I am also grateful to Pamela Sicher, another dear friend and model of a working-mother. Lucky for me, her work is psychiatry. Her profound analyses of the fears and longings underlying parenthood have been invaluable to my thinking, and to my life.

A thousand thank you's as well to a welcome new acquaintance, Jessica Benjamin, author of that brilliant analysis of gender: *The Bonds Of Love*. Not only did she bring her rigorous thinking to bear on the subject of contemporary parenting, but she rightly emphasized the limits of psychology in the face of overwhelming social pressures.

Three other psychologists gave me their thoughts on particular subjects, which in every case helped to form my own. My gratitude to Linda Carter, Mary Joan Gerson, and Kyle Pruett.

Several friends distinguished themselves for help beyond the call of affection. I am particularly touched by Honor Moore's smart reading of my proposal and her offer to "be there" just in case I needed support. And by Candace Falk, who not only read the first draft from her sickbed but, as always, steered me towards seeing the issues with greater compassion. Randy and Michael Clancy not only talked through every stage of the book, but helped me celebrate the completion of each one. Robert Hamburger, Myra Goldberg, Penny Stallings, and Amy Berkower all helped me move beyond some stumbling block or change something that needed changing. As always, Beth Rashbaum listened to me rant and responded with the good sense I have come to count on.

I also want to mention The Writers Room, which provided a clean, well-lighted, and blissfully tranquil place to work at a fee even writers can afford. I cannot actually imagine how I would have written for hours each day had it not been for this superb institution.

My final thank you to my family, foremost to my companion in life, Peter Passell, who edited this book twice and allowed me to portray him honestly as both part of the problem and part of the solution. To my daughter, who has inspired the transcendent maternal love I have tried to describe and who brightens every day with her joie de vivre. To my parents for their loving concern. And, finally, to Guadalupe Ramirez, the babysitter who made this work possible and who has shared in the pleasure of raising our daughter.

Book after recent book has examined the current work-family dilemma, but none proposes a solution. In writing *When Mothers Work*, I may have discovered why. Proponents of what are inevitably radical solutions must be unfashionably prescriptive.

While current political correctness dictates that feminists support stay-at-home motherhood as a valid choice for women, I argue that mothers *should* work outside the home. If they do not, they cannot preserve their identities or raise children to have both independent and family lives. But I also argue that women can do so successfully only if men take half the responsibility for child care—accepting the same financial and professional sacrifices women have always made.

And there's more: if women are to cultivate their independent identities along with their mothering, they must relinquish some maternal control to partners, grandparents, godparents, and caregivers. I also propose that they consider having fewer children, later in life.

Women cannot have it both ways: be equal citizens with political parity, have 50 percent enrollment in professional schools and access to the best-paid jobs, while expecting to take five to ten years off to raise their children. In short, equality means that women can no longer use motherhood as an excuse to drop out of public life and men simply cannot have it all.

This may seem like strong medicine. I hope, though, that I can convince readers—particularly new mothers and others contemplating parenthood—how much richer this approach to parenting is for themselves and their children. To make the case, I have drawn on the latest research, quoted various feminist psychologists, and consulted with four prominent therapists, all of whom have shared equally in the raising of their children.

Diane Gottlieb, a psychologist and a marriage and family therapist, is an adjunct professor of psychology at the University of Vermont. In 1974 she and her husband, Charles Gottlieb, along with associates, founded Networks, a private mental health agency. Charles Gottlieb, who has a master's degree in social work, practices marriage and family therapy. He also teaches in the Department of Social Work at the University of Vermont.

Pamela Sicher, a child and adolescent psychiatrist, is also an associate professor of psychiatry at Cornell University Medical School and an attending psychiatrist and trustee at Rye Hospital in Rye, New York. She is the director of the Center for Families in Washington, Connecticut.

Jessica Benjamin, a psychoanalyst and an associate professor of clinical psychology at New York University, has written in depth on the subject of gender in her books *The Bonds of Love: Psychoanalysis, Feminism, and the Problem of Domination* and *Like Subjects, Love Objects: Essays on Recognition and Sexual Difference.*

To illustrate how parents today manage both intimate family lives and meaningful work, I tell the stories of twelve families. Although they may sometimes appear "too perfect" to be true, I assure you they are real people. Most of them allowed me to use their names. Those who requested anonymity are starred, but almost nothing else about them is changed except a few identifying details. What I finally realized about their apparent perfection is simply that balanced, flexible, loving human beings usually make great parents.

My twelve families are also quite diverse. I cast my net wide enough to find parents who vary from house cleaner to fashion designer to electrician to corporate manager. They are urban, suburban, and rural, agnostic and devout, black and white, married, unmarried, and divorced, foreign-born and descended from the Founding Fathers. So while I cannot offer them as statistically representative, I believe my sample families do reflect middle-class America—precisely those parents who are caught between the ideals of motherhood and today's economic and social realities.

As much as I would have liked to include all social classes in this discussion, the very adversity of poverty creates a different set of mothering pressures, just as the privilege of wealth alleviates them. This is true particularly in regard to the financial burden of childcare, a subject I treat throughout this book.

In the Afterword, describing where these families were one year after our first interviews, you will see how much families must continually change and adapt to sustain their successful dual identities.

When
Mothers
Work

CHAPTER 1

The Millennial Dilemma:
Our Children or Our Lives?

We, along with other Western societies, are unique in the exclusiveness of the mother's role as infant caretaker and in our emphasis on her importance in the development of a child's attachments.

MARGARET MEAD, 1954

Soaring with joy at the birth of her first child, many a mother also finds herself with an unsettling premonition: this cherished infant, his skin so new the very air would seem too rough to touch him, his gaze more trusting than any she has known before, might someday glare at her and say, Look what you did to me. You: Mother. She may also know that however much he blames her, she will blame herself more.

Mercifully, this scene is set in some distant hazy future. But in a startlingly short time every mother realizes that should something go wrong, should the baby's father want to flee the relentless crying of a colicky child, should the snowsuit be insufficiently insulated or the stairwell gate be left ajar, all will hold her responsible.

Yet there she is, as new to mothering as her child is to the world, as eager, as innocent, filled with the same awe her infant's eyes express, more delicate in her handling than a museum curator with a Ming dynasty vase. The child molds to her body, his breath on her neck. Nothing has ever felt so warm. The snuggling infant, the smiling baby, the toddler

1

rushing into her arms, the child who can say, "I love you, Mama." That your children love you back is nearly as miraculous as their birth. That you witness so intimately the unfolding of a human being—a stage play moving from a single emotional tone to the complexity of a Shakespearean drama by the time they reach five. By ten they are the history of civilization, by twenty a cosmos.

Why should the worm of anxiety intrude so early on such pure pleasure? Why does the new mother hear whispers of self-recrimination? Why does she feel that nothing less than sacrificial devotion can ever silence them—and maybe not then? Because guilt has become a part of American motherhood, which demands a mother's total self.

Hardly a universal feature of maternity, guilt is not so much in the nature of motherhood as in the nature of traditional American motherhood. Mothers, as the primary and often exclusive guardians of their children's welfare, are held responsible for it—at times to the point of persecution.

When the cause of a child's problem is unknown, mothers are suspect. For two decades doctors believed childhood autism was the fault of the mother's coldness instead of the child's flawed neurology. Though we are supposedly wiser now, a recent newspaper article quoted a neurologist who told the mother of a boy with what was later diagnosed as a rare genetic disease that he was suffering because "she was having a hard time adjusting to motherhood."

Such social opprobrium has grown in these times of transition from woman as housewife to woman as equal partner in marriage, and with it has grown maternal guilt. Instead of reducing her maternal responsibility, a woman's new economic obligations have increased it. We now presume that the common cause of all children's woes is their mother's work, which prevents full-time nurturing. Meanwhile, we ignore the more complicated root cause: our failure to modernize motherhood, to restructure family and change society along with the changing character of women's lives.

Now considered the equal of a man, and her labor an economic necessity, a woman prepares for the demands of the job market. However, she still tries to mother the way her own housewife-mother did, as if her sole task were raising her children. For the transgression of having her own life—or simply wishing to have it—a mother is more culpable now than ever, both in society's eyes and in her own.

Mothering itself is not the problem, nor is work. No woman should have to choose between an independent life and a baby. In fact, this may be the best of times to become a mother since women have the training, inclination, and opportunity to cultivate their independence and define motherhood for themselves. That is, to redefine motherhood so that they can love their children without sacrificing self. But doing so requires that women share the management of family life and the responsibility for raising children, and that, in turn, men coparent and society rebuild an educational system in decline.

Most important, however, is that mothering differently must begin with women. For if women do not change, they cannot make the necessary familial changes or press for the requisite extrafamilial supports. Therefore, we must start with a better understanding of the psychological difficulties women face in trying to adapt to the social changes they themselves have generated.

Good mothering does not require mothers to focus so intensely on their children that they give up crucial parts of their own identities. Indeed, such sacrifice is not even in their children's interest. For if women who are reared to participate economically, socially, and politically stop doing so, they risk their sense of self, their contentment, and, therefore, their effectiveness as mothers.

The evidence shows that depression is much more common among full-time mothers than employed mothers. This is true even for working-class women whose jobs may be less varied and rewarding than those of "professional" women, whether or not they work a second shift at home.

And what about their children? A recent British report comparing 100,000 children of employed mothers with the general population demonstrated that children with mothers in offices and factories have higher reading scores than children with mothers at home. A fourteen-university American study found that children in high-quality day care from one month old on have better language and cognitive ability than children at home. Alison Clarke-Stewart's work on day care argued that if children have good day care, they have greater confidence and social skills than children of mothers-at-home. These and other similar studies suggest that mother-at-home is not the most beneficial arrangement for children, and for other reasons as well.

Children flourish with multiple attachments. Far from depriving them of full-time mothers, maternal employment creates an opportunity for children to form other close connections—not only with their fathers but with a network of caring adults who can both diffuse and reinforce maternal love, relieving it of the isolation, self-abnegation, and involution that too frequently have given it unhappy and sometimes tragic dimensions.

And what about women who *want* to stay home with their children? Many do, but often for the wrong reasons. Women are still deeply ambivalent about independence and success in the "harsh" world of business. Although they may have initially desired and even succeeded in that world, they sometimes prefer to retreat into the kinder, gentler (and safer) world of motherhood when the option arises. In fact, knowing deep down that they would do so may have made their independence more of a game than a real commitment and thus rendered it less frightening. Sometimes I hear such women say that working just didn't work anymore, or that they didn't really like their jobs anyway. But instead of finding more fulfilling work or sticking it out until they garnered more power, as men usually do, they opted out in the name of motherhood.

Many other women choose full-time motherhood because they understandably do not know what else to do. In their experience they may have only one very unattractive alternative: careers that leave no time for family.

THE FALSE DICHOTOMY: DEVOTED MOTHER OR COLD CAREERIST

Our culture offers mothers two choices. It constructs four walls around mother and child even as women gasp for space, trying to mother and also pursue careers, maintain friendships, work out at the gym, and maybe have time to read a book. Stay or go, the culture declares. If you want to be a mother, watch the bricks and mortar set around you. Otherwise, peer at your child through the window. Send gifts. Celebrate holidays together. But otherwise, leave.

The message is this: either women embrace motherhood in the traditional way, focusing primarily on their children, or they must turn their backs on mothering, relegating child care to others and carrying on as if reproduction were just a brief detour on the road of life. Even the traditionally inclined mother obliged to work to keep bread on the table may find so little support from her employer, from schools and children's services, and from her husband that she too feels shut out of her family's life.

The majority of mothers do not want either extreme. But with only two models to choose from, the devoted mother or the cold careerist, most women struggle in isolation to push back the walls and live an airier, less confining mothering life. Many, however, find the struggle worthwhile. Recently, *Working Mother* magazine surveyed one thousand working mothers about how happy they felt. Nine out of ten considered themselves "very happy" and found work to be an essential ingredient—"a challenge and an outlet," as one respondent wrote. On the other hand, most conventional media report that these jugglers are exhausted and self-destructive, ruining their marriages and abandoning their children to day care, and so conflicted that they can barely live with themselves.

The parenting gurus, while sympathetic with working mothers, essentially corroborate the media's view. In a searing critique of the bestselling baby care books, the *New York Times* reporter Susan Chira notes that "to read them is to be immersed in a world in which a mother's needs do not count." While the widely respected tomes of Benjamin Spock, Penelope Leach, and T. Berry Brazelton help women cope with what is always perceived as *their* work-family dilemma, "nowhere," Chira writes, "is there mention of the compensations even hard-pressed working class mothers have said they enjoy: self-sufficiency, social contacts, and the work itself." And nowhere, I would add, is the idea broached that a mother's self-development is an asset to the development of her children.

The result is that women contemplating motherhood or women who have just had their first child often cannot imagine a kind of mothering that doesn't require an unappealing choice. In *The Mother Puzzle*, a 1993 addition to the public discussion of motherhood, Judith Schwartz, the childless author, observes that her girlfriends scaled down their professional lives or dropped out entirely when they had children. Motherhood today, she concludes, seems "unreal, even surreal, given the way our adult lives had begun."

This outsider merely glimpses the surreal quality of mothers' lives; many mothers *live* it, unable to incorporate the person who was a lawyer, a sales clerk, a physical therapist, or a teacher into this new one who mothers within brick walls.

Naturally, since Schwartz considers only these two kinds of motherhood, one good and the other bad, she concludes that the pieces of a woman's life just don't fit together. On the one hand, women now fantasize being Jackie Joyner, Toni Morrison, Murphy Brown, or Ruth Bader Ginsberg; on the other hand, they are supposed to stay home with each child for at least eighteen months (Penelope Leach) or two and a half years (Burton White) or until kindergarten (still the conservative view). If you have two children, that can add up to somewhere between five and ten years out of your professional life.

While Schwartz probably hasn't read the baby-care books or surveyed grandmotherly advice, she has absorbed the maternal imperative they all convey. Liberal and pro-woman as even the new baby-care books appear, the subtext always reads, "Good mothers are home whenever their children are."

Far too many women are defeated by this supposedly basic rule of motherhood, including the most educated and ambitious. For example, when Shirley M. Tilghman, director of one of Princeton University's medical laboratories, assured a group of female graduate students that they could be scientists and mothers, they simply did not believe her. They claimed that science is so competitive now that they dared not leave the lab before 10:00 P.M. Yet, like Tilghman, they could avoid the fourteen-hour-a-day "macho" labs and select controllable experiments. Like Tilghman, they could share parenting and find reliable household help. At the very least, they could organize to fight the oppressive way in which science gets done. Instead, they will forgo either career or motherhood.

Many girls who were reared by 1960s feminists adopt the stay-at-home model because, according to a *Wall Street Journal* reporter, they claim to have seen in their own mothers' lives "exhaustion, frustration, working-parent guilt, and divorce." They too assume the family-work conflict is inherent in motherhood rather than a result of trying both to work and to honor the goals of *traditional* motherhood. They too assume they have only two choices—life-denying careerism or devoted motherhood.

And it's not just the daughters of 1960s feminists who suffer this myopia. Says one perplexed thirty-five-year-old New York City professional, "Eighty percent of the women I graduated high school with are raising children in the suburbs while their husbands commute to their Wall Street jobs. We all had dreams of doing something. Maybe there's nothing wrong with being a homemaker, but none of them thought that was their goal in life." Indeed, it probably was not. Although maturity often means accepting the gap between dreams and the reality of adulthood, why should so many women find that gap "surreally" large?

Even the youngest women contemplating their futures are undone by this grim choice. Among Hispanic high school girls, one survey reported that 83 percent said they did not want to be homemakers while, at the same time, more than half the girls expected they would be! Perhaps it should not surprise us that many adolescent girls see the advantages of being boys when almost no boys covet female status. Despite the equality often achieved in law, education and workplaces, our constricting kind of motherhood requires women to give up their dreams of an independent life when they have children while men can still have it both ways.

Significantly, in certain cultural enclaves women remain largely unaffected by the work-family conflict. One study demonstrated that Mexican-born women, many of whom believe it is their maternal duty to support their families financially, are largely unconflicted. On the other hand, their American-born daughters, who have absorbed the stay-at-home ideal, do feel guilty when they must work outside the home.

Another example, as the sociologist Patricia Hill Collins points out, is African American mothers, who, as a group, do not suffer as much maternal guilt. Collins observes that "women of color have performed motherwork that challenges the social constructions of work and family as separate spheres." Her term "motherwork" in itself expresses how differently successful motherhood is defined by different groups. In addition, instead of recoiling from their mother's choices, black women generally describe their admiration for their mother's fortitude and earning power.

In a recent television documentary called "Hillary's Class," film-makers interviewed many of the women who graduated from Wellesley College with Hillary Rodham Clinton. Aside from Clinton, the only one who hadn't let her dreams dissolve into family obligations was a black woman working at the Pentagon. She not only worked full-time and under pressure—sometimes halfway across the world—but had an intact marriage and a grown son who was successfully pursuing a career.

What about mothering? she was asked. "No matter where I was, I'd call my son at four o'clock every afternoon, and we'd talk over his day. He knew when I returned he'd have my full attention." She was the only woman interviewed in the film who spoke without guilt, depression, or regret.

Of course, Wellesley College graduates are exceptional women, the skeptic will say. They are understandably reluctant to give up their exciting careers. But it's different for women who are "just" wage earners. People who think in this way say to young mothers, "It's only a job. You'll get another when the children are older. You'll be giving your whole salary to the baby-sitter anyway."

Yet these mothers may also value the earning power, camaraderie, and satisfactions of work; they may even prefer relatively low-stress jobs to high-pressure professional positions. But without public validation, they often cannot justify to themselves keeping jobs they don't adore. They may not have read the latest studies showing that when people have multiple sources of self-esteem and varied activities, they feel better. So they are persuaded to give up a significant source of identity for mother-hood rather than adding motherhood to work.

Certainly some people do not derive any aspect of their identities from work, just as some derive no self-definition from parenthood. But they are exceptions. The majority need both, and as a result, women put themselves emotionally at risk when they trade in a work identity for motherhood. As much of a relief as quitting work may initially be, after six months women generally feel bereft, particularly since their husbands have not had to trade work for parenthood. Furthermore, although society pressures women into full-time motherhood, it does not value their "motherwork."

In her early mothering years a full-time mother may find herself off-balance or depressed by the loss of her former "working" self even if she cannot put words to her emotional state. Later she may suffer a feeling of unlived potential, particularly if she consciously enjoyed the bustle of the workplace and the satisfaction of paid labor well done.

For *Secret Paths*, her book on women in middle age, the social psychologist Terri Apter interviewed eighty women on this subject and found that

> virtually all the traditional women I interviewed harbored ambitions and achievement identities—a sense of themselves as potential achievers, which ticked, in counter time, to the real time in which they passed their days.
> "Not a day goes by," Mai said, ". . . when I don't think about what I might have achieved and how that would have felt. I look the part of the perfect wife and mother, and it's a part I play with all my heart. But I chose it because I did not see, for me, a way of doing more, which doesn't mean I didn't want to or don't want to."

Remember that the emotional vulnerability of the full-time mother affects her family as well. These same women who mother with all their hearts understandably grow resentful of husbands who reap the benefit of family life without giving up their dreams. Not only do children feel that tension, but they bear the burden of their mother's grief for her undeveloped self. As psychoanalyst Jessica Benjamin has written, "A mother who stifles her own longings, ambitions, and frustrations cannot tune in empathically to her child's joys and failures."

Ironically, then, to no one's advantage, the dissatisfied full-time mother may be less emotionally available than the employed mother. Linda Carter, director of the New York University Center for Family Therapy, believes that "if a mother who wants to or needs to work is frustrated in that, she is a less available mother. If she does work, the child will learn to be more self-reliant and also understand that the mother will return."

Maternal guilt is not the only impediment to employment. After all, a mother's employment, which depletes the reserve of parental attention, requires that the father replenish it. Some mothers simply cannot see an alternative to full-time maternity because the alternative requires the father to change his work patterns, priorities, and psychological orientation. Few women dare to insist on this. A pediatrician I interviewed cut back to a forty-hour week after her second child was born. She did this by exchanging a private practice for a hospital directorship with limited, set hours and other doctors to cover for her. She also cut her income in half. Yet her physician husband continued at eighty hours a week, hardly spending any time with their children. Although, she told me in a halting whisper, she had "made her peace with" this arrangement, it was difficult to believe her.

Most women make more than the necessary changes when they have children; most men make none. And when this happens, the family structure moves into a subtle disequilibrium, leaving the women to do it all and the men to pick and choose.

DANCING DOGS, FLYING PIGS, WORKING MOTHERS

The phrase "working mother" need not be an oxymoron. After all, every time we swear a woman into public office, grant her a college degree, or promote her to plant manager, we are stating emphatically that we no longer believe anatomy is destiny. Since the women's liberation movement of the sixties and seventies, women's status has definitively changed. Although class action suits may be necessary in order for women to gain their equal rights under the law, no one disputes that they should have them.

As long as no children are involved, equality between men and women generally prevails, in theory if not yet always in fact. This is largely true privately as well as publicly: most childless couples share in the financial and domestic maintenance of their homes. But when these same men and women become parents, instead of modernizing motherhood and fatherhood to preserve their equality, they unthinkingly submit to the traditional roles their mothers and fathers have struggled to expand these last thirty years.

This contradiction is at the center of the mother puzzle. Solving it requires taking a far deeper look at what stops us dead as soon as a child is born. We must finally get to the bottom of the psychological drama that

silently plays itself out alongside our conscious desire for equality between the sexes. We must better understand the emotional persuaders,
social inhibitors, and ensuing internal maelstrom that come into play
when we have children.

The enormous amount we have learned about male and female psychology simply has not been enough. Since modernizing motherhood is
harder than all the other changes women have initiated in recent decades,
we must finally turn our full attention to the locus of conflict—the hearts
of women and men. And why is modernizing motherhood so hard?
Because mothering is so much closer to home.

Only by understanding what holds us back will we be able to remake
parenthood according to our conscious beliefs. Only by changing the
heart can we live according to principles that enhance the parenting and
personal growth of both partners. Of course, such profound change is
never easy, but it is certainly well within most people's reach.

As we will see in the portraits of contemporary families, partners in
parenting must plan this new kind of parenthood well in advance if
possible, so that they can both find work that leaves time for family life
and buy the time to adjust to parenthood together. To avoid the isolation
of the nuclear family, they need to create parenting networks of relatives,
friends, and/or hired caregivers who can provide baby love when they, the
parents, cannot. They must also cultivate the psychological flexibility to
respond to ever-changing work, family, and individual needs.

Practical as these changes may appear, all of them are predicated on
the greatest emotional challenge of our times: modernizing our antiquated concept of motherhood. This is where we begin.

CHAPTER 2

The Donna Reed Makeover

Whereas the feminists of the sixties and seventies rejected the Donna Reed model of womanhood, many of their daughters, rejecting in turn the feminist model, have become "power moms" or "super-moms." Power moms may have been sales reps or run companies before their children were born; now, cell-phones in hand, they run their homes. Super-moms can spend the day trading bonds or processing words, but they still preside over their homes, making birthday cakes and Halloween costumes even if it takes staying up all night. Believing themselves to be the equals of men, and their motherwork to be more important than any job, these new moms hardly identify with that icon of domesticity who never troubled her pretty little head with bottom lines. They resemble her nonetheless.

Donna Reed, we should remember, was a power mom in her own right. Her motherhood was all-important; indeed, it was all of life. With her starched apron and her sunny equanimity, she not only embodied America's postwar hope but washed away the horrifying memory of the Depression, the war, and the Holocaust. Reduced to the borders of her circumscribed life, the world seemed a tame and welcoming place. Thus, in its collective imagination, America fled from the harsh world of men into the satiny arms of its good women. Father may have known best, but Americans loved Lucy, married Joan, and remembered Mama.

Although we today have hardly suffered the traumas of the first half of the century, we have had serious societal distress resulting from the war in

Vietnam, the civil rights and youth movements, and steady economic decline. Women, who for the first time had thrust themselves into the midst of the harsh world, now seem to be considering a retreat to home. Raising high the banner of motherhood, many are once again trying to make children the center and goal of their lives. Never mind that *The Feminine Mystique* put the lie to the myth of the happy housewife; a surprising number of young women today have convinced themselves to try it again. But with a twist.

Since Donna Reed's lack of worldliness hardly appeals to women raised "to be free to be you and me," they have remade her housewifery in their own image. Employed or not, today's women who choose traditional motherhood bring to it all the science, management, and goal orientation usually applied to work. Thus, they have preserved Donna Reed motherhood by appending worldly functions to it. To be fair, society's broader neglect of children has made raising them more time-consuming. In this respect, professionalizing motherhood is also a necessary adaptation to the increasing complexity of our lives. However, both these private and social responses seem suspiciously driven by our guilty impulse to placate the gods of patriarchy, who have become increasingly upset with women these days. As a result, rather than adapting motherhood to women's new lives, Americans have turned motherhood into a job.

OVERPARENTING: A PECULIARLY AMERICAN INVENTION

For the white middle class, the edifice of motherhood has ironically grown more massive as more mothers work outside the home. While the time available for mothering has shrunk by at least eight hours a day (plus commuting time), the job description has expanded to include ever more exacting functions. Mothers are now expected to be creative playmates, child development experts, and education specialists. Many I know practically run their children's schools. Some volunteer to teach French and computer science, do lunchroom duty, or raise funds for services and supplies no longer provided by hard-pressed school boards. And with many towns grown too dangerous for children to travel by bicycle, mothers must drive them to music lessons, hockey practice, and the Saturday matinee.

This intensive kind of motherhood is a recent, and uniquely American, creation. In the fifties—despite television's sentimentalization of motherhood—mothers were expected to take care of children and rear them, a task that usually involved keen attention to food, clothing, shelter, manners, and morals. Though some mothers headed Scout troops, played catch, and enjoyed an occasional game of Monopoly, motherhood did not necessarily include one-on-one play. Nor did PTA membership entail raising money for half the school budget. While parents may have exacted high grades, clean living, and religious observance from children, those standards were laid down without a great deal of hand-wringing about the proper way to raise a child.

In his memoir of growing up African American in the fifties, Nathan McCall sums up what for many people (including me) characterized family life, and therefore motherhood:

> My folks were typical of their generation of parents. They didn't focus much on us unless we were sick or had done something wrong. They didn't hold conversations with us. Love was understood rather than expressed, and values were transmitted by example, not word of mouth.

Of course, it is wonderful that we give so much more thought to raising children, but there may be a point of diminishing returns—for parents and children both. Today middle-class parents read books on toddler development, attend parent workshops, and learn how to talk so children will listen. They often treat applications to preschool with the reverence once reserved for applying to Harvard. It's a rare mother who now unthinkingly tells children to "go out and play." Even in safe communities, most parents are more comfortable setting up a project for the child or having an outing together.

At one time parents heard a bit about their children's social life at the dinner table. Now we have closely monitored play groups, play dates, and quality time. Parents used to feel sufficiently dutiful signing a child's report card and coming in for the annual parent-teacher conference. Now mothers are involved in every aspect of their child's daily homework from on-line research to laser-perfect execution. In my daughter's public school, mothers learn the new math in order to help their children, and they take positions on the way writing is taught. When I was growing up, children's grades disappointed or pleased parents. Today parents grade themselves according to their children's performance.

Super-parenting has become so much the norm in America that most Americans do not find it aberrant. However, foreigners observing American parenting mores often find it bewilderingly excessive. The first of several mothers we will get to know in this book offers such a revealing view from abroad. As a widely published writer and a mother of four, she is a particularly astute observer; having graduated from an American college, lived in several American cities, and married an American, her view is an intimate one.

GIOCONDA BELLI

Gioconda Belli, a Nicaraguan novelist and poet who held several important public positions in her country, became the mother of her fourth child, Adriana, after moving to Los Angeles with her second husband, an American, in 1990. With daughters in graduate school and college and a son in high school, she was quickly initiated into American parenting.

What surprised her initially were her son Camilo's high school friends, who seemed angry and alienated from their parents. Camilo, by contrast, is very close to his parents and stepparents, typically participating in their social activities and often taking care of his baby sister and any other younger children in their home. His older sister Maryam took a job in Los Angeles to be near her family after receiving her degree in architecture. Melissa, the second daughter, visits during nearly every vacation from medical school.

Gioconda wondered why such closeness should be less typical for American children. Why do they routinely move away from home after college and often reject or rebel against their parents? Why do they distrust their parents?

When we meet to discuss these questions one morning, the beguiling Gioconda, famous for her passionate love poems, is dressed in what I've come to think of as her elegant gypsy style: a long flared skirt, colorful vest, bangles, and earrings that bob beneath a river of auburn ringlets. Sitting in the walled garden of her Spanish-style home, her toddler dashing over for periodic hugs, she tells me that her experience with her two-year-old has given her some insight into the teenage alienation that shocked her at first.

"Even at Gymboree," she says, "I notice how parents are so worried about the most minute details in the child's life—whether they had enough free versus structured time, for example. Or whether their child is participating with the group. The director of a prospective preschool reflected that same preoccupation when she assured us that they didn't have any Disney books, only 'good' books at their school.

"Here, parents discuss these things as if they were going to have a profound effect on their children, with a concern that seems disproportionate considering that children grow up exposed to all kinds of influences. Whether they have Disney books or not, the children come to school with their Simba lunch boxes and their Mickey Mouse sweatshirts. Yet the parents still worry so."

Listening to her thickly accented English, I am reminded that when I first met her a decade before in Nicaragua, Gioconda had brought the then-ten-year-old Camilo with her to the garden of my hotel for our interview about her country's dire political situation. And there he sat or roamed—without toys, crayons, entertainment, or our attention—for a full two hours. Being an American, I finally found some paper and pencils "to keep him busy." In her Los Angeles home, I comment that although I wasn't a parent myself at that time, I had been surprised, and somewhat anxious, that she had left Camilo to his own devices.

"Exactly," she continues. "To me, American parents seem to regard their children as so vulnerable that they must constantly protect them. Most Latins I know rather trust in a child's basic humanity. We don't want to shield them. If something isn't perfect, or time isn't arranged for them, the child will know that life isn't perfect. If they don't learn this, then they cannot engage themselves without our help. American children are rarely left to their own devices when they are small." She gathered herself up and leaned forward, very nearly leaping, as it were, to the heart of the matter.

"The concept of 'being there' for a child is, in my opinion, taken to an extreme in this country. It forces the parent to respond to the child in a very premeditated way that's not natural or spontaneous. So many parents here seem to feel as if they must react to *everything* the child does, as if being distracted or involved in something else while they are with him will harm the child. They are very anxious around their children, and one can almost feel, in their response to the child, the effort they have to make to pretend that they are delighted by any little thing.

"I personally think children can see through this and often get frustrated because, even though they know they don't have the parent's attention, there is the pretense that they do so they feel somehow cheated. It probably ends up also being exhausting and taking a lot of pleasure out of the relationship for the parent.

"I think it creates a more honest behavior pattern in the parent-child relationship and builds trust when a child knows that he or she cannot have the parents' attention all the time, that the parents also have to think of other things and do other things, or simply that sometimes they are just not in the mood. Forced involvement has to end up creating hostility, both for the parent that has to pretend and for the child that feels drawn into this game of pretense.

"Adrianita," she calls out to her daughter, who is now leaning down to pick up a muddy stick, "no, that's dirty." Adriana considers the injunction, then scurries off for the hose instead, using the water slowly dripping from its spout to clean her stick. The garden has neither a swing set nor a playhouse. "I think it's very hard for American parents," Gioconda continues, returning her gaze to me. "They have so many tasks. Child-rearing is like another profession: knowing the right mobile to buy for the infant's crib, the right music to play, which experts to read. The spontaneity of parenting is turned into a dreadful obligation. Such a preoccupation with children doesn't seem to me to be good for the children either. It takes away from children's *self*-importance, from their ability to take responsibility for their own happiness."

When the baby-sitter arrives, an aging Nicaraguan woman who begins at once to coo at Adriana, squatting to meet her eye to eye, we leave the garden for Gioconda's home office, a tiny "tower" room just big enough for her desk and two chairs. The manuscript of the German translation of her latest novel sits on her desk festooned with yellow Post-Its. I have read all three of her novels. All the protagonists are women; none, I realize, are mothers. Well, one does eventually have a child, but the novel centers on her premothering years.

When the new novel is published, Gioconda tells me, she'll have to go on a publicity tour for three weeks. It's longer than she wants to be away from Adriana, but she must go. Such a long time, I comment. But she reassures me that Adriana has her father, her siblings, her baby-sitter. "She will cope," she says. "That's part of what I'm talking about. American parents seem to think that children learn to cope later in life rather than in early childhood. They don't give their small children responsibility. Then when the children reach adolescence, parents expect them to suddenly become responsible. These children go from being the sun in a family to being a planet orbiting around it, and they are full of resentment."

Middle-class Latin family life is quite different from the American way, she explains. "I never thought that children were the center of my life, but that they participated in my life. I felt they had to learn to be the center of their own lives. I wanted them to understand that, although we were together in life, each of us was separate and responsible for our own lives. The same way I understood they had to separate from me, they had to understand I had to separate from them. I wanted them to know that in order to nourish them spiritually I had to have spiritual nourishment."

How does that different focus play itself out in daily parenting? I wonder out loud. "Take the subject of school," she offers. "I participated in my children's schools, offering a poetry workshop or something, so I would know their friends and teachers, but I didn't supervise their work. Although I helped if they asked, I never did homework with my children. I see American parents obsessing about homework and taking over a teenager's college application process, as if where the child goes is a reflection of the child's worth. I fear that for American parents it is.

"In the States children are made to feel that their worth is going to be measured by the kind of college they get accepted to. This turns the college application process into judgment day, a judgment day that somehow will also reflect upon the parents, which makes the whole issue an agony for the teenager. It is as if the teenager bears the burden of proving to the world that her parents have done a good job of raising her. But the parents' intrusion and worry is such an emotional weight for the child that she withdraws just to protect herself. Teenagers here almost have to reject their parents in order to find themselves because the parents don't trust them to do it.

"Instead of controlling my children, I tried to create an intimacy with them. I've tried to parent while staying true to myself. We always had long talks about their feelings and mine. Even with Adriana, who is two, I talk about anger, sadness, and love in as grown-up a way as I can. I tell her if I don't want to play because I'm tired, sad, or feeling bad. I tell Camilo and my daughters about problems I have with work or with my husband so they know what life is. They are concerned about my life, and they don't hesitate to come to me with their problems. Even their American friends talk over their problems with my husband and me. They know we will help without overwhelming their own ideas or experience."

What is so striking about Gioconda's motherhood is how relaxed she is about parenting while still being very present with her children, how confident in sharing motherwork with her husband, her older children, and her baby-sitter, how she doesn't grade herself on her children's accomplishments. What is so striking about our American parenting style, after speaking with her, is our anxiety and constant supervision of children.

Gioconda, of course, is only one observer, but psychologists corroborate her view that American parents tend to be overinvolved. Among her highest-achieving clients, Linda Carter has observed the kind of overparenting that Gioconda describes and analyzes it similarly: "These parents read every new book and judge themselves by those criteria. The pressure is tremendous. They live with a constant sense of evaluation, from whether the child is eating the right foods to whether he or she can get into the right schools. This is where parenting turns into an evaluative rather than an unconditional, relaxed love in which a child's natural development can be enjoyed—with no agenda." Of course, as she explains, this overparenting impulse comes out of love, but "a child must just 'be' and evolve in its own way. The driven quality compromises the relationship, the love."

Given that such intensive parenting threatens rather than nourishes the parent-child relationship, it is all the more unfortunate that our country today—with its often-threadbare schools and extravagant expectations of mothers—has contributed to driving women to overparenting. And make no mistake, the job of parenting still belongs to mothers.

MOTHERWORK: MOTHERS STILL DO THE WORK

A lot of fathers now also prepare ten or more lunches a week and serve in the PTA. Some fully participate in the overparenting. In a *New Yorker* essay entitled "Making The Grade: Going to private school is increasingly hard work—for the parents," James Atlas writes: "Boy, am I busy! What with serving as a sommelier at the Fathers Who Cook dinner, attending 'the first Class VII Parents in Action Meeting,' lacing up my kids Chargers on Great Skate Night at Wollman Rink, attending a performance of 'Iolanthe,' and hawking raffle tickets for the school fund drive door to door in our building, who has time for work?" But James Atlas is an exceptional father.

Compared to mothers, the number of fathers who overparent is small. In any case, a father's participation in child-rearing usually involves even more work for the mother, who must stage-manage the parenting experience for him. It is generally the mother who determines that her child might like to play soccer, finds the soccer team, mails in the entrance fee, schedules the games, then suggests that the father might like to take Jesse or Jessica to the game on Saturday morning. It is the mother who so often explains father and children to one another, briefing the father on the importance of a piano recital or an essay contest. Mothers still soothe their children with whispered references to father's fatigue or frustrations at the office if he's brushed aside the child's advances.

While many fathers are involved, mothers alone are becoming super-parents. Married women do at least twice as much child-raising as men. By one recent count, they also do 87 percent of the shopping, 78 percent of the cleaning, and 63 percent of the bill-paying. Men's increased parenting has not caught up with the greater demands of motherwork, leaving mothers to organize children's activities, preside over them, stay in intimate contact with the children, and also to wash the finger paint off the kitchen floor. Mothers still bathe the children, buy their school clothes, plan their meals, and take them to the orthodontist.

Although 70 percent of American mothers are now employed outside the home and everyone pays lip service to the idea that mothers cannot do it all, most people still unquestioningly accept the two basic Donna Reed assumptions about modern motherhood: (1) that children are a mother's primary responsibility, and (2) that children need their mothers first and foremost. Untenable and historically anomalous as they are, these beliefs seem as incontestable to us as the divine right of kings did to sixteenth-century Parisians.

According to a recent Harris poll, nine out of ten women *who contributed nearly half of their family's income* "said it was their responsibility to take care of the family." Some might guess that the poll reached a more traditional population. However, even the two savvy Harvard lawyers who wrote *Everything a Working Mother Needs to Know*, an up-to-the-minute primer on problems like pregnancy rights and maternity leave, explain their premise that "for everyone's peace of mind, one parent has to be ultimately responsible for the children, and that parent usually ends up being the mother." They never explain why this should be true, or why this arrangement is better than having two responsible overseers, two emergency numbers, and two adults who know a child's teachers and friends.

Most men consider their parenting voluntary, not compulsory; they do it at their whim. Listen, for example, to the words of the *Wall Street Journal* columnist Hal Lancaster writing about overwork burnout:

> To shake off my case of the blahs, I went through the following process: I eliminated extraneous issues—the kids, household chores—that were contributing to my feeling overwhelmed (don't do it for too long or you'll face an even bigger problem: spousal wrath).

What mother do you know who would ever think, much less publicly write, that caring for her children was an "extraneous issue"! And note: Lancaster's reason for resuming his domestic work was not because it was his responsibility, but because of "spousal wrath." Men do not believe that they *must* care for their children. They do as much as they want, or as little as will keep their wives friendly. But because women dare not ask too much from them, women have taken both essential motherwork and overparenting on themselves.

The irony is that this new intensive motherhood may be no better for children than the old minimal motherhood. We may, in fact, have created the kind of motherhood that threatens mothers and children alike and still leaves fathers out of the loop. For the most part, however, intensive motherhood is precisely how all the conservative and even most liberal sectors of our society tell us to parent.

THE GOSPEL ACCORDING TO LEACH: MOTHER FIRST

Penelope Leach, the psychologist whose best-selling child-care books embody this conventional wisdom, is in part so popular with women because she is herself a professional whose thoroughly modern, brass-tacks practical approach to child-rearing makes motherhood seem anything but old-fashioned. She tells it like it is, or seems to. But she also absolutely—and with unflappable authority—asserts what she believes to be the necessity of traditional, primary motherhood: that mothers should be "ever-present, always-responsive" to their babies. And she argues that female biology dictates such behavior.

In her latest book, *Children First*, Leach writes that giving birth "makes it impossible for women to seek self-fulfillment that is separate from fulfillment of [the baby's] perceived needs and wishes." Furthermore, only women can take proper care of a child because "there is no way a working-father can be as aware of a baby's needs, moods, and feelings as a mother who is sharing their ebb and flow." Averse to considering that perhaps a father of a newborn should discontinue working full-time for a while, or that a mother may wish to continue working, she then argues that society ought to support financially a mother's right to stay home.

Leach's assumption that mothers must be "ever-present, always-responsive" may well be more an automatic acceptance of the social norm than a considered conclusion. Indeed, her insistence on the issue seems to be more a product of her unfortunate personal experience than of scientific evidence. An article on Leach in the *New York Times Magazine* reveals that her career was just taking off when her two-year-old son almost died of meningitis. She explained to the author that she naturally put her work aside to care for him, but that didn't seem sufficient. When he was better, she left him with a nanny and returned to work "knowing perfectly well the only person he was O.K. with was me." Several months later, unable to bear the guilt, she quit work entirely.

The author of the article points out that Leach's father considered children "an expensive bore" and paid his daughter little attention. Leach, we learn, was frightened of her father and close to her mother.

Given that mothering seems to be all she had herself, it is not surprising that Leach puts so much emphasis on it. With her family history, it is no wonder that Leach never seemed to consider the care that the child's father, a beloved aunt, or a friend could have given her son. Nor does it take a belief in repetition compulsion to suspect that in selecting a nanny, Leach clearly did not choose someone her child could love. She might have wanted to be the only person her child could trust, just as her own mother was for her.

Though Leach's own experience is quite unusual, her conclusions seem normal because they reflect the biases of so many of the people who were reared with uninvolved fathers. The assumption that men are not truly parents in the "mother" sense, combined with the dirth of different models for family relationships, encourages people to think Leach must be right. We mistakenly believe that to save today's imperiled children mothers must reaffirm their primary and exclusive parenting. In this narrow framework, work and family *do* conflict, and therefore women must choose one.

UNNECESSARILY DIVIDED LIVES

Although we may not realize the extent to which we have automatically accepted Leach's assumptions, most women act according to them. That is why women who refuse to choose often find themselves torn in two. Again and again, authors exploring the surreal misery of trying to mother and have a life conclude that it doesn't really work. Elsa Walsh's 1995 book *Divided Lives: The Public and Private Struggles of Three Accomplished Women* offers portraits of a breast surgeon, an orchestra conductor, and a television journalist. *Vogue* magazine called its excerpt of the book "The Hell of Having It All."

Consider Meredith Vieira, who left her job as a correspondent for *60 Minutes* to be with her children. Although her husband, Richard, was happy to do the main parenting, "she wanted to be the emotional nucleus of the family, the primary nurturer." Later she took a job for an ABC magazine show that entailed little travel and allowed her to work at home. Even so, because she believed a good mother should be "always available," she felt guilty.

Walsh, like the childless author of *The Mother Puzzle*, was herself at that "crossroads" when her husband, who presumably didn't face the same cruel choice between work and parenthood, suggested she think about the professionally successful mothers she knew who were most content. But Walsh couldn't think of any. "Too many seemed overwhelmed with frustration and stress, mired in guilt and worry." Hence, her investigative book.

Walsh is not entirely unquestioning. For example, she notes her surprise at women's willingness to shoulder the bulk of domestic responsibilities while complaining about doing so. She also recognizes that "the ideal of the conventional family with a woman at the center of the home" was driving these women crazy. But she still seems to feel that the only two choices are this primary motherhood, despite the suffering it causes, and what she describes as the cold careerism of a Lesley Stahl. Ponder her description: "Tough and relentless, Stahl was one of the iron maidens of television. She had a daughter and a husband, but that was not her primary identity." The iron maiden, you may recall, was a medieval instrument of torture, a coffinlike box in the shape of a woman with spikes inside.

The fact that motherhood wasn't Stahl's primary identity is precisely what condemns her, in the author's mind. No evidence is offered for insufficient mothering. And never mind that at close range Stahl seems quite intimately involved with her daughter. Talking with her at a gathering, I watched as she spun round toward her husband when someone asked after her daughter, registered typical maternal consternation that they hadn't spoken to her as usual the night before, and began to discuss one of her college papers with him—her interlocutors be damned. This was not the picture of an uncaring mother. But if she has not been "ever-present, always-responsive," by the prevailing logic she has failed at motherhood. If, like Gioconda, she has perceived her fulfillment separate from her child's, she is not a good American mother.

Indeed, having it all must be hell if she who has it is frightened of failing at both mothering and work, haunted by self-recriminations, and dogged by the disapproval of her own mother, her peers, and her culture. Yet the dilemma presupposes that mother as the emotional center is the best arrangement for children and for the family. From my research and experience, I have concluded that it most definitely is not. In fact, it may be among the least sensible child-rearing arrangements civilization has come up with thus far. I am not alone in this opinion.

More than two decades ago the sociologist Jessie Bernard wrote in *The Future of Motherhood:*

> The way we institutionalize motherhood in our society— assigning sole responsibility for child care to the mother . . . is not only new and unique, but is not even a good way for either women . . . or children. It may, in fact, be the worst. It is as though we had selected the worst features of all the ways motherhood is structured around the world and combined them to produce our current design.

It is easy to see what she means. Instead of maintaining extended families and close-knit communities for raising children, as they do in Asia, for example, we isolate mothers. Instead of demystifying breast-feeding in public, a practice that would allow women to continue working while caring for an infant, the way they do in Africa, we have relegated infant care, including breast-feeding, to the privacy of the home.

On the cusp of restructuring family life, we cling ever more ardently to this antiquated and ill-conceived provider-homemaker design. In spite of the economic and social incentives to change the way we mother, we feel ever more acute guilt for abandoning the old way. Just now, when we need it the most, we withhold or withdraw that portion of the social infrastructure that protects children, consigning them even more to their mother's care.

It may be obvious that change this profound is difficult for the individual, but it is just as difficult on the collective level. America now recognizes women's equality. Although women's lives have consequently been transformed, nothing has helped them to mother in a way that is fundamentally different from how their own mothers did it. In spite of our dreadful fear of modernizing motherhood, many women are quietly going ahead with their own experiments in motherwork—though, as most of the portraits here illustrate, the sacred ideal of motherhood is so strong that experimentation requires courage. That is certainly what it has taken for my husband and me. Even as I write about this new kind of mothering and try to implement it in my daily life, I am as humbled by motherhood as I am determined to break its imprisoning old rules.

Every one of the mothers and fathers I interviewed has helped me in some unique way to refine, explain, and justify a new kind of mothering. In spite of—or because of—the fact that both partners in the first couple I interviewed were, like Gioconda, raised beyond the reach of the oppressive American ideal, their parenting teaches a great deal about putting a healthier perspective on mothering, one that eschews guilt and creates well-rounded, independent children.

NEIL BROWN AND AMSALE ABERRA

Neil and Amsale have inadvertently created a model for the guilt-less blend of work and family life that sociologists observe in the black community, although Amsale, an Ethiopian who emigrated at the age of nineteen, is not exactly a typical member. Neither she nor Neil feels conflicted about pursuing their careers while raising their nine-year-old daughter, Rachel. In fact, as graciously as they discussed their work and family lives with me, they were inclined to wonder what the fuss was about—despite their own high-powered jobs. Neil is vice president for film programming at HBO, and Amsale, a well-known fashion designer, is about to open her own shop on New York City's chic Madison Avenue. Spending time with them, I too began to wonder what the fuss was about.

To be fair, I visited with them on a Sunday morning at their weekend home in Bridgehampton, New York, a place and time dedicated to family tranquillity—and fun, to judge from the jeep parked outside and the pool at the patio's edge. Inside, the sunlight softened by gauze curtains is so golden in the all-white interior it might have been artfully painted into the atmosphere. We sit on plump couches covered in white muslin, a bleached wooden coffee table between us. The only touch of color comes from the sunflower-yellow accents in the Moroccan rug and the pots of pink impatiens set about the cozy room. In the background Louis Armstrong sings "What a Wonderful World." Even their dog, a bichon frise named Georgie who lies between them, belly up, head dangling over the edge of the couch, has been lulled into deep relaxation.

Once or twice during the two and a half hours of our talk Rachel, in her red sweatpants, floats by on her way to the patio outside or tries (successfully) to make her father giggle. Despite Neil's description of weekdays spent "chasing their tails," you could not convince me that their lives were not essentially serene.

Everyone in the Aberra-Brown family is soft-spoken. Rachel, a bit shy, lights up when her parents show me her freehand drawing of Tweety and Sylvester, Daffy, and gun-slinging Fievel, each with his inimitable expression. "She can work on something for hours," Amsale explains. "She was always like that. At two, she would struggle to tie her shoes even though she didn't have the coordination in her hands. I felt terrible to watch her be so hard on herself, but it's how she is."

Amsale says all this with a calmness that would seem impervious to the rush and tumble of American life. Her looks are distinctly Ethiopian: a narrow, sculpted face, sharp black eyes, cocoa skin, and a burgundy tint to her lips. Ethiopian, too, is her style, from her dignity to her warmth to her elegant carriage. But by now, in her early forties, she is a cultural hybrid. In a tank top, denim overalls, a ponytail, and a sporty thick-soled version of what we used to call mary janes, I could picture her as an American teenager—or as one of the models for her gowns, though she is more delicate and less physically bold than the famous Somalian model Imam. Her Horatio Alger story, however, is no less remarkable.

Raised in Addis Ababa, with her mother at home and her father working as a vice-minister for economic development, she followed her half-sister's recommendation to go to Green Mountain College in Vermont. But the political turmoil that landed her father in prison prevented her from returning home. Instead, she moved to Boston, where she worked as a waitress and put herself through school. There she met Neil Brown.

Neil was not your typical Harvard Law School student. After his father died when he was three, his mother worked as a secretary and attended night school, eventually becoming a loan officer at a bank. She sent her son to a private day school outside of the black section of Montclair, New Jersey, where they lived. This was a risky move in the racially incendiary sixties of Neil's youth, but a felicitous one. Although he endured the social discomforts of being one of only five blacks at the school and the only one in his grade, he ended up with friends and largely positive memories.

With fine brown hair, dark eyes, and gold-hued coloring, Neil is as attractive as his wife. He is charmingly generous with his smile, un-guarded, and so pleasantly unaffected, I imagine him wearing the very same flip-flops, khaki shorts, and white polo wherever he might be.

"You tell it," he suggests to Amsale when I ask how they met, explain-ing in an aside that their versions differ. Hers went like this. Their formal introduction was at a party in 1976 when they were both in their twen-ties, but she recognized him immediately as a regular at the coffee shop where she worked. He had no clue who she was because, "at work, we had to wear these turbans on our heads!" I gather from the elliptical descrip-tion that follows that he began to patronize the coffee shop a lot more frequently.

Amsale, who was studying political science at the time (with an eye to activism in her country), soon realized that her talents lay in designing and making clothes, which she had always done for herself and friends. So after Neil moved to New York City for his first job, she joined him and attended the Fashion Institute of Technology. More or less at the time Neil began his career at HBO, Amsale began hers at Harvé Benard Ltd., fashions for women. With pluck and a determination about her work that too few American women possess, she went straight to the company's owner when her division shut down to ask his advice about her career. In lieu of advice, he offered her a junior designer's job in his leading division. Though attractive, the offer didn't feel exactly right. What she decided on instead took even keener judgment and determination.

It was when she and Neil decided to marry that Amsale discovered a hole in the fashion market. The bridal gowns were far too ornate for her taste. After discussing with Neil the idea of creating custom wedding gowns, they decided together to make a small investment for a model and advertising. "I was financially secure enough that she could take a risk," Neil says.

"You could support my hobby," she replies, throwing him an acerbic glance.

Amsale, who comes from a country where wedding gowns aren't even white, knew her market. The very first day her ad ran, she got a call for a hairpiece to be worn at a trendy wedding. Then more calls, including some from the editors of bridal magazines themselves. Then she got pregnant.

When I ask them how they both planned to continue working or if they

had discussed whether Neil would share parenting, they both look puzzled. "We never really discussed how we would have a family and work,"
Amsale says. "I just knew Neil would be as concerned about raising a
child as I. We've been partners in other things, like my business. We
would be partners in this. For myself, I knew I needed to work. I never
even entertained the possibility of staying home."

Neil says, "My presumption is that women work. My own mother did.
I got home from school without anyone waiting, and I was fine. I just
didn't see a problem. Maybe it's because I didn't have any negative male
model, but I just assumed that I would raise my child too. I will say that
my mother made sure I exhibited none of the usual *negative* male traits. I
remember once, for instance, I might have been eight, we were watching a
movie about some Casanova and I said, 'Wow, what a great idea, living off
women!' I was only joking, but my mother considered it so reprehensible
that her son would have even considered that an option, that she chewed
me out as if I'd contemplated murder or pillage. I had to be independent,
that was that. Like a lot of upwardly mobile blacks, I also assumed I'd be
successful in all ways. I always knew I wanted a successful family and a
compatible spouse."

He clearly has both. As culturally different as Neil and Amsale are,
they have much in common. Both were children of middle-class, educated households. Both absorbed the profiles of achievement and made
their way up the professional ladder of white America. Listening to Neil
describe his mother remaking her life after his father died, I can't help
thinking that he found a wife who had been similarly triumphant after
catastrophe left her on her own. I could also imagine the gentle but
resolute Amsale recognizing a kindred spirit in Neil Brown.

As it turned out, parenthood proved their judgment sound. They were
partners as before. When Rachel was born three weeks early just as
Amsale's business was taking off, it was Neil who delivered her gowns to
the influential people numbered among her clients. Encouraged by her
success, they dared not let her business flag. As for integrating the baby
into their lives, Amsale had a trial by fire. The first time the editor of a
bridal magazine came to do a story about her, Rachel was shrieking and
the new baby-sitter was of no use. Amsale simply continued showing
swatches of fabric and discussing bodice designs with her infant in her
arms. "I just had to work despite my embarrassment, and I got the

editorial anyway. So I realized, I can bring my child along if I need to. If someone has a problem, it's theirs, not mine."

Characteristic of their partnership, Neil continues the saga of Amsale Bridal Gowns. "There were really two stages. The first couple of years after Rachel was born, customers didn't take up much time. Amsale's job was more about finding fabric and going to New Jersey to see the dress-makers, so she could take Rachel along in a Snugli. The second stage was more difficult. The business grew from custom to wholesale, and Rachel wasn't so mobile any more. Sometimes Amsale worked seven days a week."

So they did the sensible thing and went about "creating a life that worked," as Neil puts it. Instead of living in the more comfortable Upper East Side of New York, for example, they live on the fringe of the garment district in midtown Manhattan, in the same building that houses Amsale's thirty-person factory. They purchased a weekend house for family time. They adapted Rachel's rhythms to their own.

"Mornings I'd take Rachel to preschool, a baby-sitter would pick her up, and Amsale would be in the building when she got home if Rachel needed her. I'd get home at seven-thirty, and we'd have family time by staying up till eleven. Now we can all go to a restaurant in the evening or a movie or just walk around Times Square, which is Rachel's favorite family activity. Mornings she always slept later than most other kids."

Almost unconsciously, I'm drawing lessons: flexibility, adaptability, creating a life that makes working easier. "Now that she's at Hunter"— Neil is referring to a highly competitive program for gifted students in the New York public school system—"a school bus picks her up and takes her home."

"In emergencies I can juggle my schedule," Amsale adds. "I'm in control of my hours. And Neil can always get away for something special at Rachel's school or in her life." They both travel extensively, Neil to film festivals and meetings in Los Angeles, Amsale to trunk shows every Thursday through Saturday from mid-January to mid-March. When one is gone, the other does the parenting. "And if, by chance, we're both gone, which has only happened once, Rachel stays with one of her friend's families for the weekend. It all works out."

They've even used their travel to the family's advantage, combining a bit of vacation with their overlapping work in Milan and L.A. That way, twice a year, they all go as a family and employ the same local baby-sitters. "Rachel thinks of them as her pen pals," Amsale says.

What about guilt? I ask. Reflecting, Neil answers, "Sometimes, sure, when Rachel calls me at the office at 7:00 P.M. to ask when I'm coming home. At times I wonder if I have enough time with her to listen—or just to be there—at the moment when she's really talking. But she knows we are devoted to her." Amused, he adds, "If you weren't here, she'd be sitting on one of us."

Amsale says, "If I thought Rachel had problems, I might worry, but she's a great kid who does well in school, loves to read, has good friends. I think I'm more relaxed about raising a child."

"More relaxed" raises the question, Than whom? Remembering Gioconda's words, I think I know, and ask whether Amsale finds more parental guilt and preoccupation here than in her country. Her response is as animated as it is immediate: "In Ethiopia," she begins, "parents teach their children right from wrong, of course, but that's it. My mother would never play games with children or intervene in children's arguments or supervise play. We children went outdoors and played among ourselves. I wish I could give that experience to my daughter, but it's New York City. Play dates are supervised. Children are always under adult control. Also, Ethiopian children there are very well behaved. They do not make demands or argue with parents. By six, a child does his own dishes. They do for themselves and are responsible for themselves. There it is the children who wait on their parents. If you want some juice, the child will get it for you, not the other way around. Here the combination of attentiveness and underdisciplining makes parenting much more stressful."

I am suddenly aware that, just as in Gioconda's home, kid stuff does not dominate their space. Rachel, of course, has her share. On my tour of her room I note the neat stack of games, register familiar names, like Scrabble, and wonder what Tuba Ruba is. She has her treasures, including her own rendition of a rockface, a square of Scotch tape where the nose fell off.

Rachel has that casual, unself-conscious American kid style. As we talk, she bounces on the bed. Her own bed, adjacent, is unmade. Wisps of light brown hair hang out of her ponytail; her T-shirt, with the injunction "READ" written over an illuminated eyeball, hangs out too. She is polite, but not deferential. Shy, she'd probably rather not talk, but she does so with bashful smiles. Has she enjoyed traveling with her parents? I ask. "Oh, yes." She likes Italy best, she says, but corrects herself, adding, "Not as much as Disneyland and Six Flags." Does she prefer visiting her mother's factory or her father's office? "HBO," she's quick to respond. "I get to watch movies there." Do you wish your parents were home more? Unequivocally, another "yes." Hungry, restless, excited by my attention perhaps, her strong spirit seems to rise, literally lifting her off the bed. Following behind, I watch her bound back into the living room.

Although Neil and Amsale claim that Rachel is not up to Ethiopian standards of child behavior, they are also glad she is more assertive than the average Ethiopian child, even though she argues with them (about the same things again and again, Amsale sighs). They really don't seem to mind waiting on her—as they tell me they do—or playing together. Though, mostly, Neil says, they just hang out and don't do any special kid activities.

We gather around the kitchen counter to review my directions home. The music has switched to Ella Fitzgerald. Amsale has started to fix Rachel's lunch. Rachel takes her father's hand and twirls in and out, having a fast dance with him. Ever so subtly, still chatting navigation with me, Neil accommodates, reeling Rachel in at just the right time.

Smooth as Aberra-Brown family life seems, it is not magic that makes it possible for them to combine work and family. They may not have planned overtly, but they have definitely put certain principles of partnership into practice, such as helping each other with work. As Amsale says, she knew Neil would be a partner in parenting as he had been in other things, like her business. Without being strident, she is fully aware that she chose to have a child with a parenting man. And why not? Sharing an interest in raising children together is hardly less relevant than enjoying sports, music, or politics together.

Neil and Amsale have also avoided the kind of overparenting that creates unnecessary stress. They have simply adapted their child's rhythms to their own, understanding intuitively that the reverse would have made for a more demanding child. To be fair, they seem to have had an "easy" child. Not all parents do. But to some extent, all children can be

encouraged to live the way their parents do, particularly when parents—
even busy ones—feel good about how they live.

At work they chase their tails, as Neil says. At home, in their parenting, they relax. Instead of bringing that professionalism into their parenting, overseeing every breath their daughter takes, they trust themselves to
raise their child well. When they are with her, they are very much there,
not letting experts, guilt, or anxiety come between them and their child.

Quite consciously, these parents "created a life that worked," although
it meant giving up a preferred neighborhood in order to keep work close
to home. Of course, combining work and family may be easier for them
because they have only one child, but that too can be part of wisely
planned parenthood.

Having only one child may be a difficult choice for couples because it
has been long associated with maladapted children and an incomplete
family life. However, because having one child has distinct advantages
for parents who both work, it is worth noting that only children actually
have important advantages. Long-term studies here and in China have
determined that they are higher achievers and have higher IQ scores and
more self-esteem than children with siblings. Although they also tend
toward self-centeredness and lower frustration levels, thoughtful parenting can counteract these tendencies by avoiding peer isolation.

The psychologist Diane Gottlieb, who is also the mother of a single
child—her preferred term—points out that with after-school programs,
group sports, group lessons, and community activities, it is much easier
now for children to bond with peers. As a result, their friendships are
often deeper than they were fifty years ago, more loyal, and less conflicted
than many sibling relationships.

On the other hand, siblings do form a kind of kid world in which they
work out many of their problems on their own. Then, too, some people,
including myself, simply enjoy children in groups, and some families
become more of what they need to be with a bunch of kids. And as we will
see in subsequent portraits, two is certainly manageable for working
parents, though on average each additional child increases household
labor by four hours a week for women, two for men. That labor does not
include the emotional work of facilitating the siblings' relationship with
each other and each with his parents, individually and together.

The number of children a couple has is a trade-off. As Neil and Amsale's discussion reveals, many of the strategies for planning parenthood today involve trade-offs, such as living close to work instead of in a preferred neighborhood. But sensible trade-offs made on the basis of partners' respect for each other's independent life do not feel so depriving. Neil and Amsale make them seem easy, even natural; nonetheless, the fact that their parenting works so well may help others with more constricting backgrounds to see that a thoughtfully formed family can help us taste all of life's grand pleasures, rather than having a full plate and an empty goblet.

CHAPTER 3

Sacrificial Motherhood: The Sacred Ideal

Why hasn't motherhood adapted to our vastly changed lives? Why is it that so many women feel guilty when they do not measure up to an outdated mothering ideal? The answer lies in the force of tradition, culture, and personal upbringing, which have taught women to subordinate their lives to their children's. As equal as women see themselves now, femininity is still defined in terms of caring, acceptance, and accommodation—not accomplishment. Motherhood, in contrast to fatherhood, still means providing for a child's essential psychological security and anchoring the family.

Our traditions are so strong that even when the majority of mothers fail at this devoted kind of motherhood, or feel tormented by the effort of trying, they hold fast to the ideal. Contrary to our most reasoned reflections, the majority of Americans seem to agree with the religious right that if Mother is not the linchpin of family life, the family will unravel and civilization will collapse. Better our own families fail than the myth.

With stakes this high, we have not dared to tamper with the basic concept of motherhood. Yes, a mother can have a career, we say, especially since financial realities now demand that the majority of mothers work. But our culture keeps the ideal of motherhood intact by insisting that a career be secondary to mothering, and women have taken the message to heart. How a mother manages to put mothering before work is her problem. If she can afford it, she cuts back to part-time work or stops entirely. If she cannot give up the income or just cannot bear to stay home, she often assuages her guilt by eliminating everything in her life besides work and family. She inadvertantly shackles herself to the traditional mother role because her approach to mothering springs from the most unconscious, unreflective part of her psyche.

Nina, a literary agent and mother of four, expressed it this way: "Work *was* my indulgence. I wasn't allowed any other. Even if I was traveling for work, I didn't dare enjoy it because I was so guilty. At home, in the evenings, my husband might go down to the basement to exercise. I wouldn't dream of it. While the kids were still awake, my time belonged to them."

Nor did it matter that her "indulgence" was the family's primary income. Paying work has always been acceptable for the vast majority of mothers who have had to work. Although a mother's success in the workplace may have resulted in shame for her impecunious husband, her motherhood was never called into question—especially if she worked in the sweatshop or pushed a peddler's cart. No one ever accused the African American mother who worked all week cleaning other people's houses of neglecting her children. In fact, we lambaste a poor mother on welfare for staying home to take care of her children while we praise the middle-class woman for doing the same.

A woman is labeled a careerist only if she is unusually successful and earns enough to buy her independence. Only when work is optional, highly remunerative, or competitive with male labor does it threaten ideal motherhood. After all, work, particularly mule-hard labor, is, like motherhood, a sacrificial virtue. However, because an employed mother today often comes dangerously close to self-gratification—if only the gratification of having an independent income or doing a job well—her motherhood is automatically called into question. Therefore she must *prove* her motherhood by giving all her nonworking hours to her family. She may never get to exercise, see her old friends, read the newspaper, or take a weekend away with her husband. For mothers, solitude is tantamount to sin. Not long ago I asked a friend what her children gave her for Mother's Day. With an uncharacteristic giggle, she said that her husband had taken them somewhere. "I just wanted them all away. That's what I really wanted."

Trying to please the old gods of sacrifice and the new gods of self-actualization, so many mothers are stressed, harried, and guilty that it is no wonder motherhood appears frightening to the uninitiated. Who would want to live such an emotionally fraught life? What sane woman contemplating motherhood would want to work all day and then take on a second shift at home? Not only must women work hours in the home before and after they work at the office, but they are obliged to stay home when a child is ill or a baby-sitter is absent. Mothers, not fathers, must fit the rest of their busy lives around parenting. The trouble is, the rest simply does not fit into the standard middle-class model of motherhood.

My neighbor, a woman who earns a six-figure salary buying oil drilling rights in the remotest parts of Siberia and Vietnam, was racing up our street with a bundle dangling from her arm, her neatly bobbed hair and Ann Taylor suit as disheveled as if she'd done the fifty-yard dash. Since I had just seen her an hour earlier walking her daughter to school, I asked whether everything was all right. "Monica forgot her bathing suit. I'm bringing it to school," she answered.

"No one else could do it?" I called to her as she dashed by. She turned to me and, with an expression that crossed fury with resignation, hollered, "The buck stops here!"

At the time my neighbor had both an unemployed husband and a housekeeper. Apparently neither was available. Apparently the school called *her*. Apparently she accepted that she was the primary caretaker of her children and the linchpin of family life. And yet the causes of that morning's mothering fiasco are not apparent at all.

She may well have been feeling guilty for not remembering it was her daughter's weekly swim day, and afraid that her daughter or her daughter's school or the invisible censors within and without would find her unmotherly, a careerist undeserving of the daughter she adored. Protective of a husband grappling with unemployment, she may have done more than usual so that he wouldn't feel the onus of his "free" time. As for the housekeeper, my neighbor told me on another occasion that she could not risk losing her by asking her to do anything extra. Despite the absurdity of galloping back from work as soon as she arrived, my neighbor fulfilled the austere maternal ideal to the best of her ability because, she probably told herself, that is what mothers do. It is certainly the myth of what mothers have always done.

THE MOTHER MYTH

Mothers have not always asked so much of themselves. Until the middle of the twentieth century, women commonly spent more time doing the work of survival than tending the young. Consider the nineteenth-century farm wife living with family members who took charge of her children while she made candles and clothes and soap and bread, did laundry, and raised barnyard animals. Poor urban women living in isolation did piecework at home, like my immigrant grandmother who generated the entire income for herself and five children by gluing together sheets of brown paper to make grocery bags.

Today most of the women in poor countries work the land. Anthropologists point out that within the great majority of agricultural communities grandmothers and older children take care of the young. For most mothers, then, motherhood is characterized by providing the essentials of life, not by being "ever-present, always-responsive" parents, as Penelope Leach would have them.

American motherhood, the kind that sends mothers panting from their offices to bring children their bathing suits, does have historical roots. It is a particular version of "maternal instinct" in which a mother's devotion to children is as extreme as the children's perceived need for it. My Great-aunt Paulie describes it in her favorite story from the old country:

> A young man had fallen in love with a woman who refused to marry him. "I'll do anything," he begged her. And she relented. "If you love me as much as you say, then kill your mother and bring me her heart." Immediately, he returned home through the woods and killed his mother. However, as he ran back along the forest path with his mother's heart in his hands, he tripped. "Be careful," said the heart, "don't hurt yourself."

This was not a joke, Aunt Paulie would protest when the laughter began. Where she came from, this story explained what it means to be a mother.

What motherhood meant to my Great-aunt Paulie—and what it still means to women who have inherited this tradition—is that not only do mothers gladly give up their lives for their children, but that *their children's happiness requires that sacrifice*. Fortunately, we are rarely called upon to sacrifice our lives literally. But all too often a mother sacrifices an important aspect of her being because she assumes her children need more of her.

As the psychologist Shari L. Thurer has argued, the core of our concept of motherhood is that it transforms women into patient, self-sacrificing, eternally loving people who alone know what is best for their children. Even the great child psychologist D. W. Winnicott's supposedly liberating concept of the "good enough mother," notes Thurer, "left little room for a mother to do anything else," what with having to be "exquisitely responsive to baby's needs."

The aura surrounding motherhood is hallowed. Motherhood is still evoked as a religious calling, a state of being that elevates women above the human condition. A mother is "the holiest thing alive," as Coleridge put it. Like the Virgin Mary, who, historically speaking, was a Jewish mother from the same tradition as my Great-aunt Paulie, a mother should be goodness and giving personified. Only in her soothing hands does true peace reside.

If a mother fails to provide that peace by failing to be ever-present and always responsive, she is a monster. As mythically powerful as the good mother, the lethal mother delivers instead a hell from which the child must flee: whether the kind of mother portrayed in *Snow White*, *Portnoy's Complaint*, or *The Bell Jar*, she is the obverse of the sacred devoted mother. Literally or metaphorically, she is a murderer of her children— that is, from her children's point of view. Mothers do not offer their own.

With the mother's perspective so rare in Western literature, the Pulitzer Prize–winning novelist Jane Smiley suggests that we have filled in the blank with fantasy: "If mothers never speak in a literary voice, it means, for one thing, that everyone in the culture is allowed or even encouraged, to project all their conflicting fantasies, wishes, and fears onto the concept of motherhood and onto their individual mothers." Thus, we sustain the dichotomy by separating good and bad mothers into distinct categories. As one critic has pointed out, even mothers themselves project all their own "bad" mothering feelings onto a demon character, such as the homicidal baby-sitter in Mary Gordon's novel *Men and Angels*, in order to preserve the fantasy of the unambivalently good, devoted mother. Films like *The Hand That Rocks the Cradle* or even *Fatal Attraction*—whose careerist antiheroine tries to destroy her lover's "good" traditional family—do the same.

Men and women alike are so hooked by the myth of the sacrificial mother that we are quite capable of punishing a mother who acknowledges a wish to have her own life. Not long ago a Michigan judge awarded custody of a three-year-old girl to a father who rarely visited her and would not make support payments until forced to do so by the court. The judge's reason: the girl's mother, Jennifer Ireland, had enrolled her daughter in day care three days a week so she could go to college. The father was also attending college, but because his own mother agreed to take care of the child, he was deemed the better parent than the one who had done all the nurturing. A year later—an inevitably agonizing year for mother and child—the decision was reversed on appeal. However, not all mothers win such battles. In most cases, fathers win custody suits because mothers are held to a higher standard of parental care. Such was the Ireland case: Jennifer's crime was to put her needs on a par with her child's, an act that, unlike the self-improvement efforts of her similarly disposed ex-boyfriend, threatened the myth of the sacrificial mother.

This may be the moment to state emphatically that I am not advocating maternal selfishness. Selfishness is not the only alternative to complete sacrifice. I have no sympathy with parents who largely ignore their children, are too busy to spend time with them, or use them to gratify their own thwarted ambitions.

Parenthood does call for sacrifice: getting up in the night when you are bone-tired, giving comfort when you are in need of comfort yourself, putting your life on hold when a child is gravely ill. It requires maturity: an ability to give nonreciprocally, to accept the incessant demands of a small child, to empathize with a whiny toddler, a quibbling ten-year-old, or a critical adolescent. However, if a parent isn't too emotionally damaged to feel it, children also call forth a depth of love that astonishes, disarms, overwhelms, and gratifies so fundamentally that it offsets the servitude and frustration. If a mother or father has sufficient time away from parenting to pursue individual goals as well as parent, then after the shortest absence the very sight of one's child can be rapture, longing, an ache.

I see an immense latitude between selflessness and selfishness in parenting. A new kind of mothering exists between these two extremes, at the locus of self. My Great-aunt Paulie placed motherhood at the selflessness end of the continuum. Most women now oscillate between selflessness and self, guilt driving them in one direction, desperation in the other—like my neighbor with her daughter's swim bag. Some unlucky ones, like the many Jennifer Irelands, move toward self and are punished for their presumption.

Our present definition of motherhood is so self-denying that one mother, discussing the exhaustion involved in working and mothering in the current style, warns that if we don't change, "we are going to have a nation of comatose women."

Unfortunately, no matter how much most women would love to mother differently, they find it too painful to try. We have only to think about what anguish it causes most people to change their relationships with their own mothers, to look at how they prefer to pretend acquiescence, keep their distance, or reenact the same battles for years rather than take on a different role.

Acting differently, stepping out of the invisible skin that has molded us into our familiar shape, is so frightening we starve or stuff ourselves to maintain it, loathing that shape all the while. In the same way, our customary style of mothering is so confusingly, confoundingly ingrained that we don't change for fear the whole house, or one's whole self, will come tumbling down.

Women are drowning in the obligations of their lives. But as Diane Gottlieb explains, changing something as basic as how we mother means redefining who we are in the world, and that may seem more frightening still; it may generate more guilt than the guilt that presently drives women to fulfill those obligations. We prefer to endure impossible demands rather than risk our familiar identities. And not without reason: even the smallest changes in mothering have created a formidable backlash.

THE REVIVAL OF THE MOTHER MYTH

It is no accident that the mother myth is almost as strong now as it was before women's liberation exposed its contradictions. I don't mean there is an actual conspiracy to wrench mothers from the workplace and send them back home. However, the current trend in custody settlements, abortion restrictions, and curbs on affirmative action does add up to backlash, a reaction to the dramatic increase in women's independence. Just as individuals resist the unknown and revert to the familiar, so does a society: the devil you know is better than the devil you don't.

Similar resistance and reversion occurred after World War II. As the birth rate declined and freed women from lifetime child-rearing, psychology began to emphasize the crucial importance of the mother-child relationship, noted the groundbreaking sociologist/psychoanalyst Nancy Chodorow. Two steps forward, one step back.

The emphasis on the mother-child relationship now dominates parental attitudes in the form of "attachment theory." This is the idea that a child's sense of security depends entirely on a mother who is his primary nurturer and is never away from him for more than a few hours. The theory originally developed in the fifties from the observations of the physician John Bowlby, who, astonishingly enough, seemed to be the first to notice that children separated from their mothers for prolonged stays in hospitals or orphanages became severely depressed. Just as astonishingly, no one suggested that the children's depression was obviously a result of several simultaneous traumas—illness, family crisis, unfamiliar surroundings, insufficient adult attention—not just maternal deprivation.

An extremely subjective test later devised by a colleague of Bowlby's to ascertain "secure attachment" turned the underlying belief in an exclusive mother-child bond into a "science." In the test, done on a handful of first-time mothers, the mother brings a child into a room with a stranger, then leaves for a short while. How ardently the child greets her return establishes the child's rating on the attachment scale. Of course, children used to strangers and used to mothers who come and go may not be as ardent as those who rarely leave their mother's side.

Despite the fact that attachment theory amounts to a flimsy set of assertions, it has such a strong hold on our national psyche that contradictory evidence made front-page headlines in the *New York Times*: "Study Says Babies in Child Care Keep Secure Bonds to Mother." The federal study, which followed the children's development from birth to seven years, is the most comprehensive ever done. It showed that it did not matter how many hours a child spent in day care or even if the care was of good quality. The child still bonded securely with his mother "if the mother was sensitive and responsive to her infant."

Ignore for the moment the startling lack of concern for the child's relationship with his father. Suffice it to say that attachment theory holds such power over us that the study accepted the premise that the mother-child bond is central, attacking only the standard conclusion that day-care separation disrupts that bond. In other words, mothers need not be "ever-present, always-responsive"; "sensitive and responsive" will do fine.

News though this was to many, numerous psychologists had already discarded attachment theory. Diane Eyer recently devoted an entire book to proving that there is "absolutely no research to prove the existence of a special 'bonding' period . . . or to show that women's employment interfered with mother-child relationships." An earlier study established that day care enhances child development and that "at whatever age [children] enter day care, they develop attachments to both their mothers and to their caregiver and their attachment to their mother is much stronger."

The idea, disproved many times, that children cannot abide their mother's absence is the contemporary incarnation of the sacred mother ideal. Now, a mere twenty years after women declared themselves the equals of men, they are told to be ever more vigilant in their maternal devotion. Women have made substantial inroads into the public world, flooding graduate schools and filling positions formerly reserved for men. No one can tell women that they cannot be good surgeons, CEOs, or Supreme Court judges. Nor is the "you're taking this job away from a man" line of reasoning effective. But like the standards of female beauty, the norms of traditional motherhood continue to unsettle women sufficiently to make their manipulation possible. If beauty is the chink in our perilously thin female armor, motherhood is our Achilles' heel.

America is glorifying devoted motherhood today because of ongoing social and economic change. Nearly three-quarters of the mothers of schoolchildren are now employed, and that number is still increasing. What's more, stagnation of wages and the risk of losing a job in midcareer have forced men to confront greater challenges than they have in the recent past.

It's now harder for everyone to earn a living wage, but men still expect to. They compare themselves to their fathers, who may have earned a more satisfactory living with less work. The real threat to social stability today, argues Lester Thurow, an economist at MIT, comes from the inequality between the rich and the rest of the population, a degree of inequality America has not seen since the 1920s. But economic inequality is an abstract, untargetable enemy; women are not. That is why the narrowing of the gender gap is much more threatening to men today than it was during the prosperous seventies when the women's movement flourished.

The wish for the stay-at-home mother may well reflect a nostalgia for the imagined simplicity of earlier, less anxious times when gender designated fixed roles, expectations were humbler, and economic goals were easier to achieve. Like the Islamic fundamentalists whose principal act of "revolution" was to put women back under veils, the American fundamentalists, unable to accept or adapt to their changing world, propose a version of "family values" that requires mothers to stay at home.

We are constantly confronted with the suggestion that unselfish mothers are not women without professions but women who give up their professions to take care of their children—like Marilyn Quayle, the woman who trained to practice law but became a "partner" to her husband instead, as if the two roles were mutually exclusive. These women are often designated the "wise" ones who dropped out of the rat race to do something so much more fulfilling . . . to do their duty.

The backlash against women who value their careers comes in numerous guises. We read stories about women over thirty-five who, having deferred motherhood until they had job security, can no longer bear children. We watch commercials for pregnancy testers that warn women to remember their biological clocks. Having children has been wrapped in the gauzy romanticism of Madison Avenue and sentimentalized by Hollywood in baby movies from *Look Who's Talking* to *Three Men and a Baby*.

In all of these depictions, parenthood is romantic, rollicking fun in which men are integrally involved. Parenting *is* romantic and fun, but it is also very hard work. And however much men seem to be involved in the movie versions, women are the ones doing it. The more they mother, so the unconscious cultural logic goes, the less space they take up in the economic, political, and social sphere of men. As Jessie Bernard put it, "Rocking the cradle has been precisely what has prevented [women] from ruling the world."

Although the majority of women are not giving up, giving in, or dropping out, they nearly all feel the pressure of the American mothering ideal. Even Neil Brown and Amsale Aberra, who circumvented that pressure by virtue of their outsider status, are aware that most of their peers feel it strongly—so strongly that only the very lucky or very determined ones find their way to an unconflicted family life that combines the desire to nest with the desire to earn and achieve.

Among those lucky ones are men and women raised by parents who had already broken the rules themselves and, by example, inspired their children to do the same. In this second family portrait we'll meet just such a couple. Both partners grew up believing that parenting does not require sacrificial motherhood. They also had some excellent ideas about how to structure their family life to avoid it.

MADDY AND PATRICK O'CONNOR*

Maddy and Patrick have one of those rarest of gems, a truly 50–50 marriage, which they maintain in a seemingly nonchalant way. Both of them take care of their four-year-old son Liam and his six-week-old baby sister, Dierdre; both have work they love. Patrick, who completed his first short feature as he turned thirty, is a scriptwriter; Maddy scored his film and writes her own music but earns her living composing for commercials. They met at Oberlin College when they were eighteen and have been together ever since. He's an easygoing, winsome Irishman, handsome enough to have earned a living as a teen model; she's an intense Italian, earthy as the garden she plants every summer at her parents' summer home and solid as the family business she works for.

Today, because she will go to the office, Maddy has exchanged her usual jeans and Doc Martens for a flowered sundress she can slip off her shoulder to nurse, her silky brown hair falling to its scooped neck. Dierdre is contentedly nestled in the crook of Patrick's arm, her own small but plump one dangling over his. They are sitting on their soft gray sofa, Patrick's legs up on the coffee table, Maddy's resting on his shins. One of Maddy's tomato sauces simmers on the stove; the mountain of papers in Patrick's study overflows into the living room where we sit. No one seems worried. It's a beautiful June morning.

Their son and my daughter, who screech in the background playing hide and seek, are dear friends, as we are. We live a few floors apart in a building whose halls are often clogged with strollers and dogs. Mornings Patrick and I walk our kids the seven long blocks to school, which is on the way to both our offices. My husband or Maddy will often cook dinner for all of us. Whoever has a free hand sets up the kids' paints, plays monster, changes their dance music, or referees their spats. Occasionally we spell each other in child care. And daily, it seems, we discuss every new child-rearing challenge that comes up—practically at the same predictable time—in both households. Our interview isn't very different from our usual talks about how to work, parent, get enough couple time, and honor at least some of the hedonism we all enjoy.

Most couples have to work hard at having a 50–50 marriage, tamping down deeply felt Ozzie and Harriet impulses about who does what. What's so unique about Maddy and Patrick's marriage is how unconscious their partnership seems, evolving naturally from their own parents and being supported by the liberal segment of our culture they have both lived in. They never had to plan their shared parenting; it was a foregone conclusion. As Maddy tells it, "Our relationship started as best friends, and we never imagined that should change. I knew Patrick was a kindred spirit, not just someone to fall in love with."

Maddy knows absolutely that she would never have married a man who wasn't going to be involved with his family in a major way; she simply wasn't a person who would ever have been in an unequal relationship. Growing up, she didn't know women with second-class status. Girls ran her high school; her college was ultra "p.c." Her own parents were business partners, though her mother didn't work full-time when the children were very small. "My father baked and my mother cooked. To me, it was normal to have parents who worked *and* were devoted to their children. In fact, I thought having a family made it easier to have a career, not harder."

Her parents' work was in no way a deprivation for Maddy. "Our caregivers were wonderful. We had dinner with our parents every night, spent weekends together, went on trips together. I *knew* family was a priority for them: once, when they had practically no money, they spent the last of it taking us to stay in a fancy London hotel. Whenever my father had to travel, no matter what, he'd never stay overnight. He wanted to spend the night with his family. That's why he started his own business. My mother, who was a lyricist, wrote with her partner one evening a week in addition to working at their company every day, but we thought that was exciting. I don't know anyone closer than I am with my parents. All my friends envied me. Our house was where they wanted to be." In creating her own family, Maddy wanted to perpetuate what she had.

Patrick always knew he'd be a good parent. Although he didn't have as harmonious a family life as Maddy, his parents ultimately separating when he was twelve, he knew they both adored him—that *he* was the best thing in their relationship. From the time Patrick was eight, his mother worked and his father, who had lost his job, stayed home to take care of him.

"I didn't know other dads who gave their kids the friendship, love, and attention my father gave me. Other kids would have *one* special day with their dads. That was every day for me. He was a great friend, the ultimate companion—older and wiser, someone who could teach me things. The price was that he wasn't responsible: he didn't pay bills, he didn't look for jobs. That's why I wanted my career in place before I became a father. But I never imagined I wouldn't be totally involved."

The extent of Maddy and Patrick's planning was knowing they were in the parent business together. When Liam was born, they figured that since they were freelancers, they didn't need help; instead, they'd just trade off the responsibility, as they'd always done with everything. It took them less than three months to realize how wrong they were. As enamored as they were of their new baby, they were also in shock.

"Suddenly the amount of responsibility escalates tenfold," says Patrick. "This child needs you twenty-four hours a day, and you're two exhausted people constantly negotiating whose turn it is to give. You might not be giving each other anything. There is no preparation. Also, you don't ever know what kind of baby you'll have, and ours needed a lot of attention. He wasn't a great sleeper, so we lived in terror of waking him. The phones were off, the TV was off; we were on edge. When he was awake, he could cry five or six hours a day. If you were in charge of Liam, you might not get ten minutes to have a shower. Once I didn't shower for a week!"

Although their extended family mobilized—Maddy's sister flew in from California to stay with their parents' dogs while their parents moved in and slept on Maddy and Patrick's pullout couch for two weeks—parenting an infant like Liam was still a considerable challenge. They understood that an extraordinary ability to concentrate, for example, underlay his ability to reproduce particular musical sounds by the age of two months. However, it did not make him a docile infant. Says Patrick, "Getting comfortable enough to leave Liam, even to go to a movie, was so hard because we couldn't think of *Liam* as comfortable."

In addition, Maddy says, "I felt total fear that I couldn't just walk out the door when I wanted. I always imagined a cute little baby, you know, and suddenly there was a person who would be with me my whole life. I wished I could go back to the other way, when we could just do whatever we liked. I never experienced anything as exhausting or consuming, even though I was the one who picked up jobs fairly quickly and Patrick took more care of him than I did. All my wires were crossed. My energy was gone."

Maddy and Patrick are no martyrs, however. When Liam was three months old, they put an ad in the paper for a caregiver. "With good help, things calmed down. By six months our lives had a rhythm again." With their second child, Dierdre, things calmed down in just a few weeks. Patrick says, "By a second child you have already transformed your life. If you can't go out, you know it's no big deal." Maddy says that although even a second child pulls you back into the chaos of infancy, it's not as scary; you know it will pass. Also, Dierdre is a docile baby. Finally, as Maddy is quick to point out, they now have a caregiver they trust.

Since I spend so much time with Maddy and Patrick, I know that while they both do the hands-on parenting, they do it very differently. For example, in matters of discipline Patrick is a great believer in diversion and Maddy in reason, responsibility, and talking problems through. When I ask them whether their differences create friction between them, Patrick flashes his great smile and says, "Only several times a day."

"We're getting better at it," Maddy counters.

"Maddy," I ask, "do you ever want to just quit work and take over at home to avoid such conflicts?"

"I've definitely thought of staying home completely, especially since I'm happiest when I'm cooking and making Christmas tree ornaments, but I just couldn't do that. I wouldn't be me. I don't even think I could like myself if my world got that small. Besides, right now we need the money I earn, and if I work, we have to both take care of Liam and Dierdre. Sometimes I don't get home until 7:00 P.M. Sometimes I have to work all night."

Patrick adds, "I couldn't *not* take care of Liam and Dierdre. I can't stand to miss anything. Part of me wants to watch him even when he's at school. And also, the other way, one person is doing everything and hating the other one for *not* doing it. I know that from when I have to take over completely."

Patrick feels that in their case the everyday friction of shared parenting is more a matter of style than intention. "Many of our disagreements are that Maddy sees things coming faster than I do, so I don't think of the thirty things that have to be done. She's already done them and is ready to hit me." What saves them, he realizes, is that "she knows I don't expect her to cook and clean for me. I'm not actually avoiding doing the work. I'm just on a different learning curve."

Patrick points out that he gives Maddy that same benefit of the doubt. "I sometimes feel that because Maddy's the lawgiver, I parent without the power. But things do naturally polarize with couples. If one has the strength, he or she takes over that function. I'm more of an anarchist; Maddy's naturally organized. But her parental lawgiving isn't because she's the mother. When I'm the one on, I make the rules."

Maddy concurs. Although she's the family organizer, she doesn't feel like the emotional center or the primary parent. In fact, unlike most women, she can say that if she were to die, she knows Patrick would nurture their children as fully as she would. She knows they are in good hands.

In other words, for Maddy and Patrick, whatever their daily division of labor or different parenting styles, they feel deeply that they *both* nurture their children, and they *both* want professional success for the other. As Patrick puts it, "I never thought caring for a child was gender-specific. I just parent. The kids want their mother for some things and me for others, but that's fine. I'm there for them. I identify as much with Maddy's career as she does. Right now, I've gotten a chance to write and direct a feature film, so soon I'll be working more and Maddy will be covering the home. But if she got a chance to score a feature, I'd do the sacrificing. If we get our chances at the same time, we'll call on relatives. But neither of us wants to work sixty hours a week, at least not for any extended time. We want to raise our own kids."

Of course, good intentions aren't everything. Maddy and Patrick have an ideal situation: flexible, paying work they love, great child care, and extended family nearby. That means, in addition to daily support, they also get time off to relax together—alone. When any of the grandparents take the kids for a weekend, they have a weekend to themselves. When Liam was a year old, they took two weeks off and went out west. That felt a bit long, so their next vacation was only five days—but they went to Paris, where they'd been for their honeymoon.

As fully as they give themselves to their children, Maddy and Patrick do not begrudge themselves couple time, work time, or even solitary time. Patrick is famous among the children of our neighborhood, a Pied Piper whose antics and games enrapture them; Maddy is as well loved for her great cookies as for her hugs and understanding. Yet Maddy and Patrick go off every morning to work, have their Thursday nights out, and guiltlessly pack their bags for their private vacations knowing their children are safe and happy with their grandparents. Having defined parenthood for themselves, shaped it according to their respect for each other's work and their desire to remain the closest of friends, they have the family life they truly want.

Maddy, with her cooking, her gardening, her beautiful home, and weekends gardening at her parents' country house, could pass for a classic earth mother. The difference is that Maddy doesn't believe mothering—even her wonderful homemaking kind—precludes her work or her own pursuits. In fact, in explaining her beliefs, Maddy brilliantly defines and defends the self-nourishing rather than self-sacrificing motherhood that has allowed her to mother and to remain herself: "The fear of not being there is based on a lack of respect for your children. If you are always home, you're really depriving them of other relationships and experiences, of the opportunity to separate. I feel sorry for people who think you have to be a martyr to mother. You have to respect yourself and your children enough not to have your relationship with them become so important that it blocks other outlets. You expect your children to grow. Why not you too? It's not my goal for my kids that they only do mothering or fathering when they grow up. So I too have my dreams."

Gioconda would heartily agree on the basic premise, un-American as it would also seem to her. Neil and Amsale assume it. This sense of entitlement to self-fulfillment is the underlying maternal perspective of all the mothers depicted in this book, including those who have not been able to arrange a 50–50 family life at present. Entitlement is what differentiates a truly new kind of motherhood from the old and sustains a mother who is "doing the sacrificing" at one time or another. It is what saves a mother from losing her self.

Maddy's ability to work and mother also underscores how important it is for young women setting out today to chart their courses carefully with their mates, agreeing at the beginning to parent equally. The problem is that the subject of raising children is usually not discussed. Romance, whether the wacky, decorous, or incapacitatingly voluptuous kind, rarely includes attention to the practical details of a future domestic life.

Our culture also cautions women not to raise pesky issues of parenting lest they frighten men off—men being notoriously reluctant fathers. Even Patrick talks about his own "male" hesitations: "I was saying, I'm not ready; she was saying she was. But I'm not sure men ever feel as ready. Not to generalize, but men want everything and want to commit to nothing. They want all their options."

Women are better off raising the issue and working through differences or even getting counseling before having a child. Often, says Diane Gottlieb, even a man who had not wanted to do child care is motivated to compromise if for no other reason than to stay close to a woman he loves. Nor does he have to love child care. Gottlieb points out that "we all accept parts of our professional lives that we find tedious or difficult because we value the jobs themselves; the same is true of our family lives." Despite his initial hesitations, Patrick is obviously a parenting man, but one senses that even if he had not been, he would have adapted.

Finally, the O'Connors' experience emphasizes how much a couple gains when both take time off after a baby is born, no matter how impractical it may seem or how forcefully a man may argue against it. Most do argue, because such leave is unprecedented in their workplaces and money is often tight. But a new father's arguments may actually be an expression of his anxiety about nurturing. Money is not always prohibitively tight. Just as couples save for a vacation or a larger home, they can also save for a month's parental leave, as Maddy and Patrick did. Some may have to forfeit a newly outfitted nursery, but all the baby's gear can be bought at tag sales and consignment shops or acquired from others. Hours spent together are far more valuable than $500 worth of Babar wallpaper. That time can set the tone for an entire parenting life. Both partners get to know the baby, give one another the assurance that they are both parenting, and grow accustomed to respecting each other's parental authority.

Of course, some mothers accept their husband's arguments against paternity leave, feeling covetous of their new, privileged relationship with their infant and with peers who honor their motherhood. Some experience an authority they may never have felt before, even on the job. But like Maddy, they can resist the impulse to be a primary, full-time mother in order to cultivate other parts of themselves.

If both partners simply cannot take parental leave and the father returns to full-time work, as is usually the case, they can maximize the father's time with his new child by having him be in charge before and after work—even if he isn't as responsive as the mother or even if the baby has been fussy or feverish. Caring for children under *all* circumstances is what builds parents' confidence. The fact that Maddy was the one who had to go back to work first may actually have helped Patrick to be as comfortable with nurturing as he is.

Finally, romance may be the strongest argument for tending a newborn together, for it means that the parents can share one of life's remarkable adventures. No one tells parents what *really* to expect in the first parenting months, but it is wild exhilaration and exhaustion. In fact, it is an exhilaration and exhaustion that feed off one another, producing rapidly alternating emotional combinations, such as happy stupefaction followed by manic anxiety. Of course, some new parents glide through without a hitch. But for most, everything changes, including the chemistry between the parents.

Consider the simplest physical impact: sleep deprivation. Most people are aware that infants eat every three hours, but few know what it means to wake from sleep every three hours, or even more often. Staying up for a week during final exams is nothing compared to months of interrupted sleep with an infant. The difference lies in walking around dizzy with fatigue, a permanent goofy smile on your face, and a numbing chill at the rim of your brain, where only one or two— instead of two dozen—thoughts now coexist. Sometimes you sink into unconsciousness—sitting on the rim of the bathtub, on the kitchen stool, on the couch.

With an infant, you do not move through a day at your own pace. You cannot live your former life. You don't dine; you eat. You don't sleep; you nap. You don't stroll out of the house; you organize a mound of equipment and set off. Every move is punctuated by the baby's far more pressing need. In this earliest period, parents live to serve the house's new potentate, for that is absolutely what every infant is—shrieking for quicker service and inspiring fear in the hearts of his body servants.

It is difficult to focus on anything outside the infant's orbit. You are so busy with her care that you might not manage to read a newspaper, as one astounded friend told me. And if you do manage, the world's problems often seem peculiarly irrelevant and remote, the way they do while waiting in a hospital emergency room. An infant illuminates the foreground so brightly that the background fades. Only she, and you as her parents, have any sharply defined reality.

Caring for newborns often leaves parents amazed by how great their human capacity is. They no longer wonder at people with infants in tow who have scaled mountains to escape invading armies or crossed the Atlantic on rafts. They understand what it means to run on adrenalin, the result of a panic to keep this unbearably delicate child alive combined with the pure excitement of its new being.

Yet sleepless adrenalin energy, like sixteen cups of coffee, makes for a certain wackiness. Waves of blurry delight can come close on the heels of despairing fury for any small imperfection: putting the baby's pajamas on backwards, buying the wrong size crib sheet. Then comes the desire to stare at this child as if she were the eighth wonder of the world, a status that no one else quite sees, save perhaps for her grandparents, who will also tell you to put another blanket on her. Their suggestion, of course, often leads to a wave of despairing fury, which soon subsides, if only because you can't quite focus on any one thing for too long.

Wackiness being the natural condition of early parenting, it is wise to plan for quiet time—time to keep the world out so you can wander around your happily demented (and sporadically miserable) universe with no one to take it personally. The self-protective woman plans to inhabit that universe with the child's father, preferably so that he too has the same blotto smile on his face. Remember how Patrick didn't shower for a week? Whatever wonderland Maddy and Patrick found themselves in, they were there together, able to spell one another, make room for each to return ever so briefly to the world, if only to go to the gym or stroll to the corner for an ice cream cone. Neither one had to be alone.

The great value of starting out parenting together, whether both of you continue to work part-time, both stay home for a while, or you take leave consecutively, is how much easier it is to maintain a marriage of equals. How important is it to start out together? The sociologist Scott Coltrane uses the words of one of the fathers he interviewed to caution men, "If you don't start at the beginning, you get left behind."

New parents rarely anticipate just how difficult unequal parenting is on a marriage. Psychologist Ron Taffel, author of *Why Parents Disagree*, asserts that the major disagreements a couple will have are over who is doing more, not enough, or too much for the children. Patterns get set, so why not set them with foresight? It is so clearly Maddy and Patrick's planning ahead to both parent that has made it possible for them to stay close as a family throughout surges in first her work and then his.

CHAPTER 4

Real Mothers Are Good Enough

Because women in the workforce cannot be "ever-present" and "always-responsive" to their children, they all too often try even harder than stay-at-home mothers to fulfill the holy mother role—particularly if they grew up with a mother at home. The psychologist Rosika Parker observes that "the hectic round of extracurricular activities does not constitute a new ideal, but is an attempt to achieve the old ideal sense of total devotion to children." Or assuage the guilt for abandoning that traditional ideal.

With our fantasy of what motherhood should be—idyllic maternal bonding and blissful embraces in spotless white matching mother-daughter ensembles—the mother in the workforce is primed for disappointment and self-hatred. It is she who blames herself for every shadow on her child's happiness, from the first tantrums of the terrible twos to the last slammed door of adolescence.

In a *Redbook* column aptly titled "The Secret Life of Mothers," (for these backlash times) one busy working mother laments, "So when I do spend time with my daughter, I expect and want it to be fun, enriching, and rewarding. Sometimes it is. Other times, I'm just going through the motions—and I know it. That's when I worry that maybe I'm lacking in some critical maternal gene."

Employed mothers worry that if they aren't experiencing the idealized motherhood on parade in those same magazines, they are not maternal. However, if our culture didn't promote the saintly image of motherhood, mothers who do not choose to be "ever-present, always-responsive," or who do not *always* enjoy parenting, wouldn't feel the guilt. If child-care experts, social critics, and politicians did not put stay-at-home mothers on a pedestal, those with jobs outside would not feel so insecure. If mothers were not trying to live up to the myth, we would not need columns about the secret lives of mothers.

If, like Gioconda, Amsale, and Maddy, the majority of women honestly described their parenting lives, their mothering would inform the discussion at large. But most mothers are still too afraid to voice their real feelings.

Once, when I was sitting with a group of mothers waiting for my daughter's preschool to let out, I mentioned that I was sending my daughter to day camp that summer. The woman across from me curled up her lip. "*I* want my kids with me during the summer. They're in school all the rest of the year." Instantly I felt shame. I saw my own daughter alone, desolate in a crowd of indifferent "strangers," and imagined this woman moving through a day of thrilling summer child-care activities: at the pool, making clay ashtrays, riding bikes. Then a woman behind me whispered in my ear, "Let her take mine if she likes it so much." She too was a housewife. They all were except for me in this section of the small California town where my family spends vacations. Mercifully, not all of them were as intimidated by the mother myth. As it turns out, there is no reason to be.

One new study that gives the lie to the myth establishes that stay-at-home mothers don't actually manage all those thrilling activities. Faye J. Crosby, head of the Psychology Department at Smith College and author of *Juggling: The Unexpected Advantages of Balancing Career and Home for Women and Their Families*, a compendium of the research on employed mothers and their children, reports that "working mothers and at-home mothers and children both spent three hours per week watching television together, less than two hours per week in teaching and learning activities, and both kinds of mothers read aloud to their children for an average of one hour per week."

How is it, then, that most women remain unaware that stay-at-home mothers are no more giving to their children than employed mothers? How come we imagine that other mothers love every minute of their child-tending days and only we cold careerists don't?

Because, as I mentioned earlier, mothers in Western culture have so rarely written or spoken from their maternal point of view. But noting this bizarre reality does nothing to explain it.

THE SILENCED MOTHER TONGUE

It has become commonplace to assume that we don't know how mothers feel because real mothers have no time to write. Indeed, most of the great women writers of the past, like George Eliot, Jane Austen, and the Brontë sisters, were childless. But not all were, and some, like Austen, lived with and knew intimately at least one mother her own age. All *had* mothers and might, like Virginia Woolf in *To the Lighthouse*, have assumed their voices.

An omission this flagrant points to something deeper in our collective unconscious. Shari Thurer offers a theory: "Once she attains motherhood, a woman must hand in her point of view. Midcentury psychoanalytic thinking assumed that motherhood is essentially the child's drama, with mom in a supporting role." That is, to be a good mother is to be too child-centered to write about mothering as if your own experience counts. The result is that we have no "mother-tongue."

At the risk of making a whipping girl out of the otherwise sensible Penelope Leach, her prose is rife with maternal platitudes that exemplify this absurd cultural standard. In *Your Baby and Child: From Birth to Age Five*, for example, she says: "Your interests and [the baby's] are identical." Most mothers are painfully aware this is not true. A mother's interests—if only to sleep through the night and have a moment's peace—are frequently in conflict with her child's. Yet we believe we are not supposed to feel our "selfish" desires, and so, in public, we do not.

That taboo derives from our wish to believe that mothers feel all-giving toward their child. Telling the truth about mothering—when it does not refer to the oneness and bliss—means breaking the rules. The distinguished novelist Jane Smiley, also a mother of two, believes that "to write about our own experience could lead us into, God forbid, analyzing our children and husbands, to belying the idea of maternal love that they depend on. To write about the world could reveal in ourselves despair, alienation, fear, anomie that could communicate itself to our children and damage them."

Yet while that maternal taboo has grown stronger, women have grown stronger too—financially and psychologically. Women can now *afford* to create a language for mothering that embodies the full, complex experience. In the tradition of Adrienne Rich's 1976 book on mothering, *Of Woman Born*, "the masks of motherhood are cracking through."

The novelists Louise Erdrich and Anne LaMott each recently published a memoir of their child's first year. Mary Kay Blakely's *American Mom* is a scathing (self-) portrait of motherhood. The accounts are as different as the women. Yet what they all describe is the fluctuating reality of mothering, the bliss and the breathlessness as well as what Blakely calls the "bad mother days" and the "bad children days."

How incredibly hard it is, how wonderful and how awful—often in the space of a few minutes. In *Operating Instructions*, Anne LaMott writes:

> He falls asleep and I feel I could die of love when I watch him, and I think to myself that he is what angels look like. Then I doze off, too, and it's like heaven, but sometimes only twenty minutes later he wakes up and begins to make his gritchy rodent noises, scanning the room wildly. I look blearily over at him in the bassinet, and think, with great hostility, Oh, God, he's raising his loathsome reptilian head again.

At first, reading this passage I let out a gasp: I had never seen maternal ambivalence described on the page. Everyone I know is sending the book to new mothers. This is the truth, we tell them. This is what you'll be thinking in your shriveled, sleep-deprived, love-sodden brain. What blessed relief from the platitudes.

It is all the more important that women today tell the truth about motherhood because few young women now have much personal experience with babies. We have been reared like our brothers to develop our potential, not to mind younger siblings and learn about infant care. Anne LaMott also writes, "I just can't get over how much babies cry. I really had no idea what I was getting into. To tell you the truth, I thought it would be more like getting a cat."

Her surprise is not unique. We are probably the least prepared generation to become parents. The Quechua Indians of Central America call babies "wa-was"; they know how much babies cry. We, on the other hand, picture a serenely content woman with a baby in her arms. The baby never has colic, thrush, diaper rash, infant acne, or cradle cap. The mother is never sobbing, fighting claustrophobia, or screaming at her husband. Our fantasies about motherhood are as disproportionate as the disappointment and self-recrimination that inevitably ensue.

A woman might love her baby but discover that she is not a "baby person." She may not have a sensitive feel for infants, who can seem like "feeding tubes" or "blobs," as I've heard them called in candid moments. Another woman might adore helpless, cuddly babies but find the activity and demands of toddlers nerve-wracking. Women can love their children but not like particular aspects of mothering or specific developmental stages. They may have so many contradictory feelings about their children—not to speak of moments of real distaste—that they distrust their love and thereby undermine their mothering.

One-third of all mothers today experience some kind of depression or postpartum blues after giving birth; at least one in ten cases endures for a full year. The lower the family's income, the higher the incidence of depression. In one large study of new mothers, researchers found that half the mothers with incomes less than $20,000 were significantly depressed.

Women are at highest risk for severe depression after having a child, and not only because of hormonal changes. When fantasy confronts reality, when a woman is exhausted by interrupted sleep and shaken by the unanticipated emotional complexity of mothering, she is most vulnerable to the legacy of maternal imperatives. Unable to disappoint those closest to her who tell her she should be feeling glorious, or even to admit to herself how she feels, the gap between fantasy and reality can become a chasm at whose edge she holds a helpless child. And if she is poor, she is more likely to lack support when she needs it the most.

Diane Gottlieb reports that therapists frequently discuss the 3:00 A.M. desperation of a mother with a screaming infant, a mother who has given more than she has and longs for help or escape. But who is the mother's best friend at 3:00 A.M.? they ask. And where can she flee? All too often, Gottlieb reminds us, the in-laws have gone home after a week's visit and the husband is fast asleep. The new mother feels she *has* to have the resources and competence that no one would be expected to have on a new job or in a new sport. Filled with shame, she rarely tells a friend how inept, depressed, or restless she feels.

Those unvoiced maternal feelings come out in the baby-loss dreams new mothers are so prone to: you forget to take him when you get off the train; you can't remember which room in the castle you left her in; you misplace her in the office building where you used to work. To some extent, these dreams express anxiety about losing one's precious new child. But dreams are wishes too. And some part of most new mothers would like to give the little howler back—and with it all those uncontrollable, frightening emotions. This is even more true for a woman who is alone all day with the baby after her husband has gotten into his car and accelerated back to his regular life—another reason it is so important for couples to be there together.

Even when women have help, they may feel the desperation. I saw one of the hardiest women I know burst into tears of self-loathing because her daughter had diaper rash. Incorrectly believing that she could have prevented it had she been a "good mother" and not gone back to work, she now had proof that she was a hopelessly bad one—for not seeing the rash, for having a baby nurse who could not cure it, and, most probably, for wanting to go back to work despite it, as she did the next day.

For some, the briefest postpartum confinement can make them feel as if "the walls are closing in," as one friend confided. The president of a small women's sportswear company, she was used to varied responsibilities and engaging adult company. But it wasn't only missing her work life that unnerved her. Looking back, she said, "I realize that I was so frightened all the time, I didn't know what I was doing. Every move I made with my child scared me." At work she was a supremely confident executive; with her first child she was a skittish novice. It is upsetting enough to believe that you are not having a transcendent mothering experience, but then to also feel a nauseating anxiety about caring for a child can subvert the mothering itself.

TRUTH IN MOTHERING: AMBIVALENCE

Ambivalence—not serenity—is the fundamental maternal experience. In *Mother Love/Mother Hate*, Rosika Parker postulates that this is true because "motherhood is governed by frustration." A parent must comfort a child who cannot be comforted and, to some extent, control a child who does not want to be controlled. Along with love, argues Parker, the mother experiences "anger, irritation, disapproval, antagonism, and a depletion of healthy narcissism."

Of course, maternal bliss certainly does exist. Most mothers, myself included, gush to anyone who will listen about the wondrous passion they feel. However, as Parker says, our culture makes women believe this bliss—or oneness—is a permanent state of being when, in fact, most women experience not oneness but "at-oneness." Not the mother-child unity that Leach describes, but an intermittent mutuality with their child. Whole days or whole summers may be filled with this mutuality; it can even dominate an entire developmental stage. With an infant, a mother often feels at-oneness when her nursing calms the baby. By the same token, a father like Patrick may feel at-one with his child when his cooing elicits a responsive cooing. But when a teething infant cries ceaselessly, few parents feel at-oneness.

The ideal of parental bliss has such currency that I remember being struck by a friend's report that he and his eight-year-old daughter had played hooky and had a "wonderful day." I was surprised that every day was not so wonderful and discovered from his ecstatic description that the mundane can take over a relationship with a child just as it can with lovers. Sometimes the chemistry is off or the distractions are too great.

I treasure my times with my six-year-old daughter when we just click. We may both be in the mood for giggly play, or, taking a walk, we may just spontaneously begin to talk of things with an emotional depth that takes my breath away. She and I like to recall those times, fondly describing how we sat on the front porch and watched a summer storm or hiked deep into the woods, as if recognizing our at-one times. We both strive to ensure that such times occur, but they are just that, special times, not the routine of life.

Once, when I hurt my back, she came with me to the orthopedist, held my hand when I got an injection of cortisone, and later, while I rested in bed, said, "Mommy, I feel sorry for you." She was just four; that was her first real expression of empathy, and I was immensely moved. However, a year later when I was in bed nursing a badly infected foot during her first week of kindergarten, she was angry because I could not take her to school. And though I tried to respond, I was mostly preoccupied with my pain. While my first injury had been an occasion of oneness, the second put us at odds.

When it is suppressed, maternal ambivalence does not only come out in dreams. It can also surface in a mother's fury at the child whose misbehaving is, in her mind, evidence of her maternal inadequacy. As Parker describes it, some of these guilty mothers react by trying to control the child into exemplary behavior in order to prove their own "good motherness." Others attempt impossible levels of *self*-control instead. For example, a mother who feels too afraid to leave her child for a day's outing may in fact be reassuring herself that she is not the bad mother who wishes to be separate. By denying her desire to leave, her unconscious reasoning goes, she will not have to "hate" the baby for preventing her from enjoying her independence.

When parents do not expect to feel endless love, they more fully enjoy the love they do feel. When they allow themselves to experience the negative times—the times when parent and child are just off—they can use those feelings to resolve real parent-child conflict. As Parker puts it, "It is in the very anguish of maternal ambivalence itself that a fruitfulness for mothers and children resides." If, for example, you recognize your frustration with an infant who cries ceaselessly, you can give yourself time away to calm down.

Diane Gottlieb vividly remembers an incident some twenty-four years ago in the midst of a blizzard, waiting for her husband to return from work to take over when her infant would not stop crying. Unable to bear it a minute longer, she left the baby alone in her crib while she went outside and stood in the snow. However, Gottlieb did not punish herself with guilt. As Parker advises women to do, she used her negative feelings to "allow her to distance, to affirm her boundaries and separate needs."

Gottlieb adds that we must disabuse ourselves of the assumption that frustration, anger, boredom, and disgust are alien to good mothers. "If we accept that we have multi-faceted relations to all things, we will know that ambivalence is a function of a healthy relationship. But in all charged areas of life, not just motherhood, we dichotomize into good and bad rather than accept our ambivalence." By acknowledging this ambivalence, she says, we can make healthier decisions in all aspects of life.

The first challenge of real (as opposed to ideal) mothering is to accept that having a baby is a part of life, with extravagant ups and downs. Like marriage, it is never a panacea. Babies can deepen your life, enrich your marriage, and engage your soul. But they cannot make an unhappy person happy, a neurotic person balanced, an empty person full, a bad marriage good. Mothers will not find a way to change their lives until they acknowledge these straightforward realities.

If mothering really were accepted as part of a larger life, and women planned carefully enough to continue developing the other vital parts of themselves, a new mother would be far less vulnerable to depression, isolation, and depletion. If a mother can hold on to the things that define her—acknowledging how hard it may be—and embrace this new experience as well, she has a much better chance of mothering contentedly. While practical issues of meshing motherhood with modern life loom large, the greatest challenges are still psychological.

Unlike the old image of motherhood, which overshadowed the real experience, a new image can prepare women for it. In part, this means accepting ambivalent feelings about motherhood; in part, it means accepting ourselves as complex individuals who have other lives as well. Louise Erdrich, Anne LaMott and Mary Kay Blakely all revel in motherhood, but their delight isn't forced or saccharine. If anything in my pre-mothering days could have convinced me of how gratifying mothering can be, it would have been these very books written by these complicated women. None of them stopped being everything else when they became mothers. In fact, they all record the other parts of their lives as lovingly as they depict their children: a friend dying of cancer, a book getting published, a winter in New Hampshire. All three are doing the hardest kind of mothering—two with infants and one with adolescents—while expanding their own sense of self by recording the experience.

For Angela and Matt, the next couple we'll meet, ambivalence has been a learning tool. Their honesty has made it possible for them to break the rules of traditional parenting, even as they thrive within one of America's more conservative church communities. Unlike Neil and Amsale or Maddy and Patrick, the Sopers had no model for how to sustain their previous lives after becoming parents, nor were they fully able to invent one. Perhaps as a result, their parenting isn't 50–50. But in that sense they are far more typical than the other families I portray. Indeed, their story may be all the more important because it shows that parents can reap the rewards of equality just by striving toward it, by holding to an ethic of fairness, and by accepting an unsentimental, honest attitude toward mothering.

MATT AND ANGELA SOPER

Matt and Angela Soper are not your typical minister and wife. Trim, muscled, and handsome—Matt with regulation blond hair and blue eyes, and Angela with a disarming Texas smile and long russet bangs that fan out with her animated talk—both could easily be among the personal trainers or aspiring actors who populate Los Angeles. Their life revolves around the Culver Palms Church of Christ and their two children—five-year-old Morgan and two-year-old Alexandra. But Matt doesn't work the seventy- to eighty-hour week they tell me most ministers do. Honest with the church elders who hired him, he told them that his family is his first ministry. He usually works forty-five hours a week.

Mornings they take turns: one presides over the children's routines while the other has time alone to jog or sleep. Then by 6:00 P.M., Matt is home again to parent with Angela. When Angela, who is a social worker and therapist, works—typically from one to two and a half days a week— Matt becomes the primary parent. Recently they have relieved some of their personal parenting duties by hiring a part-time baby-sitter.

I first met Matt in the children's section of our local bookstore when we both lived in Connecticut. Our then three-year-old daughters had struck up a conversation, and I, charmed by a man doing child care on a Monday afternoon, struck up one with him. Monday was *his* day on, he told me, as if it weren't unusual at all—though later, at the playground, he was the only dad among us moms. He handled Morgan with such enthusiasm and confidence, we were soon discussing toilet training techniques, then work, then life. Over the course of that summer we had enough play dates and dinners for both families to get to know one another. As different as we are—they, deeply religious southerners, my husband and I, secular New Yorkers—we found we had a great deal in common, not least of which was as passionate an involvement in our children as in our professional and personal lives.

How is it possible that, coming from such traditional backgrounds and living in such traditional circles, Matt and Angela are committed to an unconventional equality within their family? Well, as it turns out, even more traditional circles have begun to welcome and support couples who both work and parent. The Sopers' friends Dave and Debbie Casson even share a ministry at the First Presbyterian Church (U.S.A) in Chattanooga, Tennessee, each working half-time. But that's still rare. Most couples, like Matt and Angela, have to cut, paste, patch, and scrape in order to nurture two sets of professional goals and their children. Why is it so important to them? I ask at the beginning of our first interview.

Matt cradles Alexandra in the rocking chair since she is having no part of her planned bedtime. With the conviction of a preacher, he starts by stating unequivocally, "I always wanted to be an involved father and equal parent." The reason? He ruminates for less than a second and answers, "My mother."

Matt's mother raised him to be fair, he says, and that included being fair to a wife. His brother, a naval officer, also married a "strong woman" who works outside the home. His mother was one of the first woman dentists in Maryland, he says with filial admiration. After her four children were born, she continued to practice, if only a few days a week. However, although she was ahead of her time in her professional aspirations, Matt says, his father was very traditional. Like most men of his time, he didn't go out of his way to help her pursue her goals; she had to do it on her own. As Matt puts it, "She had an ideal she couldn't quite meet. When she reflects back, I think she would have liked to arrange her life differently."

Perhaps that's why supporting Angela's career is an absolute for Matt. "It's important to me that Angela has what she wants. That she is the most she can be." Somewhat shyly, he adds, "That's what love is."

Angela, like Matt, had created an untraditional definition of married love for herself before she ever met Matt. Angela's mother was a homemaker, and Angela loved it that way—her mother's singing in the kitchen, filling the house with the smell of her native Brazilian cooking. Angela even admits she was angry the whole year of high school that her mother worked. But she remarks that "my mother was very aware she was too dependent on my dad. I thought, 'I will never love like that!' Also, my mother pressed me to be independent, to have a career. The problem was, she never told me how to do it."

How, indeed? Both Matt and Angela had mothers who urged them to break out of traditional gender roles, both of them wanted to break out, and each had helped the other to earn higher degrees. But like most young people, they didn't think through to the implications of their desires. Nor did they understand the depth of our cultural assumptions about gender roles.

For example, neither of them questioned that Matt's career came first, Angela's second. As much as Matt wanted to parent, he and Angela both assumed that children are primarily a woman's responsibility. As professional as Angela was, she also headed straight for full-time motherhood.

"I assumed I would stay home full-time," Angela exclaims, "until I *had* kids. After six months at home I said, 'Forget it!' I *had* to go back. I needed the distance from Morgan."

As Matt and Angela so eloquently explain, the difference between the fantasy and the reality of babies is vast. "I had no idea it would be *that* disruptive," Matt says. And then there was Angela, who kept saying to him, somehow astonished, "My life is completely changed, and yours hasn't changed a bit." Still, they didn't question the arrangement.

Angela found motherhood grueling, despite the thrill of it: "I felt like there was this person who was literally and figuratively attached to me. She would forever be part of who I was. I couldn't just walk out to the gym anymore, or anywhere. It was as if I would never be alone again, ever, and I couldn't deal with the feeling of losing myself." Fortunately, her sister, a veteran mother, comforted her by saying, "Nobody will ever be able to tell you how overwhelming it will be. But it's going to get better. All mothers feel this way."

By the time Morgan was six weeks old, Angela recalls with the precision of someone given a reprieve, she slept through the night. Little did Angela know then that most parents must wait until their babies reach six months! Angela said, "Then I began to catch my breath a little bit. I also went back to work then."

But she was too ambivalent to keep working—probably, she thought, because as a social worker she saw a lot of people who weren't available to their kids. So she stopped working altogether when Morgan was a year old.

"It didn't go smoothly. I was so much less patient and so much more irritable. I knew I had to go back, and I worked two days a week. I was a much better parent when I began to work again. I could appreciate Morgan growing up. I was more tolerant of her developmental stages. With some distance, I just enjoyed her more."

Matt, who knew firsthand about baby care, understood Angela's decision. "Five days a week with a small child *is* really hard," he corroborates. "You can't get anything else done. I remember once having my textbooks open and clocking seven minutes of reading time in two hours. Children demand your attention. And the hardest thing is to be with them emotionally instead of just getting them busy and reading your own book. With a small child, there's no intellectual stimulation. Even sitting in the park is boring. Some of it is certainly laziness. It's very difficult to get into a child's world." On the other hand, Matt is also a great believer in spending time with children, not just quality time. "I had two whole days a week with Morgan when I had to do everything, plus taking my turn on my off days. I couldn't pawn her off." Hard as that was, he's not sorry. "Now I know her extremely well. We're very close."

Angela adds, "He's a much more confident father than many men I know. Nothing flusters him. And he's learned. For example, at first, when Morgan fell, he'd jiggle her instead of holding her tight. Now he's as good as most mothers when the kids are hurt."

Looking over at him, their daughter now asleep in his lap, I ask Matt, "Can men nurture?"

He takes a moment to ponder carefully, then says, "I think I nurture. I mother."

Angela smiles lovingly and in obvious accord, says, "There aren't a lot of Matt Sopers in the world."

"Does he get a lot of flack for being Matt Soper?" I ask.

"Everyone notices," Angela says, knowing exactly what I mean. Matt adds that he doesn't hide it. Often, during the coffee hour after the service, he's holding the baby. He makes a point of letting his congregation know he takes care of his children. He makes public his belief that a man serving his family is the essence of manhood.

Matt doesn't hesitate to counsel his parishioners that if a man can spend more time with his family by working at a less prestigious job— say, teaching high school rather than college—there's no shame in doing so, and there may be benefits. "People tend to think the demands on their time are temporary and opportunities to be with their children are permanent," he says, "but the opposite is the case." He also believes that family time is more important than piling up possessions. Although he doesn't tell people what to do, he does advise that if a family has to do without in order to have time together, then give it up—new furniture, clothes, travel, whatever.

In one sermon, as a way of calling attention to how hard parenting is, he exhorted men to admit that, "if given the choice between our worst day at work and our best day at home with the kids, we would choose the worst day at work." He also sets an example for the emotional and material sacrifice that he believes parenting requires.

"Angela and I have a comfortable life, but we haven't hesitated to simplify if that means more time with the kids," Matt says. Angela points out that they don't have a lot of furniture and decorations, which she loves. "On the other hand, we have the family we want. And we're very happy," she says.

Their happiness is apparent. Yet, I wonder out loud, is the sacrifice greater for women than for men?

Angela answers indirectly. "I don't for a minute feel I won't get the career I want. When the kids are in school, I'll practice therapy until three o'clock, then again one or two evenings a week when Matt's home to take care of them. I don't feel that a career conflicts with a woman's role. The Bible is clear about being a person of integrity, a loving person whose own gratification is not of the highest importance. But it doesn't say anything about a woman staying home."

When Matt goes to put Alexandra down in her crib and Angela and I are by ourselves, she continues. "Matt and I both want to get our Ph.D.s. He's really eager. But only one of us can pursue it at a time, and it's my turn now."

Matt overhears as he returns; he obviously accepts her decision as part of the fairness he believes in.

Weary now, the three of us are saying good-night and I ask my last question, going to the heart of the assumption they've used to structure their family life. "Why is a woman and not a man primarily responsible for raising the children? Why is it she who must limit her professional life to care for them?"

We talk for a minute about Angela having felt a "calling" to motherhood, but when I comment that she was raised to feel this way, she adds,

"I think a partnership is ideal. The children are richer for having two parents so involved. But how do you do that in real life?" Day care is apparently repellent to her; she thinks of it as an unsanitary situation in which children are treated like cattle. Yet now that they have a part-time baby-sitter they trust, she's warmed to the idea of child care.

As to *why* the children are more her responsibility than his, this gives them pause. They both think about it. Then Matt, who has studied similar questions deeply in his years of preparation for the ministry, rests his chin on his hand, stares straight ahead, and with his characteristic thoughtfulness says, "There are no hard and fast rules. It's true that women have a more powerful 'mothering' instinct, and historically raising the children has been their role. But I think the most important thing is that they both agree on a fair plan."

"Fair" and "plan" are the keys to the Sopers' successful shared family life, plus their acceptance that men and women can both nurture. Because Matt does real daily child care, he understands and supports Angela's need not to do it full-time. Because they admit their ambivalence about child care, they both continue to work and feel they are better parents for it. What is so interesting is that although their own parents could not show them how to create a new kind of marriage, both their mothers inspired them to do so.

Perspective and coparenting can mean all the difference when a woman or a man must temporarily stay home, even part-time, with the children. Alternating child-care responsibility is a far cry from asking a woman to postpone her career to raise her children. As another woman put it: "At this time in our lives, my husband is working outside the home while I stay at home with our son and daughter. He did his turn while completing his studies at night and will again." If both partners commit themselves to taking turns and placing equal importance on both their careers, then neither has to completely sacrifice personal goals for family life.

For Matt and Angela, postponing parenthood also had significant advantages. Of course, making a rational decision about when to have children is asking a great deal of lovers. So many unconscious drives affect so basic a desire: the wish to feel truly united with another, to please one's parents, to achieve adult status, or, simply, to be a parent. But wearing her therapist hat, Angela explains that, "if parents are immature, anything the children do is a reflection of them. Parenting is more about what the child does for the parent. Younger parents tend to care more about what 'I' do, what 'I' feel, not what the child feels. I was a lot more mature after I got my master's degree and had a career. At age thirty, I knew my child wasn't going to meet my needs. The most she says is, 'I love you,' and gives me a kiss."

For women especially, such maturity is insurance against losing one's self. According to Scott Coltrane's study, "Early-timed mothers were less autonomous than late-timed mothers, derived more of their identity from their mother role, and were less likely to recognize and talk about their own needs."

People assume that younger parents have more time and patience, but this is not necessarily true. I once had a conversation with Dr. Jerome Kagen, a prominent Harvard developmental psychologist, in which I expressed my concern that as an older mother I am less playful and have less physical energy than mothers in their twenties. He responded by saying that "young people spend enormous energy on finding themselves. They may have less energy than you imagine. Even less than you have." That, apparently, was an opinion he took to heart. I later learned that one of his children was four and the other twentysomething.

Clearly, early motherhood can work very well for some people. We all have heard of impressive women who developed themselves *by virtue* of having children early. Also, younger parents will be generationally closer to their children. Maddy was just twenty-six when she had her first child, and it was undoubtedly the right choice for her—but not by virtue of her desire alone. Maddy's career was set, and she is a self-described homebody with no yearning to try everything, or everyone.

Patrick wanted to be a young father. His own parents were nineteen and twenty when he was born, and he felt it was a great advantage to have parents who were generationally close. His friends with older parents wished they had had his luck. His father, however, was not terribly responsible; when he lost his job, he never bothered to find another, frittering away his talents in play. So warned, Patrick is vigilant about being responsible to his family and his career.

Their situation, however, is fortuitous. Both Maddy and Patrick were professionally successful at an early age, secure, and surrounded by helpful family. It is worth noting, too, that at thirty-plus, they are still both as energetic and as playful as they were five years earlier. So I'm not sure much would have been lost had they been forced by circumstances to wait.

Biologically speaking, the right time to have a child is probably in one's late teens, when fertility is highest and the body is most resilient. However, we don't live our biology. We have vaccinations, antibiotics, blood thinners, and Prozac. We also have contraception and fertility technology. The point is that the choice is really each individual woman's if we can escape the external pressures and inner compulsions to conform.

Thus, partners who value their equality can plan parenthood by timing children when both partners are ready to parent and when they have the best chance of maximizing their individual fulfillment. Once they have children, they will be better able to brace themselves for guilt and to use ambivalence as a tool for finding a comfortable parenting role.

CHAPTER 5

The Work-Mother Nexus

I used to think that having a child would feel like a vacuum sucking me out of the world, and I was not entirely wrong. When I was in college, there were few women professors, and none with children. Women were either in the world or home with children. In the seventies, as an instructor in English at Middlebury College in Vermont, I replaced a woman who had been dismissed by the department chairman because, as he explained to her, "If you have a child, you should teach at a junior college, not a four-year institution." This sounds hilarious now; no college administrator would say such a thing for fear of a sex discrimination suit.

Officially, children no longer relegate women to some less valued domestic sphere. Children and their mothers make appearances at political rallies, swearing-in ceremonies, restaurants, even college campuses. However, the department chairman's prejudice still lurks under the politically correct surface. No one tells a pregnant woman she must leave the job, but a supervisor will often quietly assign her to the mommy track. As documented in a study of women graduates of Harvard's medical, law, and business schools, mothers have to fight much harder for promotion and lucrative accounts—in short, the right to be considered a serious player. If she is to thrive, a mother will attribute an absence from work to the flu or a flat tire rather than a parent-teacher conference.

The authors of *Women and the Work/Family Dilemma: How Today's Professional Women Are Confronting the Maternal Wall* concluded that most professional women returning from maternity leave find their colleagues "blatantly hostile." Such workplace discrimination is a major legal problem. But just as important is the emotional issue—the debilitating fear that babies will pluck women from the world they previously inhabited, never allowing them to return.

Babies are not a distraction from the world. On the contrary, they pull you further in, grounding you more firmly than ever. Not only do their schooling and social lives bring the community closer, but they provide a fixed point in the fragmenting swirl of life. They are, after all, passionate and permanent attachments like no other. For most parents, children are, if not sacred beings, then a source of a kind of spiritual experience. Their magnetism is so powerful they draw us ineluctably, the way sexual longing draws a lover.

When I returned to part-time teaching at Sarah Lawrence College six weeks after my daughter was born, I remember having to restrain myself from running to the parking lot, screeching onto the highway, and speeding home. Once, when I was late, I arrived nearly hysterical with worry that I had passed some absolute point of emotional safety for my infant— that in divine retribution for my absence, something awful might have happened. I was so upset that I snatched my daughter from my babysitter's arms and sank with her on the couch, holding my coat around us both. We both fell asleep in an instant: I, exhausted from anxiety, and she, I assume, from the shock of being in the arms of her hyperventilating, sweat-drenched mother.

A singer tells of having accepted an engagement when her son was three months old; the money was too good to pass up. But at rehearsal, with her husband and baby waiting in her dressing room, she began to sob "because I couldn't *see* him," she said. In the end, both the hysterical teacher (me) and the sobbing chanteuse (her) did their jobs—and the babies were no worse for the wear.

Much of a new mother's anxiety, explains Diane Gottlieb, is a fear of being unable to inhabit two worlds at once. Many people are afraid that if more than one important thing is going on, chaos will ensue. But as Gottlieb points out, parenting can actually teach adults to play several roles at once, such as being a parent, a dermatologist, a dressage champion, and a distance swimmer. (I'm describing my sister-in-law here.) It can encourage our multidimensionality.

Remarkable as it may seem, mothers do still perform in the workaday world despite the powerful magnetism of, and their prodigious concern for, their newborns. Since new mothers are often bleary and preoccupied, they may not do their best work at this time; on the other hand, perhaps because of the heightened excitement, determination, or sensation of power, some of them do. The Nobel Prize winner Toni Morrison wrote her highly acclaimed first novel *The Bluest Eye* after a full day's work and often with her infant in her arms. Once, when the baby spit up on her legal pad, she continued to compose sentences around the stain.

As if exchanging war stories, mothers tell each other about carrying on with their lives while they were vomiting all day from morning sickness or had milk dribbling from their breasts. My neighbor left for Siberia to buy oil rights with tears of maternal anguish streaming down her face. But just because she was crying didn't mean she would have preferred to stay home. With infants it *is* difficult to carry on, and no one should be forced to. But later, when children are a little older and their fragility is no longer such an issue, motherhood can be a terrific activator.

Another writer defused my initial fears of motherhood by telling me that she worked more efficiently after her child was born. There's no time to waste, she said, so you don't waste it. And it's not just writers and artists who find this to be true. After interviewing dozens of working mothers for *Everything a Working Mother Needs to Know*, the authors remarked that "virtually all the women said that they did not feel that they performed less effectively at their jobs. Yet, most of them also said that they reduced their hours at work."

Yes, there is certainly a desire to lose oneself in maternity, to drift on the cloud of cherubim, the sweet smells of baby flesh, waking and dozing with a baby's rhythms. The siren call is so strong that many mothers, in order to return to work, unconsciously deny hearing it. Nina, the literary agent with four children, was the editor-in-chief of a publishing company when she had her first baby. "I'd leave in the morning and work all day without a thought of her. But as soon as I left my office and pressed the elevator button to go downstairs, I'd sometimes burst into tears because I wanted to be home with her so badly. I couldn't let myself feel it during the day, so the feelings flooded me." It would be nice, indeed, for new mothers and fathers to nest with their newborns awhile. In more civilized countries like Sweden and Canada, which guarantee paid leave for all new parents, they do.

As agonizing as it can be for mothers laboring under the myth of motherhood to leave small children, it may in the end be emotionally harder to withdraw from their work in order to be at home with them. Admonishing mothers not to lose the opportunity for a multifaceted life, Gottlieb suggests that when a woman turns mothering into her sole focus, it may offer her the intensity of playing a violin sonata; however, without the rest of the life she has cultivated, she will rightly suspect that she is missing an orchestral richness that was once available to her.

As much as some women want to be home while their children are young, they may well find a purely domestic life unsatisfying. Quite simply, Gottlieb adds, not all of us like to hang out exclusively with small children; not all of us can comfortably shift to a child's rhythm or switch from a busy job to an environment offering no social recognition or companionship. In the fifties, when most women prepared to be house-wives, they thought their real lives began when they got married and had children. Today, when women spend their lives preparing to participate economically and socially, they should not be surprised if they simply don't feel like themselves when they drop out. On the other hand, if we did not pressure women to withdraw from their work lives to mother, they would not imagine that a child could fulfill their high expectations of self-gratification. They would be less likely to overparent by transferring to their child their own stifled wishes for achievement.

Some mothers do make child-rearing a satisfying vocation. But many of them amplify their motherwork with other work. They may bring work such as farming, weaving, or sculpting into their domestic sphere. They may more fully partake of an avocation like horseback riding or teaching Sunday school. They may actually earn money from selling their home-made jams and cakes, or they may do more than twenty hours a week of unpaid work, as the head of the PTA does in my daughter's school, sometimes rising at dawn to prepare. These are not stay-at-home mothers in the Donna Reed mold.

Some traditional stay-at-home mothers have such a large brood they are more like the director of their own day-care center. One mother of three I know became a nursery school teacher when her youngest started school. She had had three children in four years and, as she put it, she was already doing the job. Nor was it a coincidence that she had "a bunch" of children; she is truly gifted in child care, which she loves. In fact, so many women come to her for advice that she contemplated setting up a 900 "motherhelp" line.

Most women, though, find the walls closing in if they are with a baby constantly. The world "out there" begins to feel distant, irrelevant. Or they themselves feel distant and irrelevant, a feeling that communicates itself to the child. Like lovers who do everything together, mother and child can grow overly dependent, clingy, irritable. As Adrienne Rich wrote,

> Like so many women, I waited with impatience for the moment when their father would return from work, when for an hour or two at least the circle drawn around mother and children would grow looser, the intensity between us slacken, because there was another adult in the house.

Rich longed for "even a quarter-hour of selfishness, of peace, of detachment from my children," knowing, if she had it, she could love better.

The same psychological scene is acted out today, even among young women who can choose other ways to mother. One acquaintance, a trendy Generation X mother with a nose ring and leotards revealing the contours of her second pregnancy, dropped to the floor when her three-year-old daughter ordered her to pick up her toy. She paused, holding her head. "This is about where my self-esteem is," she whispered to me. "On the floor. I better take a class or something before I disappear entirely."

Instead of disappearing, some stay-at-home mothers turn the baby world into everything. I remember a colleague mentioning how surprised he was when, meeting the wife of his department chairman at a shop, she asked him to help her choose the color of tights for her toddler. The woman had been a historian, like my colleague, who in no way begrudged her the pleasure of selecting her children's clothes. What surprised him was her assumption that it was worth prolonged consideration—not to mention a friend's time.

The examples are purposely petty because tiny details of everyday life do preoccupy parents and consume—even distort—their judgment and self-regard. The details take mothers out of the world. The details involve them so intensely that the rest of their identity can become submerged.

The pediatrician-psychiatrist team Marilyn Heins and Anne M. Seiden, authors of the unfortunately neglected book *Child Care/Parent Care*, feel obliged to warn new mothers, "Don't get so involved that there is no 'you' left." Ironically, when children are a part of a woman's life rather than its center, they can strengthen a mother's connection to the world, focusing and motivating her. Like lovers, children illuminate the world.

Ideally, children bring a healthy perspective to life. When a woman I know lost her job, she was devastated, but, as she put it, "I'd kill myself if it weren't for Anna." Her daughter was a constant reminder that a job, no matter how coveted, isn't life or death, at least not for an educated, middle-class American who can reasonably expect to find another position. Another friend, whose husband left her for one of his high school students, had no money, two small children, and a part-time job an hour's commute away. When I offered my sympathy for the burden of motherhood that seemed to keep her from studying, dating, or living better, she responded, "My kids are my roots," as if I were a fool not to have known how they grounded her. And I was.

For my friend, and for many of the mothers interviewed in this book—including single mothers with no help or money—children provided a powerful inducement to enter or reenter the world. "I have to do well, for Anna," said the woman who lost her job. She was not motivated by the myth of the sacrificial mother, but rather by a desire to support her family and to be someone who could teach her daughter how to live in the world. Both these mothers—one a journalist now, the other a librarian—did better in the world than they previously imagined was possible.

As much as children deplete mothers, they give them energy and a clear sense of priorities. On becoming mothers, women do not automatically turn into muddle-brained bovines. As Jane Smiley writes in her essay "Can Mothers Think?": "Far from depriving me of thought, motherhood gave me new and startling things to think about and the motivation to do the hard work of thinking. For me, much of that thinking has been done through narrative fiction."

That post-maternal zest, to paraphrase Margaret Mead's famous description of "post-menopausal zest," needn't go into something as lofty as fiction writing. Take Eva Pina, a thirty-two-year-old Mexican American mother of five who earns $16,000 working full-time as a job counselor at a refugee center and $5,000 working two nights a week and twelve hours on weekends at a bakery. Her husband earns six dollars an hour making dishwashers. Is it just to provide for her children that she does all this? No, she says, "I want to improve myself."

Babies don't take you out of the world. Logistics do: getting dinner, keeping house, overseeing child care, buying equipment. To stay in the world, parents have to solve the practical problems. No one should ever blame the quagmire of motherhood on the baby. It's not the baby that causes it; it's the faulty parenting arrangement and the economic pressures.

MOTHER AS MANAGER

To say that management, not motherhood, is the problem sounds less fundamental, and therefore less difficult to change. But a mother's compulsion to manage her home and the lives of her children is so basic it feels inborn; it is so powerful that it can blind the most sensible and otherwise ambitious mothers. The novelist Mary Gordon, while admitting that her husband is tremendously helpful, says, "I'm the one that knows what everybody's shoe size is and who everybody's friends are and who you call to invite and what two kids you can't have in the same room at the same time and what would be a good thing to do with the children so that they don't sit around watching the VCR."

That *is* the problem. Like most mothers, Gordon cannot stop herself because running a household is the kind of mothering the culture has taught her—the kind her own mother probably did. No matter how Gordon may see it, her identification with the maternal ideal runs deep. Managing children and household is a reflex for most women, more automatic than adorning oneself.

While most couples try to share the parenting to some extent, the largest survey on the subject found that one-quarter of the tasks are performed *only* by mothers. The psychologist Diane Ehrensaft, author of a book on shared parenting, found that no matter how willing mothers and fathers were to divide the responsibilities, mothers inevitably took on the three major management functions: wardrobe manager, psychological counselor, and social director. The reason: a fundamentally different parenting orientation.

Applying the traditional gender categories of "being" versus "doing" to parenting, Ehrensaft concludes that "women *are* mothers, while men *do* mothering." She found that while men may willingly and caringly put in their parenting time, most think no more about it when they are off-duty. "Parenting," she says, "is a set of activities they are doing, defining a relationship in which they are involved, but which does not reside at the very core of their being."

This is certainly true of the *Wall Street Journal* columnist Hal Lancaster, who described parenting as "extraneous." But it is also true of all the deeply involved fathers portrayed in this book who lived with their children's mothers. None seemed to parent as intensely as their wives.

Men's mothering has clearer limits than women's, even among men who embrace the role. To some greater or lesser degree, it fits in the parenting section of their life. Women, on the other hand, feel as if they are on duty all the time because mothering is a "way of being" that permeates their lives. Because of this difference, men keep a greater distance from their children. As Ehrensaft documents, men simply do not let children intrude as much; they can tune them out, let them cry more, and separate without guilt, even when they are loving, hands-on parents.

My husband, also a writer, works at home with no difficulty. Kiddie mayhem outside his study door or beyond the periodical he is reading doesn't bother him. And while he is usually there to greet our daughter when her baby-sitter brings her home from school, she does not disrupt his day. On the other hand, I must plan to do all my work at an outside office because the moment I walk through the door, I am hers. If I have a telephone interview that can only be scheduled for after-hours, I am distracted and anxious to get back to her. Whoever is caring for her during this time generally has to take her out of the apartment. Otherwise, she will tiptoe in and whisper, "Excuse me, Mama," at which point I melt.

She doesn't do this to my husband. Why? Because he can ignore her while I cannot, and she knows it; because he perceives her as more self-sufficient while I find her needy. In short, because he is not afraid of being a "bad mother." As a result, although he loves her bountifully, he would buy more child care than I feel comfortable with, take more couple vacations—and for longer—and go to less trouble to organize her social life.

The specific kinds of management a woman controls, mundane as they may appear, reflect this difference between "being" and "doing" parenting. "Wardrobe manager" may sound superficial, as if women were just too fussy to delegate the responsibility. But most mothers resist strenuously, offering a story of their husband dressing a child in yesterday's stained T-shirt or putting the baby to bed in her street clothes. Few can simply say, So what? Soiled clothes do no harm. Pajamas aren't as important as father and child spending time together, or the mother having more time to herself.

According to Ehrensaft, a woman wants to control what her children wear "because the child is both a reflection and extension of her." Judged by their children's appearances and identified with them, their efforts can reach compulsive proportions. A child's disarray might suggest to others that her mother is negligent—undevoted.

A former colleague of mine who is herself casual about her appearance was called into her daughter Emily's school to discuss another parent's concern that Emily, whose favorite leggings had holes in them, was neglected and therefore no doubt responsible for the latest epidemic of head lice. My colleague, a very loving mother, was understandably shaken by the accusation.

Seeking to avoid recrimination, the author Mary Kay Blakely recalls that once during a Michigan winter,

> with a pulmonary tube wheezing between my ribs, I had walked three miles back and forth to town after the Dodge had broken down to get two new shirts for the boys' school pictures the next day. My behavior was completely crazy and dangerously self destructive, but the self I once was had been so obliterated . . . it was hardly recognizable.

Is this what we want? Any reasonable woman would answer that a child's clothing is not important enough to make us ill with anxiety. But women cannot easily give up the management role. In addition to not feeling entitled to do so, a mother's self-image is too bound up with her child's image. The result is that she suffers when her child does not seem to her to reflect her, or her good mothering.

This identification explains why a mother may be unable to let her husband dress their child, no matter how much sense it makes. It also explains why many women unwittingly relegate their husbands to the role of assistant manager, the one who carries out her orders. In the process, they reduce a father's essential parenting role. As anyone who has cared for children knows, dressing them is an intimate and delicate part of parenting, as is feeding, bathing, and putting them to bed. A considerable proportion of parenting is in the mundane details that women are raised to manage.

Fortunately, many mothers, particularly employed mothers who want to share parenting, do eventually realize that such management is not an essential part of their identity. Nina, the agent, was about to take a five-mile run late one Saturday morning. "Go," her husband said. "I'm doing lunch."

But with her jogging clothes on and her four kids waving her off, she noticed her husband practically emptying the Hellman's jar into the bowl of tuna fish. "That's too much," she told him. He tartly asked if she wanted to run or fix lunch. In a second she was out the door and jogging down the road, assuring herself that no child ever died from an overdose of mayonnaise. By the time she was two miles out, she was sufficiently exhilarated by her run to recognize that his lunch versus hers didn't matter at all.

Tuna fish manager is what sacred motherhood all too often comes to. Yet we cannot make ourselves stop even when we must, as reasonable people, believe that men can figure out their children's shoe sizes and make it their business to recognize their children's friends. What often upsets women is that their husbands won't do any of these things in the way they themselves do.

A mother may require new shoes when her child's old ones look shoddy; the father may wait until they are too tight. Yet if the mother feels the world finds her wanting as a good mother because her child has scuffed shoes, she may ache at the sight of them. Without thinking of the implications, she may spend a free lunch hour shopping for shoes, then cheerfully announce to her husband, "I know you were going to do it, but I saw these great boots in Teddy's size and. . . ." Having his judgment second-guessed and overridden, he is probably resentful. But also re-lieved to have one less task, he lets wardrobe management revert to his wife.

Management, whether it's about tuna fish, shoes, or how a child spends the afternoon, is never a superficial issue. A mother's investment in managing her children's daily lives is one of the most difficult aspects of traditional motherhood to change, roughly equivalent to the former So-viet Union converting to capitalism. It isn't that we do not want to change, it's that we do not know how to *be* different parents because we do not understand the psychological mechanisms that compel us to manage.

Jessica Benjamin explains that mothers are obsessed with manage-ment because this is how they reassure themselves they are good mothers. It is their report card. If they receive constant proof via the child's clean fingernails and balanced meals that they are good mothers, they can hold their underlying ambivalence about mothering at bay, an ambivalence they often cannot admit. Men do not have to make reparations for their ambivalence; they are allowed to feel it.

The obsession with management, she continues, can also compensate for the deeper feelings of inadequacy, of not being a good enough mother or, perhaps, more generally of being empty or even filled with badness. Feeling like a good mother is how women make themselves feel okay.

The problem, however, is not that women are fine, then have children and became anxious creatures. Like Amsale, Maddy, or Angela, if they were fine before they will not be so anxious about being good mothers. But women who have always had difficulty tolerating ambivalence or separation may now feel *acute* difficulty in relationship to a child who wants to be separate.

Some women never acknowledge how much they resented being "good girls" growing up and cannot as mothers admit how much they resent having to subordinate themselves to take care of a child, as they believe they must. Or they may be jealous of their children, who get to talk back and be separate as they themselves never did. When women have accepted the idea of femininity, they pay for it by micromanaging their children in order to have "perfect" children. That way, their own anxiety gets transformed into anxiety about their children's performance.

Obviously, giving up the management of our homes and children requires the deepest level of psychological change and the soberest sort of confrontation with inculcated female fears. The change is also so unprec-edented that it necessitates a genuine leap of faith. For somehow, in the end, we must try to "be" mothers less and "do" mothering more. Al-though this means that we must live with (instead of placating) the anxiety our mothering generates, anxiety can be a great learning tool. It forces us to differentiate fear from need. And with every small advance, we disentangle ourselves a bit more from the oppressive mothering im-peratives that dog us.

To the extent that we do less child management, we may also allow men the experience of "being" mothers, involving themselves more emo-tionally by virtue of attending to more of the details of a child's life. Until a parenting balance is achieved, mothers and fathers can benefit from switching roles on occasion, so that male identification with children grows stronger as female identification relaxes.

A recent parenting study corroborates the benefits of such role rever-sal. The developmental psychologist Robert Frank, himself a stay-at-home dad, found that fathers at home spend twice as much time nurtur-ing children as employed fathers while mothers do the same amount either way. "When a working mom gets home," he explains, "she dives right into the family's activities." She is "doing" parenting whether she works outside the home or not. As a practical matter, the more we reverse roles, the better the parenting balance.

Twenty years ago, the sociologist Nancy Chodorow argued that as long as women did the mothering, girls would learn the nurturing quali-ties necessary for mothering by identifying with them. By the same token, boys would avoid those very qualities or even dominate women to prove their masculinity. Only by sharing parenting, she wrote, could we break the cycle.

A lot of couples did try to share parenting during the seventies. But even during that culturally and economically supportive era, most could not. Shared parenting worked only when both partners had part-time work or could make their own hours, the way professors, therapists, or mom-and-pop shopkeepers can. Even then, women still played the cen-tral parenting role because everyone underestimated the strength of our psychological orientation.

You cannot just take two well-meaning people, give them a baby, and expect them to parent equally. It takes a particular psychological orientation, practical planning, and a lot of ingenuity. Nor can we just invite women to be freer mothers and expect a revolution in the domestic sphere. Changing the way we mother is just too freighted for that.

In the next portrait I introduce a man and a woman who achieved a work-family balance for both by reversing traditional roles. Jennifer works full-time and also mothers intimately; she may retain more authority about her child than similarly employed fathers simply because her mothering authority is unquestioned. She is also likely to do more when she is home, and Mike, like most men, feels less ambivalent than stay-at-home mothers about ensuring that he has time to cultivate himself personally and professionally.

JENNIFER PROST AND MIKE LASER

When Jennifer and Mike thought about having children, they assumed they would find day care and both continue with their careers. But six months after Helen's birth they settled on quite another plan: Mike would stay home with the baby after Jennifer returned to her job.

As unexpected as such role reversals are, they often turn out to be very successful adaptations to family life in these transitional times. Why? As the story of Jennifer and Mike illustrates, couples make such an arrangement because it truly suits their needs better than falling into predetermined roles. Also, role reversal creates two involved parents for the baby instead of one; that is rarely the case when Dad works and Mom doesn't. And finally, such an arrangement can succeed because a man's parenting, unlike a woman's, is rarely taken for granted. Underlying this recipe for family happiness, however, is the key ingredient: partners who are flexible enough to do what is best for them both, regardless of social pressures or their own preconceived ideas.

Mike's choice to be the primary parent is emblematic of such flexibility. For most of his adult life he never thought of himself as a nurturing person, nor did he want children. In graduate school he was influenced by a popular book among his peers at that time, *Epitaph of a Small Winner*, which convinced him that the world is too harsh a place to bring children into. It may well have seemed so to Mike. His own parents were miserable, as he put it, constantly arguing with one another. His father, haunted by the financial fears of a Depression childhood, worked two jobs. Between his duties at the post office and making rosaries—an unusual job for a Jewish man—he was rarely home and rarely happy.

Having observed his father's bleak dedication to work, Mike decided that he wanted neither a family nor "a real job." With a master's degree in writing from Johns Hopkins University, he worked on his novels while earning a living—most recently, writing grant proposals for a non-profit social service agency. However, since "hormones and happiness" changed his mind about having children, he has been able to find a preferable work niche. At age forty-one, he's publishing his first children's book, developing a freelance business out of his home—and raising his daughter.

Jennifer says simply, "I always knew I'd work. When I met Mike, he didn't make a fortune, but as my sister said to my worried parents, 'It doesn't matter. Jennifer has a good job.' " Indeed she does. At age thirty-five, Jennifer oversees the work of several others as the publicity director of Addison-Wesley Publishing company, the publisher of this book. When I met her at their Christmas party, we began to talk of mothering, work, and how she and her husband found their way to an unusual parenting arrangement. Their story, we both soon concluded, belonged in a book about breaking the sacred rules of mothering.

Becoming a parent turned out to be very different from Jennifer's fantasies of leisurely strolls in the park with a newborn. Helen's birth broke Jennifer's pubic bone; for the first month, she "was basically paralyzed from the waist down." In weekly shifts, Mike, her father, her mother, and her sister stayed with her and Helen during the days. Although she could nurse Helen, she was otherwise quite helpless and in pain.

"It was as if Mike had two new babies, not one," she says, looking at him empathically. "It was horrible. I had this perfect baby, and I was a wreck. What had happened to me was so unusual medically, the doctors didn't know if I would be okay. I was eventually, but even after three months I still had to use a cane."

Jennifer explains this with an equanimity that characterizes her. She speaks matter-of-factly, without self-pity or a trace of the misery I imagine I would feel recalling such an ordeal. Neither she nor Mike exaggerate or embellish. For accuracy's sake, they confer on dates, time, degrees of difficulty. It *was* difficult, Mike concurs, adding that they had just moved from their small studio apartment in Manhattan to Montclair, New Jersey, where they knew only one other couple. At the same time they were renovating their new home—and the baby had colic.

With a smiling shrug, Mike remembers that it was just as they had always heard. "I'd come home from work, and there was Jennifer with her hair standing on end, frazzled because the baby had been crying since 2:00 P.M."

It's hard to picture. Their home is the calm, spacious place they sought when they moved—a solid, sun-lit old house on the pleasantly humbler end of a street of stately, sometimes columned mansions. A cheerful neighbor minds Helen along with her own toddler upstairs while we talk in the living room below. Jennifer and Mike look relaxed in their rocking chairs, almost too gentle to have weathered such a crisis and designed a mutually acceptable parenting life: Jennifer with long, feathery, butterscotch-colored hair, freckly skin, and willowy body; Mike with soft brown curls, wire-rim glasses, easy smile, and slender frame. Yet it takes no time at all to see they are both very firm, self-aware people.

Even before Helen was born, they had planned for Mike to take three months off to care for her after Jennifer's maternity leave. That way Helen would have six months of full-time parent care before day care. But again, things didn't go as planned. When Mike took over at the three-month mark, he found himself on constant overload: taking care of Helen (who, though no longer colicky, was a fussy baby), fixing up the house, and overseeing contractors.

"Each morning when I woke and knew I'd be alone with the baby, I was terrified. Although I'd been around, I hadn't been in charge." He clung to "the list" Jennifer left for him. However, "at the end of my three-month shift, I *wanted* to stay home with her. I had adapted to it."

While heartfelt, the decision was not impulsive. Mike explains: "It was always in the back of my mind that I might stay home with a baby because I was a writer. I figured I could write grant proposals freelance and still have time to squeeze in my fiction writing, just as I had always done." This time things turned out exactly as planned.

The decision was good for both Jennifer's and Mike's careers and suited both their personalities. From the beginning of their relationship, the two had been comfortable with her ambitious career goals and higher earnings. Although her own mother was a contented traditional house-wife, both her parents expected Jennifer, the younger of two daughters, to have a career—maybe even become a dentist like her father. She too assumed it, having excelled in school, come of age with feminism, and attended a prestigious college with other career-minded women. Yet after Helen was born, Jennifer and Mike both found themselves loath to leave her with "strangers."

What might have become a work-family conflict for Jennifer instead became a sensible solution. "With Mike at home, I rarely feel guilty about leaving Helen, and I don't arrive late for work feeling jangled and rushed." At the same time, unlike many full-time working men with stay-at-home wives, Jennifer doesn't feel left out of a parent-child duo.

As soon as she gets home, it's the changing of the guard. "I come in and take over. In the mornings it's me who gets up with her and dresses her." And Helen must feel just as confident as Jennifer because, as Mike describes it, "Helen's thrilled to see Jennifer when she gets home, but she's rarely upset when she leaves."

Helen's acceptance of her mother's time away at work is obvious the minute I walk through their door. Perhaps having been told that my arrival had something to do with Mommy's work, or somehow sensing the connection, the toddler Helen brightens with understanding and says, "Mommy Choo-choo!" With her mother's butterscotch coloring and her father's wonderful curls, Helen is very much a combination of the two. "She knows I go to work on the train," explains Jennifer, flushed with pride at her daughter's obvious intelligence. Equally pleased, Mike adds, "She loves trains, just going to see them whether we're picking up Jennifer or not."

You cannot tell from watching who is the primary parent. When Helen cries, Jennifer and Mike each cock an ear, offer interpretations, and decide together who should run up to check. (*She* was concerned, there-fore *she* went.)

How, I ask Mike, did you learn to parent growing up with an unhappy father who was rarely there? From his mother, comes the instant answer. "The way I am with Helen—affectionate and loving—is the way my mother was with me." Parenting, not fathering, then, is what Mike practices since, as he says, "I don't know exactly what fathering means beyond disciplining, teaching, and taking the kid fishing." Still, being a man, he worries that perhaps he's not giving Helen what a mother would give her. He "lets her be" more than a woman might, he tells me. Or, as Jennifer thinks, perhaps he doesn't notice her changing needs as quickly. But Jennifer and Mike both agree that he is far better suited to staying home with Helen than Jennifer, who would have been restless. "It's not so easy to stay home with a baby," Mike cautions. "You have to overcome the isolation and have the discipline to make order of your day so you're not completely at sea; and you have to be able to transcend the association of staying at home to do child care with professional failure."

Mike can do all that because he has often stayed home to write. And, as he says, he's having as much success now as he ever did. With a baby-sitter fifteen hours a week, he gets as much writing time as before, though Jennifer points out admiringly that Mike has such strong discipline and motivation, in a pinch he's willing to write at 2:00 A.M. "Being with Helen complements my work," Mike comments. "I feel much more positive and enjoy my time with her."

Mike also seems to have the advantage of male confidence. He parents in a way that's comfortable for him, not according to some maternal ideal. For example, while most of the other "mothers" he knows take their toddlers to organized classes, Mike doesn't. He doesn't think Helen enjoys them, and he knows he doesn't. As much as he'd like to meet other fathers who do primary care, he doesn't seek out the various support groups available. "I'm not a joiner," he says, adding firmly, "I don't need support."

Ironically, the one play group Mike and Helen do attend grew out of a group called FEMALE (Formerly Employed Mothers At Loose Ends, or At the Leading Edge, depending on who you're talking to, says Mike). I can't help but think that Mike may be one of the few parents there who *isn't* at loose ends. He does, however, share some of the stay-at-home mothers' problems. On their first vacation alone after Helen was born, Mike, not Jennifer, was guilty and preoccupied with the baby. For unlike Jennifer, he had never spent a week, or even a few days, away from her.

When I ask Mike whether being a primary parent has changed him, he says with a laugh, "I don't know. I haven't had time to reflect."

As for Jennifer, she concludes the interview by saying, "I feel so lucky. I don't know how two full-time working people do it."

From Mike and Jennifer's unusual role reversal, we can see how important it is to customize a parenting arrangement to fit the partners' real lives and proclivities. With conscious planning and honesty about their needs, Mike and Jennifer avoided what, for them, might have been a disastrous adoption of traditional roles. Had Jennifer been the one to stay home, she remarks, she would have withdrawn socially. With her people-oriented job, she is forced out of herself and away from her tendency toward isolation. They both agree that Mike, though not a joiner, is the more social of the two. Had Mike been a traditional father, he might well have had to struggle to shoulder the entire financial responsibility for the household. And that may have put him too close for comfort to his father's bleak two-job life.

The parenting that Mike and Jennifer designed works for all three family members. Disproving Leach's central mother rule, Helen is well adjusted and deeply attached to both parents. But both, we should note, give her intimate, primary care. Jennifer is in no way like the traditional father who just plays with the children. When she is home, she parents, doing whatever is needed. Thus, Jennifer's relinquishment of child-care management has gained for her daughter two deep parental connections instead of one and has allowed Mike to become a competent, contented parent. Jennifer has also learned to respect Mike's unique style of "letting Helen be" more than she would have otherwise. Having overcome his "terror" of taking care of an infant, Mike is also proof that with sufficient commitment, fathers do adapt to child care.

Naturally, adopting nontraditional patterns creates some conflict. Although Jennifer and Mike had no trouble reversing their roles, many mothers find it painful to relinquish any degree of management of their children, particularly of newborns. Many men cannot easily work through the "terror" Mike described. However, as Diane Gottlieb reflects, the conflict and possible estrangement that ensue will be short-lived if there is a real bond between the partners. Far better to risk it at the beginning of a parenting life than to fall into patterns that violate the spirit of each partner, and of the marriage.

CHAPTER 6

The Critical Mother, the Absent Father Within

As the previous chapter suggests, both women and men have to overcome the limitations of gender training to modernize mothering. Reared so differently—to value certain qualities and not others, to fear some deficiencies over others—most men and women develop only half of their capacities. And that half is usually given disproportionate importance in our lives.

Shaped by the American ideal of femininity, women tend toward dependency and submission, finding it difficult to create boundaries and assert their own desires. In her 1981 best-seller *The Cinderella Complex: Women's Hidden Fear of Independence*, Colette Dowling struck a nerve by describing the female "wish for a full-time emotional protector, a buffer between me and the world." The revelation here was that dependency did not disappear once feminists repudiated it; it went underground, beneath the more equal surface of things. Over time it has crept back to the surface. Indeed, it has even become fashionable for women to choose dependency by repudiating ambition and gainful employment once they have children.

The danger of this choice is that dependence on a husband rarely remains solely financial. Eventually it weakens the active self, fostering a further confusion of boundaries by moving the center of identity from oneself to another, from her to him. His work and its stresses, his success, and his daily contacts are the important news. His paycheck is now crucial, giving him a new power within the home. Her desires and concerns generally take second place.

Men, many by their own description, are insufficiently dependent. Constantly guarding their rather distant borders of self, they become emotionally disconnected, often enduring the consequent loneliness for a lifetime. This disconnection, explains the family therapist Charles Gottlieb, also evolves through a man's adherence to universal codes of mastery and fairness—"the rules of the game." Instead of educating men to respond to internal emotional cues, we teach them the culture's idea of fair play, how it's done, the way things work. For many men, their own feelings do not count. Often they do not even know what they feel.

If men can be said to have an equivalent male "complex," it might be called the Odysseus Complex. Although Odysseus was ostensibly trying to return home after the Trojan war, for ten years he was actually pursuing one thrilling adventure after another, often among enchanting (and decidedly unwifely) women. In this respect, Odysseus represents the male flight from domesticity and intimacy in quest of independence. The "Iron John" phenomenon, celebrating men's retreat from the purportedly feminine sphere in order to feel their true masculinity is certainly a part of this tradition.

Given what our maleness or femaleness signifies in this culture, we have to expect to feel a subtle but tidal pull back to traditional masculine and feminine roles when we become parents. At this time of emotional upheaval, the accepted roles soothe anxiety. Not only do they suit our ingrained, if unconscious, tendencies, they satisfy ideals we may not even realize we hold. By their very prescriptive nature, set gender roles provide an easy way to forestall criticism from others about how we parent, not to mention harsh judgment from our ever-critical selves.

Having a child is such an overwhelming emotional experience that we retreat to the safest, most conservative version of ourselves, and to the kind of parenting most of us have known all our lives. Meredith Vieira "thought her mother had been too available, tending to her every need and living out her ambitions vicariously." Unhappy in her maternal role, her mother always told Meredith to be self-sufficient. Nonetheless, Meredith followed her mother's model, not her advice. That's how strongly we are pulled toward the familiar when a child arrives.

Caring for a new baby is a breathless whirlwind, leaving no time for reassessment of self. Yet it requires a profound shift in identity from son or daughter to father or mother, a shift that quite suddenly pulls you back into the depths of the psyche. In fact, a major source of parenting anxiety derives from the revisiting of our own childhoods, and therefore our most painful unresolved issues. We saw this in the case of the mother who quelled her ambivalence toward parenting by taking on the totally devoted mother role. She could not allow herself to experience maternal resentment lest it recall her childhood resentment of having to be a "good girl."

Women are even more vulnerable than men when they become parents because motherhood is the touchstone of female identity. Yet their assigned role is also in conflict with their desire for a professional identity. As Rosika Parker explains, "Long-buried fears, desire, resentment in relation to competing with her mother may be reactivated by her own motherhood. Her sense of identity and autonomy may have developed in determined opposition to the [mother] with whom she now feels drawn inexorably into identification."

This unexpected identification with one's mother, along with the often painful childhood memories that surface in motherhood, create fears that are frequently displaced into guilt about work. Pamela Sicher, a child and adolescent psychiatrist, explains that since having a baby vaults a woman back into her own childhood, she confronts all her residual emotions about how she herself was mothered. If, like Maddy, a woman was well nurtured, particularly by a working mother, she may be unconflicted about continuing her own work. But this is a transitional generation. While work is now an integral part of female identity, many women had frustrated stay-at-home mothers or "careerist" mothers who had little time for family. Insufficiently nurtured themselves, they may reduce or renounce the role of work in their lives, mistakenly believing that keeping a job means depriving their children the way their own mothers deprived them. Other mothers assume the "cold careerist" role, withdrawing emotionally from children they "turn over" to a caregiver in order to avoid feeling the painful memories and the guilt.

However, it is not work that deprives children or alienates them from their mothers, says Sicher, herself an employed mother. It is a mother's avoidance of the painful childhood memories that mothering evokes, and her wish to avoid confronting the resentments and longings that may surface at this time. She may also fear that she will fail as a mother, the way her own mother did. Whether she fears the separateness that working entails or the intimacy and responsibility that authentic parenting requires, she is still reacting to the pain of her own childhood deprivation and thus diluting her capacity to respond to her child.

To illustrate how the anguish of one's own childhood gets displaced into guilt about work, Sicher recounts a mothering scene typical of this pattern. A woman she calls Elena felt so terrible when her work prevented her from taking her daughter to summer camp that she broke into sobs of shame, "confessing" to her daughter that she felt as if she'd never "been there" for her. The daughter, feeling compelled to calm her mother, told her that she would be glad to have her older sister take her to camp, so there was no problem at all. While the daughter may actually have been comfortable with her solution, ultimately she was forced to soothe her mother's guilt at the expense of her own feelings.

Elena unintentionally put her daughter in a caretaking role toward her that was all too familiar. Her own mother's chronic "neurasthenia," resulting in several hospitalizations, had made her "too delicate" to bear any anger. Thus, all three generations reflected a difficulty in expressing or responding to anger.

Like Elena, her mother was essentially concerned with her own feelings, not her child's. As a result, whenever Elena feared she was not doing enough for her daughter—as in the summer camp incident—she was overwhelmed with guilt for being like her own inadequate mother. At the same time, though, she was remembering her unacknowledged rage at her mother and imagining that her daughter felt the same rage about her. So she cried for forgiveness in order to neutralize it. Then, to compensate for the feeling of "never giving enough," Elena overdid her parenting by offering her child too many choices, indulging her daughter because she could not bear her feeling of need without personalizing it. That is, Elena had to prevent her daughter's needs or gratify them so as not to feel her *own* childhood deprivation.

Sicher further explains that when a mother "apologizes" for working by making it up in overindulgence, the child experiences the mother's guilt, not the mother's love. When a mother expresses her sorrow that she has to work, Sicher continues, she is looking to the child for forgiveness, thus putting the child in the parent role. When a woman feels good about work and also gives her children a sense of security, the children are able to bear the occasional disappointments that her working creates.

Many women do feel good about working. But so many feel guilt about it, Sicher theorizes, because they are not feeling like "good enough" mothers and therefore are not gratified by their role. Many women are also guilty because they find work more narcissistically gratifying than mothering, "which puts you right back into your child." It is ironic, she notes, that mothering, the site of a woman's own narcissistic wound and a primary means of healing that wound, fails to fulfill its promise. Mothering, it seems, is the opportunity to heal or to be hurt a second time.

Women's vulnerability to this second hurt in motherhood may be a result of historical circumstances. Sicher points out that many women today were raised by mothers who suffered a series of societal traumas: growing up in poverty during the Depression, enduring losses during World War II and the Holocaust. These women, who mothered during the forties and fifties, were often too wounded emotionally to mother effectively. As a result, they passed on their sense of inadequacy to their daughters, the way Elena's mother did to her.

Thinking over the dramatic childhood stories of many of my friends' parents, Sicher's theory strikes me as all too true. My own mother was raised in an impoverished immigrant family that lost its meager savings during the Depression. Her father coped with disappointment by going to the movies instead of work and by taking out his frustrations on his wife. Once, my mother remembers, he turned over the dinner table because her mother had forgotten the salt. Her mother, who was illiterate and never learned English, washed ballroom floors in return for leftover banquet food; six of her ten children died before adolescence. The four who lived quit school at fourteen to support the household; the sole son continued his studies at night. None of them parented comfortably, though they all dedicated themselves to the task. My mother bravely launched herself into her days from a base of depression, alleviated only by being busy. Yet with material security and a stable culture, all of them parented more successfully than their own parents had. Not surprisingly, their children have mostly fared better in life than they did.

Today most American women, at least those who are not members of a marginalized group, are not preoccupied by childhood pain the way Elena or my mother is. Though they may have some narcissistic traits, they are not usually traumatized by societal ills. Yet Sicher believes that as a culture we are still deeply affected by the economic, political, and societal miseries of the twentieth century. She finds it significant, for example, that like our own parents we are now "killing ourselves" to survive. As much as we think we are escaping the fate of our parents, we are willingly, if unknowingly, perpetuating a narcissistic wounding similar to the wounding that earlier generations could not help but inflict. Work, in other words, has become the vehicle through which we express our inherited suffering. It is the way the pain of our parents' lives echoes in our own. Women are driven, but conflicted; they want success in the larger world, and they also want the traditional motherhood their own mothers rejected. Most men are just driven.

THE ABSENT FATHER WITHIN

While men may be less emotionally vulnerable as parents, they still experience a parallel pull into gender roles. That pull does not usually create as much immediate conflict for them. Like women, they slide back into childhood memories; however, instead of identifying with their mothers, men often "disidentify" with them in order to reaffirm their independence.

As the Harvard psychotherapist and research psychologist Sam Osherson observes, fathering is hard for men precisely because of the demand for intimacy and the need to connect. The strong feelings of love that children evoke, he suggests, can be very disturbing: "Men are used to loving from a position of strength, yet children lead us into a new kind of vulnerability." Men distance themselves, Osherson tells us, to flee the intense feelings of family life, often experiencing them as claustrophobic.

The main difference is that men do not blame themselves for their ambivalence toward parenthood. In fact, they often find a certain degree of fellowship in acknowledging how much it all drives them crazy. At the very least, men generally assume their ambivalent feelings are normal. Often they have fathers who felt the same way, as well as wives who expect them to withdraw. The culture validates them, so they are less prone to parental self-doubts than women: they are, after all, playing by the rules. But, of course, men have their own kinds of self-doubt—about the part of themselves that only their wives know and validate.

Just as a woman may act out her childhood problems upon becoming a parent, so too may men. Jessica Benjamin explains that a man may wish for a stay-at-home wife because he cannot tolerate the anxiety of knowing that the person he desires isn't always available for him—an anxiety that is intensified by his wife's preoccupation with a new baby. By identifying with the baby, he is reassured that he will remain the center of her universe if she mothers full-time. That is, he may feel jealous of her attention to their child, even as he identifies with the child getting constant maternal attention.

Charles Gottlieb puts another spin on this particular paternal response: its ironic counterproductivity. When the mother stays home, she deepens her relationship with the child. Meanwhile, a father who spends his time at work increasingly feels lost in this new universe, like a distant moon that only occasionally comes into full view.

In full view, the new father feels exhilarated, says Gottlieb. But when he is far away, when his wife and child seem like a world unto themselves, he feels distant and competitive with the child. To some extent all men feel this when confronted with the biological symbiosis of mother and child. Explains Gottlieb: "When my daughter was nursing on one of my wife's breasts, I wanted to be on the other!"

But Gottlieb, who shared the parenting with his wife, had many ways to feel close to both his wife and daughter. The traditional father who turns the parenting over to his wife, seeing his children an hour or two a day, feels their loss every day of his life.

Gottlieb notes, too, that the man who must be center stage feels himself in jeopardy; he's always eyeing the hook ready to snatch him from the limelight. In his new—and unstable—universe of three, he may question his importance and competence in all spheres of his life. Before having a child, he most likely worked in order to make money and gratify himself. Now he feels he has to work that much harder, not only for money but to prove that he is still capable, worthy.

Of course, a man's most strongly *expressed* anxiety on becoming a parent is about "providing" for his family. Most men will take on full financial responsibility for the family without question when a baby is born, although they may have shared financial responsibilities with their partners until then. Suddenly they have to get serious, hunker down, and bring home more bacon than ever, with whatever personal deprivation that effort may entail. But this provider frenzy is also a pursuit of the love they think they lost.

One of Gottlieb's clients, Dennis K., who owned a small convenience store when his wife gave birth, began to act out his sense of displacement immediately. Before they had a child, he and his wife worked in the store together. With her at home, Dennis doubled his own hours, then opened another store. Feeling abandoned, his wife was constantly angry at him. For his part, every time he felt the distance between them, he distanced himself more: he drank heavily and had an affair, claiming that his girlfriend really cared about him while his wife no longer did.

In therapy Dennis finally expressed how much he wanted to be a part of her life with the baby. Hearing this, his wife began to reach out. Although their resolution was not the best, Gottlieb adds, they were able to move on by having a second child. With two, the couple bonded as parents, and the wife was able to distance herself a bit from the children. While Dennis had had difficulty relating to one child, he was more comfortable with the somewhat diminished intimacy of "the kids."

While we associate this anxiety-driven reversion to gender with traditionalists, it often happens to seemingly contemporary couples, even when the woman had been financially independent. Typically the new father spends most of his time working and commuting and is not a central part of his child's life. Meanwhile, the new mother cannot figure out what she is doing with her own life but feels compelled to play the traditional mother. This is exactly what Melanie Meyers, a young, suburban stay-at-home mother, expressed in a wellspring of words that flowed from her like an oral history of Everywoman. She describes exactly the kind of anxious motherhood that Sicher finds so common in these times.

MELANIE MEYERS*

" 'What am I doing here?' I ask myself. I lived in New York City all my life. For six years I was the marketing manager of a major men's sportswear line. To me, that was an accomplishment. Here I am in the suburbs talking to other mothers of small children, and I mention that fact. They look at me and go, 'Oh.' It means nothing to them. I go to Gymboree, and it's six nannies and me. I go to my son's music class, and the teacher tells me, 'There's a problem here. Jake isn't sitting in the circle.' I think, he's barely two! What, is she kidding? Get a life. But here *I* am in a big house with my son, or driving down these suburban roads being honked at by women trying to beat me out to a parking space and I think, 'Get a life, Mel.' I love my son, and I've loved the chance to spend so much time with him, but this isn't me."

We are sitting on the back deck of Melanie's home of three months overlooking the flowers her husband planted around the rocky rise that extends to the woods beyond. Jonathan's desire to re-create his own suburban childhood carried them here, despite Melanie's reluctance. "Look at this. I'm in a forest," she sighs.

She's perched in her chair with her bare feet against the rim so her knees reach her chest. Thirty-two, athletic, naturally lean, she looks, in her denim shorts and tank top, as if she's ready to cruise the campus. But the wild black curly hair that usually hangs seductively past her shoulders is pinned on top of her head, and she blows her swollen red nose between sentences. Still, I catch glimpses of the same atomic energy she has always had, the same joie de vivre.

We talk while her son, Jake, is occupied with the baby-sitter who works for her two days a week and for me on the other three days. Only because I am Melanie's cousin did she trust my child-care recommendation. Until recently, she took care of her son by herself. Only because I am her cousin—albeit second cousin and from a different generation—did she offer to tell me how "weird" suburban motherhood is for her. More than offer: I had barely mentioned what my book was about when her lament came pouring out.

Melanie opted for the American dream version of motherhood: she quit work and moved to a lovely home an hour north of the city with roads named Harmony Lane and Friendship Street. Her husband leaves before seven in the morning, returning home around 6:00 P.M. She and Jake are by themselves most of the day.

"In Manhattan, even as a full-time mother, I sort of felt that I had my life: I would take Jake to the stores, the restaurants, visit my friends. I still felt I was in the center of the world, like *New York* magazine was all around me. I felt the beat. Here, in this house, the beat's not around me. I'm trying to get the beat for myself. But instead of having people all around, I'm dealing with carpenter ants one morning and driving twenty miles to find Lumiline lights another. I try to keep running just to do things. Before naptime I take Jake to classes. After his nap I just take him to one of the towns around here and do errands."

Aware of the luxuriousness of her life, she hesitates to complain. At the same time she is as eloquent about the shortcomings of her life as any of the 1950s mothers that Betty Friedan described in *The Feminine Mystique.*

"All the time I keep asking myself, When am I going to be thrilled? The other mothers around here are thrilled just going to Stu Leonard's, the crazy food store with talking bananas, or double-coupon day at the supermarket, like I'm really going to think about that! The whole suburban thing weirds me out: the quiet, being alone in the house, the constant driving in cars, the exhaustion of motherhood."

Yet despite her palpable alienation from suburban stay-at-home motherhood, she is determined to make the best of it. As much as she preferred working, she denies herself the possibility of continuing to work. "I'm very hard on myself," she explains. "When I set a goal, I stick to it. I just have to get used to being in this part of my life." For this part of her life, however, her goal is an unnecessarily exhausting, solitary kind of motherhood.

"Motherhood," she says, "is the most draining experience I've ever had. I don't even look good. I remember feeling so 'hot,' dressing for the office, feeling so powerful. Even if I wasn't feeling great, I was making decisions, answering questions, in control. Every morning at seven-thirty I'd be at my desk ready to take over the world. With a baby, it's totally different. Work is a delight compared to motherhood. You don't want to deal, you shut your door or go to lunch. Working in men's sportswear at the height of the season's craziness, with deadlines, people screaming, was *never* like this. You never shut motherhood off—that baby monitor is always in my ear, even when I'm sleeping. Even my sleep belongs to the baby."

Melanie created her own rigid rules about motherhood, then adhered to them, no matter what. "For one thing, I was tired the whole six months I breast-fed. And because I never gave Jake a bottle, I felt chained down. But the second six months is even more demanding. You have to keep the baby busy, keep him learning, take him to the park. The older they get, the more you have to do for the child. I never even had a chance to exercise, which was always important to me. It's my own fault—I wouldn't have a sitter, and I had to fulfill my goal of breast-feeding him. I was determined to do it all myself."

Melanie and Jonathan have fallen into traditional roles without really knowing how it happened, at least on her part. Melanie explains, "When you stay home, I don't care what any woman says, you just fall into that role. It blindsides you."

She tells me that Jonathan says, "You're a great mother, but you are just not a wife," because she doesn't cook, shop, and make the house gorgeous. In her defense, she says, "I never cooked. I don't want to. We just picked up whatever we were going to eat or ordered in. Here, there is no place to pick up things, so Jonathan brings home sandwiches or Chinese food from the city."

As frustrated as Jonathan is with Melanie's refusal to be a "wife," she's frustrated with his refusal to do more child care: "Jonathan's a great father, but if he plays with Jake for a half-hour when he gets home, I hear, 'Mel, I need a break.' But I've been doing it all day. His attitude is a problem with me. He says, 'I work. I have to go to Manhattan for a living. I have to deal with people. You can stay home and look like shit. I have to be alive, alert.' "

True to the old roles, Jonathan feels he can "play" with the baby when he likes, then hand him back to Melanie when he's tired. She complains that he says he doesn't know what to do when Jake cries, even though, as Melanie sees it, she's "no more wondrous than Jonathan at figuring it out." Like many traditional mothers, Melanie feels Jonathan has no idea what it means to take care of a baby all day long. "It upsets me that I have to review my day to prove to Jonathan that I did something all day. He thinks I can nap or flip channels."

"Did you ever consider leaving Jake alone with Jonathan on a Saturday, so he would know what it means to take care of a baby all day?" I ask.

She shakes her head. "Jonathan's offered, but I'm so guilty all the time. Like this morning, when my cold was really bothering me, I left Jake alone in the crib crying for seven minutes when he didn't want to nap. I felt so bad I had to call Jonathan to confess. Even he wonders why I'm so hard on myself. He says I put these demands on myself, it's ridiculous. And it's true, but I can't help it."

In moments like those, Jonathan is still Melanie's best friend, her "reality check." But she doesn't feel as if they are partners anymore. He's head of the household, and she's "only" the mother. She says that he second-guesses her decisions about the baby, telling her, for example, that she should have taken him to the doctor. "I feel like I'm answering to the teacher when he comes home."

Because, as cousins, we both know her background, we guess at why she chose to mother in this traditional way. Melanie's own mother adored staying home and caring for her children. But as I scarcely have to point out to her, motherhood was her mother's life goal; she never went to college and had hardly worked. Melanie elaborates: "Nowadays, being in your twenties means dating, living on your own, working, independence, money." In her mother's generation, women never experienced that.

"I *had* that wonderful experience," she exclaims, but then immediately mentions that she didn't come from an intact or prosperous family. Her father died when she was ten, and her mother didn't remarry until she was in college. What she saw around her in the neighborhood where we both grew up was divorce and the struggle to make ends meet. In response, she and her friends wanted a lot of money. They wanted "the dream," as she calls it, quickly adding, "It's pretty disgusting that I was thinking that way."

Thinking that way cost Melanie. She made a series of choices that precluded combining her former life with motherhood. In fact, as she saw it, she had no choice. She worked twelve hours a day and her job paid only $42,000, although male colleagues with lesser positions in the same prestigious company earned more. Child care would have taken one-third of her salary, and she felt she would never see her child. Mostly she didn't want to return after maternity leave "because it was a dead-end job, and they were exploiting me."

Why, I ask, hadn't she insisted on a raise or discussed the company's obvious sex discrimination? Why hadn't she looked for another job where she would earn more for fewer hours?

"Yes," she reflects, "I could have found a position in marketing that would have been better. I heard of a fine women's department store that wanted me, but I wouldn't even talk to them because I made my decision. I knew how to juggle photo shoots, prepare catalogs, everything. I kept telling myself I'd have to start all over."

If she'd been a man, would she have thought that way? I ask. She knew exactly what I meant.

"I never really took myself seriously enough for that. I just kept thinking I'd meet a guy and that would be it. I never considered the consequences. I have a lot of regrets about not being directed enough. I was only thinking of my career with 60 percent of my energy."

Regret, however, doesn't automatically impel one toward change. As easy as it would be for Melanie to change her life— to sell the house she doesn't love and move back into the city, which she adores, even to work part-time or to start her own marketing business, to live a life about which she could say, "This *is* me"—she cannot do it. I ask, if you could wave a magic wand, what would your life look like? But she cannot even fantasize a different life.

"Isn't it sad," she concludes. "I'm like a cartoon character who's been hit over the head and I'm sitting there with the dizzy circles around me."

When I ask her how she sees the rest of her life, she says she doesn't know. Beyond wanting to get pregnant again in time for Jake to have a sibling exactly three years younger, she tells me that thinking about the future scares her because "I'm so out of touch with my past. I know these mothers who play tennis, maybe do a little work at a travel agency. They find that fulfilling. I wouldn't. But I'm so out of touch with where I was. Why would anyone want to hire me? I don't feel I have anything to offer. I try not to think about the future. It frightens me. I just *have* to accept where I am now."

Melanie's story is shocking. Her guilt is extreme, as is her self-sacrificing maternal devotion. But it's not as if she was fine before she had a child. Melanie was always compulsive. At work, she told me, she gave 100 percent. That's why she had to quit. She didn't know how to do two things at once.

Before having a child, however, her compulsivity interfered less with the rest of her life. Her mother, a housewife, was always strongly focused on Melanie. Her father was a salesman who was always anxious about money—"a nervous wreck," as the family called him. Melanie's husband is a salesman too, though a more successful and confident one.

While a psychologist could easily piece together the facts of Melanie's childhood to explain the nature of her guilt and her compulsion, Melanie is by no means a neurotic oddity. Her strengths are impressive: her competence in the world, her highly developed social skills, her humor, her warmth. Were I opening a new business, I would not hesitate to hire her. The truth is that Melanie is all too typical of women today, if more honest. As much as her personal past contributed to limiting her adult choices, so did her social past—and present. That is why she offers a cautionary tale about the parent traps facing all women.

AVOIDING THE PARENT TRAPS

If Melanie had not seen her choices as so extreme and incompatible, she might have felt less obliged to choose devoted motherhood over cold careerism. Had she been motivated to find a way of combining work and family, and encouraged by her husband, family, school, and culture to do so, she might have planned her life quite differently. Had the culture helped her to cultivate several skills at once, she might not have ended up focused on motherhood alone. If society did not marginalize and devalue women, Melanie might not feel so bad about herself that she so easily assumes she is a bad mother.

How different would Melanie's life be now if her self-worth had been reinforced? Long before marrying, she might have found a less pressured, more congenial position in her field. She might have insisted on buying a house closer to the city or even staying in the city. She might have involved her husband in child care from the beginning. She might have found other caregivers. However, such plans would have required Melanie to want to preserve her former self. But Melanie, like all women, is caught between worlds and identities. The strength to swim against the cultural tide cannot come entirely from her personal reserves. It must also come from a new social awareness.

If we are forewarned about the inclination to regress to this emotional safety zone, or to be catapulted into a profound identification with one's own mother, we are in a better position to grow with parenthood. If we think carefully about how our own parents taught us to parent, we can more consciously choose patterns of behavior that suit us, or at least recognize when we have simply become our parents. If women understand the reasons they feel anxious and guilty about work, they can use parenthood as a vehicle for growth, experiencing themselves as expanding on their inherited identities.

Parenthood can bolster the parts of the self that society and our families may not have supported—female independence and male nurturing. Psychological growth generally reinforces itself: the exhilaration of doing something that is right for you, as Amsale, Maddy, Angela, and Jennifer all demonstrate, staves off the unconscious fear of abandoning the mothering ideal. For men, the satisfaction in caring for a baby reinforces their inclination to nurture, helping them to overcome their fear of the feminine.

Of course, saying it and living it are quite different. Confrontations that result from shared parenting do not always feel straightforward or solvable. My husband, who did not have the strong nurturing figures in his past that Neil, Matt, Patrick, and Mike had, was deeply shaken by our colicky infant. On one occasion, when I had gone to take a sorely needed nap, he kicked on the bedroom door howling—louder than our daughter who had just spit up all over him—"I can't do this!"

I could see he was at his wits' end. Half-asleep and silent with anger, I took our daughter in my arms while he went to clean up. Somehow we got through the day. Over the next week his medical interest was engaged by reading the passages from the baby book on colic. He took our daughter to her next doctor's appointment, alone, and became the expert on how and when to use Mylacon drops.

Although I can't say how the change took place, we never had a comparable incident. One evening we talked about his own father, who spent months away looking for timber for his furniture business or seeking better climates in hay fever season—a pattern of flight he taught his sons. But my husband's sense of fairness has impelled him to keep fathering.

Also, he has the confidence to let me know when I use my maternal prerogative to automatically overrule him. When I lashed out because he put her to sleep without a diaper, he simply assured me that the room was warm enough, there was a towel underneath her, and that was the fastest way to cure diaper rash. But we bickered—constantly, it seemed sometimes—as he tried to come to terms with child care and I tried to take it over. Now, however, we rarely argue over child care, and we have the closeness we both valued so much before our daughter's birth.

In everyday terms, the greatest emotional challenge for women is to allow men to nurture children in their own manner, not simply as assistants to mothers. While relinquishing management takes more self-control than many women feel capable of, it pays off in unanticipated ways. One man interviewed by a sociologist makes this point in explaining why he is so much better a father to the child of his second marriage than of his first: "She [his wife] lets me have my time with just me and him. She gives me my space with him."

With infants, men must be allowed to feed and comfort in their own way, not encouraged to hand the baby back to the mother as soon as he cries. With older children, the issues are more complex and may truly reflect differences in male and female attitudes.

For example, my own mother-rule on television is none at all. Videos are a treat reserved for times when our daughter is ill or alone with the baby-sitter while we're out for the evening. In my view, vegging out in front of the tube dampens a child's imagination and self-reliance. And as in most households, my child-rearing beliefs generally prevailed at the beginning, even though my husband would have been happy to let her watch TV every morning and have a video every night. Once, though, after a difficult day with a bossy playmate had unhinged our daughter, my husband plugged in "Winnie the Pooh," then whiled away the late afternoon watching with her.

Once she was asleep we had it out. I argued that he was opening a Pandora's box offering her television when she was unhappy. He said, "Sure, she was escaping. What's wrong with escape when you feel bad? I do it. You and all your women friends want to *feel* everything, never miss one emotion. The worse you feel, the more you have to dwell on it. You all make yourselves crazy and end up hurt all the time. Well, I don't want her to be as vulnerable as you are. I don't want her to be a girl in that way. I'd rather she had more of a buffer."

I was stunned by the idea. The truth is, I didn't know he had a reason, no less a compelling one. I assumed he was just looking for the easiest way out of really parenting. And though I could still have ripped into my tirade on how men were as sensitive as oxen and their collective repressed feelings were responsible for hundreds of homicides at that very minute, I thought instead about the truth in what he said. My women friends and I *are* often mired in feelings. We are sensitive to every slight, to our own failures or insensitivities. We are often paralyzed by setbacks or altercations at work or with friends. We often talk among ourselves about developing thicker skins.

I do not believe that female dependence is only a matter of masculine versus feminine values. I have always valued women's ability to connect and to feel deeply, but I also know many women have too hard a time turning off feelings when it is appropriate. "She has no dimmer switch," explained Meredith Vieira's husband, a description that could apply to a lot of women.

Neither my husband nor I want our daughter to be as emotionally unaware and cut off as most men are. However, I do agree that women's present level of emotional sensitivity is a liability—and not just because we must conform to the dominant male mode. Teaching at Sarah Lawrence College, I found that the majority of my women students at this liberated, predominantly women's college still suffered terribly if criticized. They were far more reluctant to speak in class than the men and usually needed three times the encouragement to overcome obstacles in their work. After the video argument, I changed my mind. Though I want my daughter to value connectedness and be a sensitive human being, I don't want her to be as vulnerable as her predecessors, including her own mother.

It is terribly important to understand that much of women's vulnerability is due to our social position. Teachers favor boys; employers, mostly men, hire and promote men first and fire them last. Most of the people below the poverty line are women (and children), and most women still have "pink-collar" jobs that hardly pay for a middle-class life. One out of ten are victims of domestic violence, and nearly 500,000 are raped annually. So, yes, women have a lot to feel vulnerable about. And still, some of that vulnerability is psychologically generated.

Chodorow explains that because most women see their daughters as extensions of themselves and not as separate people, the daughters never experience themselves as separate either. My friend Jenny's husband used to joke that when their daughter Nora falls down, Jenny cries. Although he was describing empathy, he was also describing the way mothers overidentify with their children. By the same token, this kind of overidentification may lead a mother who is depressed to project that depression onto her daughter. And the daughter may introject the mother's state of mind, blaming herself for her inherited depression. If a mother is fright-ened of the world, she is likely to infuse her daughter (though not necessarily her son) with her fear. She may require that her daughter be a particular kind of person because she cannot see her as a separate indi-vidual.

Some of the new "psychologists of difference," as they are called, are critical of Chodorow, believing that she tows the Freudian line on the importance of the child separating from the mother. Jean Baker Miller argues that "the child can move on to a larger, but more articulated sense of herself *only because of* her actions and feelings in the relationship [with her parents]." Miller does not believe in a "separate" sense of self, but rather a "more complex sense of self in more complex relationships to other selves."

Like Miller, I do not want to substitute the male "separate" self for the female "connected" one. However, the psychologists of difference cer-tainly don't mean for women to suffer from overdependence. As one of Miller's coauthors notes, "In clinical practice we see many adult women who experience difficulty in delineating, articulating, and acting directly on their own needs and perceptions." This is the overidentification and dependence I am referring to, the very identity problems, I believe, that get in the way of a healthier kind of mothering.

However critical some of the now-fashionable psychologists are of Chodorow, much of the give-and-take amounts to academic quibbling. Chodorow set forth what is still the most revolutionary idea: if mothers continue to be the primary nurturers, they will create daughters who will do the same. Such mothers, says Chodorow, "are liable to overinvest in and overwhelm the relationship" with their children. They may fulfill their emotional needs with their children instead of finding their own fulfillment. Again and again in therapy, Diane Gottlieb hears women blame themselves if their children do not do well in school. They are often overwhelmed with shame, she says, for their children's failures. By the same token, a child's accomplishments can be so important that the mother pushes him too hard to achieve.

Mothers overinvest, overidentify, and overparent more than men be-cause motherhood is too often a woman's only province. In a sexist culture, it's harder for women to find fulfillment outside of mothering. Fewer women are rewarded for their talent or work. It is no accident that

Patrick, not Maddy, "got a break" first, or that Melanie was so brashly exploited by her company while her husband did so well at his. Few women have the confidence for political action, and until the rise of special female funding organizations like Emily's List, few had the backing. Then, too, women so rarely feel the freedom to invest themselves outside of their families.

So the vicious cycle continues: we create daughters who have difficulty articulating their own needs and perceptions. As the Harvard psychologist Carol Gilligan has shown, even if they are spunky kids, girls eventually censor themselves to fit their gender roles. By adolescence, they veer into selflessness and fear the criticism of peers.

If there's been one great change, it's that mothers identify more with their sons than they previously permitted themselves. Women now are less afraid of instilling "feminine" virtues in them. Also, the culture has eased up on men. They get enormous praise for fathering.

Dave Casson, the man who shares a ministry and child care with his wife Debbie in Chattanooga, Tennessee, says, "The public price for being a full-time father isn't big. When I'm the only dad in a place, like I was when I registered my daughter for kindergarten, it made me feel great, like the progressive person I want to be. My mother-in-law absolutely canonizes me." Mike Laser, who is the primary and at-home parent, does feel that child care for men is associated with professional failure; however, as he points out, he is respected for the parenting he does.

The result of this change is that while men still suffer the isolation of their independence, many are now comfortable nurturing and having close relationships. Nevertheless, the greatest stumbling block to equal parenting is the cultural assumption that, except for a few saints, men cannot nurture—and that they should not be required to. As we'll see in the next chapter, nothing could be further from the truth.

PARENTING TOGETHER

Women like Melanie never assume that men should nurture, though even she knows that she is no more "wondrous than Jonathan at figuring it out." She is far too respectful of a man's right to continue his pre-fathering life. At the same time she is so overwhelmed by guilt she cannot allow herself to be apart from the baby. If she had structured their parenting lives to better support joint parenting and her own ability to separate, she might have avoided the anguish.

Even women who have been home with a newborn while their husbands returned to work might try a break at the three-month mark. Diane Gottlieb talks of an institution that grew up among her friends: whenever a baby reached three months, the women would all go on an overnight with the new mother. Not only does an exhausted mother get a chance to sleep through the night, return to herself, and reconnect with her friends, but it helps her to separate from her child enough to allow her partner to deepen his connection. This outing is more cumbersome if a mother is breast-feeding, but hardly impossible. If it works well, it can become a monthly ritual.

Also, time by themselves helps to reestablish the new parents' own primary connection. If they do not want to spend a night away, they might do something that symbolizes their shared interest and equal partnership—playing tennis, taking a hike, or visiting some old friends who live a few hours away. Meanwhile, another person, a grandparent or godparent perhaps, will get invaluable alone time with the baby. These gestures help to forge a calmer attitude toward parenting than Melanie, in her isolation, was able to find. It helps to bring parents into closer communication about the baby, and about themselves.

However frightened a new mother is of abandoning her child, in the view of Marilyn Heins and Anne M. Seiden, authors of *Child Care/Parent Care*, "there is nothing wrong with leaving an infant for a few days, understanding developmentally when it is harder and easier for your child to tolerate your absences." In fact, it is much easier to leave a three- or six-month-old than it is to leave a three-year-old, who is struggling with issues of independence.

Diane Gottlieb also suggests that couples who find it hard to share parenting acknowledge the other, traditional parent they expected to be, perhaps even writing down his and her characteristics. She believes that for some women, giving up the person who would mother like her own mother did is a tremendous loss, one comparable to the loss of a dear friend. It should therefore be handled with respect, patience, and some appropriate recognition, perhaps a commemorative act such as burying a written description of that other parent within.

Whatever small steps they can take toward breaking the bonds of tradition, parents must recognize that they will be using new "muscles" that might hurt at first but soon grow stronger. Remember how Matt had to learn to hold his babies tight when they cried and had to overcome the boredom he felt? How Patrick came to terms with Maddy's organizing and found a way to feel his own importance to his children when they wanted Maddy? She nursed them, but they talked to him, vocalizing in direct response to his cooing—even as tiny infants. And consider how Mike overcame his terror of caring for his infant.

Fearful as she was, Melanie could not contemplate separating in order to return to work even part-time. However, when both parents do work, they can more easily adjust to the inevitably longer absences by knowing when to be there when the baby needs them most. That is, they can frame the night with their presence.

Night is when most creatures sense danger. Parents want to be there at night for their children, getting up when they cry, and making necessary appearances in between. If they frame a child's night, they need not feel so anxious about missing his days. Being available at these important times builds the intimacy children need; listening when *they* most want or need to communicate is preparation for the future, when communication is so much more complex, and often more difficult.

Mornings and evenings are equally important. Since most babies wake at dawn, parents will find it is a time when babies are most playful and alert. Most parents, unfortunately, are bleary. But if they prepare—the way a farmer does—by retiring early, they may well feel they have spent enough time with the baby to last the workday. An alternative is to trade off, one parent getting up with the baby while the other sleeps in. If a nursing mother has to get up to feed the baby, she can go back to sleep while the father takes over at six-thirty. If one parent is working outside, his morning time with a child is a way to balance the parenting—and reduce resentment.

Of course, spending time with a baby can be mystifying for some parents. While everyone tells you they'll be grown before you know it, one of the mixed blessings of babies is how they slow time to a turtle pace. You sing a song, you roll a ball, jiggle the baby up and down for what seems like an hour, and find that four minutes have passed. The day vanishes before you have had a chance to shower, but it has been composed of moments magnified to ten times their normal length. Some babies will happily study a mobile for a quarter of an hour; others won't. They want your attention—and are very effective in getting it.

Fathers especially find it difficult to spend time with an infant. But they are often quite creative in figuring out mutually interesting pastimes. Matt told me he used to take his small daughter to the hardware store, where they would both indulge their fascination in the aisles of tools. One restless father I know bundled his baby and headed for an all-night diner at six o'clock every morning. He did this so often that he and his son soon became regulars and made acquaintances who cooed at the baby while the father ate his pancakes. And no, the baby never froze to death.

Intimate evening time is equally important. If parents dedicate evenings to child care, they can build rituals that make a child feel secure and connected. Arriving home between five-thirty and six, parents have at least an hour with a small baby in which to bathe him, read a story, and tuck him in. The bath is an excellent way to signal that the day is over; it is also a place where small children are often at their most open and expressive. Even before they can use language, they communicate non-verbally and learn to rely on your being there when they are most relaxed. Having at least one parent home for the child's pre-bed rituals helps immensely to reestablish intimacy after the day's absence.

If we are going to cultivate our full potential, including men's stifled needs to connect and women's suppressed independence, we must identify our resistance to change as just that—resistance—even when it feels like fear of leaving a child or an incapacity to pursue other interests. Anticipating women's tendency toward maternal domination and men's tendency to paternal withdrawal, parents can move beyond these rote responses. If they do not, parenthood will blindside them, leaving them stunned and lumbering down paths that, for so many, have led nowhere.

CHAPTER 7

The Father Problem

At the annual meeting of the American Psychoanalytic Association in 1985 a colleague introduced the results of the Yale psychiatrist Kyle Pruett's study on nurturing fathers: "Well, gentlemen, Dr. Pruett's research has taken away a major male excuse for not being involved with our kids. We can no longer say to our wives, 'Look, it's better for the kids if you do it, dear.' " The six-year Yale study of families in which men were the primary parents had one particularly startling result: although all the men had expected to be traditional fathers, when economics or health put them in the primary parenting role, "all the fathers had formed the deep, reciprocal nurturing attachment so critical to the early development of a thriving human baby."

Not only did the children thrive, they had higher test scores and better social skills than mother-reared children. Pruett describes them as having "a comfortable dependency, flexibility, a zest for life, assertiveness, and a vigorous drive for mastery." In his eight-year follow-up study, he found that the children sustained these strengths. This was all the more remarkable, Pruett notes, because most men are reared to be ineffective nurturers.

These successes do not mean that men are better nurturers than women. To begin, all the couples involved apparently had the flexibility to accept a dramatic role reversal. That flexibility itself is generally associated with more harmonious households and less anxious child-rearing.

Also, because women are reared to want intimacy with their children, these mothers jumped right in when they got home from work, just as Jennifer did. As a result, the father-reared children have two nurturers instead of the one-and-a-quarter that most mother-reared children have. And clearly, a child who learns to respond to two kinds of intimacy and two parental styles is usually more flexible than those who learn only one.

However, as Pruett and other researchers have discovered, men also nurture differently than women. In one study of couples videotaped while bottle-feeding their infants, fathers burped, soothed, and fed as successfully as mothers—but more playfully and with less intensity. Other observers have noted that fathers speak more rapidly when their infants make sounds, while mothers are more likely to touch their infants. They also noted that infants do respond to their father's voice pattern, but they respond differently: they lift their brows and hunch their shoulders in what is perceived as an anticipatory way.

As different as men's interactions with babies are, though, their fundamental response to infants is the same as women's: their blood pressure rises when they hear their infant cry, and they adjust their speech and focus to them. Only later, when their skill has begun to develop unequally, will the mother—and not the father—be able to distinguish among the different kinds of crying.

Hence, while a nursing mother provides a special, incomparable bond for a newborn, fathers provide a different but integral bond as well. For if infants are given the opportunity, they "attune" to both parents more than to strangers. Jessica Benjamin believes that "play interaction can be as primary a source of feeling of oneness as nursing or being held." Remember Dierdre "talking" to Patrick, her vocalizations mimicking and responding in distinct harmony with her father, together creating an unmistakable music of love.

The Yale study suggested that primary fathers allow older children more freedom than primary mothers and praise their independence more. Ironically, a primary father may offer a special benefit to his children. Never having experienced the discomforts and "physiologic symbiosis" of pregnancy, a man is less conflicted about fostering his child's separate identity. I would add that most men have not experienced the psychological symbiosis with their mothers that is so common among women.

Because men have been taught to value independence, they betray no one by encouraging it in their children. And they instill it in daughters as well as sons. In fact, another advantage of primary fathering is that, more than mothers, fathers treat sons and daughters equally, probably because they are less closely identified with them.

SOCIAL RESISTANCE TO FATHERING

I do not argue that men should all become homemakers and couples should reverse roles. I do, however, believe we must recognize the enormous psychological resistance to the idea that fathers can nurture their children. When they must, they do. Even when fathers are initially more awkward with children, even when it takes a bit longer for intimacy to grow, the requisite intimacy does indeed grow soon enough. Necessity being the mother (or father) of invention, men do figure things out on their own. But because men lack the experience and confidence, infant care training can help. In fact, it can be a necessity for a new father who feels his baby is "a strange, foreign, or inanimate body on its arrival, random in its movements and unrelated to them"—"a thing," as one father told the psychologist John Munder Ross, "that ate and defecated a lot." It is not surprising that in Berry Brazelton's hospital nursery, where men are taught how to "read" infants, they respond far more to their babies than do untrained fathers.

In one of the recent studies on fathers, most of the fathers talked of having to learn how to nurture. All of them stressed the importance of doing it from day one. As one of the fathers said, "If you don't start at the beginning, you get left behind." The researcher concluded that "when fathers are involved in early infant care, they seem more responsive to cues from the child." Both their confidence and commitment increase. Charles Gottlieb adds that men need the early bonding that comes from participating in the birth and infant care to counter the physiological reality that babies grow in the wombs of women.

Unfortunately, this crucial shared participation in infant care is precisely what most parents forgo, on the assumption that only women can nurture infants and that someone—namely the father—must work to pay the bills. Surely, though, it is just as important for men to take parental leave when they become parents in order to create the parent bond that a mother's "natural" nurturing engenders. As difficult as taking joint parental leave may be, nurturing an infant together is a strategy worth every penny sacrificed and every vacation lost.

Most women undoubtedly do find nurturing easier because of their biological bond and the feminine values that have been inculcated in them. But that does not invalidate men's nurturing; in fact, male psychology and values make it more effective at this historical moment.

When men are flexible enough to do child care, and do it unresentfully, they are every bit the "mothers" that women are. But women as well as men are threatened by the idea. As a culture, we are sometimes even angered by the very suggestion that men can nurture—or be taught to nurture—children.

Penelope Leach writes of a mother's "hormone-driven vigilance," which the father does not have. His role, according to her, is to "facilitate the female's mothering and shield her." In Leach's view, equal parenting "distorts the parental roles and creates competition."

But where, apart from the opinions of the "experts," is this gender rule written? In the stars? In our genes? Nowhere except in our history. And it is specifically *our* history. Scott Coltrane, a sociologist of fatherhood, discusses how anthropologists have long acknowledged the immense variation among cultures in definitions of male and female, mother and father. The most bellicose, aggressive tribes differentiate the genders the most; more pacific ones, such as the Tahitians, have almost no differentiated roles. Women there are no "softer" or more "maternal" than men; both sexes can choose whatever activities they want—including competing to becoming chiefs. In another tribe exhibiting what Coltrane calls an "intimate and egalitarian pattern," mothers do more child care but fathers sleep with their infants, give them their first solid food, and have contact with them throughout the day.

Coltrane concludes from these cross-cultural studies that the more men are involved in child care, the less misogynist they are and the more political power women have.

As much evidence as there is for the personal and social benefits of shared parenting, mother as primary nurturer remains a cornerstone of our culture. Replacing that foundation, we fear, will topple the edifice. Fathers have so rarely done the nurturing that their attempts are either portrayed as heroic or summarily dismissed. For every support we give to men's nurturing—inviting them to attend Lamaze classes, putting changing tables in men's bathrooms—we also discredit their nurturing. I heard one father comment, for example, that when his daughter spent five weeks in a preemie incubator, the staff recorded his wife's visits as "mother in to bond" whereas his appearances were written off as "father visits." He noticed, too, that he, not his wife, became "guilty of the stereotypical vices of motherhood—neurotic worry about Hannah's mental and physical well-being . . . excessive emotional demands and general nudginess."

Sometimes personality alone dictates nurturing ability. But we often do not notice because we see what we expect to see: mother's devotion and father's reserve. Only when the father is doing far more than expected do we see him as a hero, as family and friends see Dave Casson, the minister from Tennessee. I would argue, though, that it is easier for men to take on the nurturing of children than for women to give up some of it.

PSYCHOLOGICAL RESISTANCE TO FATHERING

Although the culture may not support men's nurturing, it does not condemn it as doggedly as it does a woman's failure to follow the mothering rules. Men's resistance is largely internal rather than socially generated. It's not that men cannot nurture or that society won't permit it, but that most men simply will not. Most refuse to defy the cultural definition of masculinity, to overcome their fears, or to relinquish their male privilege.

Time magazine recently ran a cover story based on a survey showing that men want more time with their families; many said they would even give up their fast-track jobs to get it. But the survey also showed that most men do not follow through: "When they are not talking to pollsters, some fathers recognize the power of their atavistic impulses to earn bread and compete, both of which often leave them ambivalent about their obligations as fathers."

Pruett believes that most men "strangle their nurturing qualities" because they experience children as a trap. He adds that, "while men are more ready to nurture than they were previously, they still have deep anxiety about whether their nurturing will get them in trouble with women, both for competing with women in the nurturing sphere and for revealing the nurturing side of themselves that women may not like."

Charles Gottlieb adds that men dichotomize: they are afraid they will lose their closeness with their wives if they get close to their child, as if the total amount of love were a fixed quantity.

The psychoanalyst Sam Osherson theorizes that fatherhood threatens the very structure of male psychology. Because children blur the boundaries of self, men, who guard their boundaries so vigilantly, feel claustrophobic with them. The claustrophobia expresses their sense of the children being too close. Also, children don't automatically respond; they must be wooed. And many men are too afraid to let themselves feel enough need for a response to do the necessary wooing. However, they don't necessarily experience this emotion as fear. Instead, they feel "bored" or "dead-ended" when they are taking care of their infant because the deeper emotions, like fear of how much they need the infant's response to them or sadness for not having been intimately nurtured themselves, threaten their basic orientation. Avoiding such painful feelings is all they know to do; experiencing them, especially with a newborn, may feel "too feminine."

Children put men in touch with longings they have often carefully suppressed—longings not only to nurture but "to be charmed by children, to be passive, sexy, sensuous, feminine," explains the psychologist John Munder Ross. In his book *What Men Want,* he shows how boys under the age of six express their desire to be mothers. Even in middle childhood, he says, many boys "enact and express an avid interest in caretaking," either directly or indirectly in growing plants or tending pets. If they have a nurturing father, they eventually "want to be neither mothers nor 'just men' but quite specifically, fathers." If they do not, they are more likely to suppress their nurturing desires.

On becoming fathers, men experience those often long-hidden desires very strongly; however, they also fear that if they "do what [women] do, they risk becoming female." After all, when they were small and they felt their feminine urges, they did want to be just like mother—hence, the danger of nurturing. These fathers will often hang back from play, absent themselves, or tyrannize in "an effort to fortify a masculine identity in the face of maternal and symbiotic pressures."

Parenthood, by taking men back into their childhood just as it does women, often puts them in touch with their sadness about their own fathers. Charles Gottlieb says that many of his patients cannot give him any details about their fathers; they simply do not know them. His own father would lie down after dinner, light a cigar, and listen to classical music. No one bothered to tell him that for a year of his early childhood his father lived in a different city on weekdays. Of his own daughter, he says, "She would call out from her crib "mommydaddy" as if we were interchangeable. Now, I'm very important in her life. She knows me and I her, as well as my wife does. If I retreat, she'll struggle with me and won't give up. Had I been a traditional father like my own, I wouldn't have been that important."

Unfortunately, men must pass through all those repressed feelings before relationships with children feel rewarding to them. Simply put, they must create themselves anew with children because, as Osherson says, "they do not have a language for father love."

But men can come to terms with their suppressed longings. Even men who have been accidentally thrown into primary child care do get over their resistance. They reinvent themselves, often without a model for their paternal roles. Usually they had good relationships with their mothers and, like all the fathers Pruett interviewed, do not mind modeling themselves after maternal nurturing. That was true as well of several of the fathers I interviewed, notably Matt and Mike, who didn't hesitate a second to say they learned their nurturing from their mothers. Some, like Patrick, had one of those rare, loving, intimate fathers they sought to emulate—though they may also have to eschew certain of their fathers' destructive characteristics. With all these men, however, their egos are clearly strong enough to overcome any residual fear of the feminine. They also are able to confront whatever sadness they feel about their fathers.

Despite the evidence that men can raise their children, most women still do not trust them. Most women feel they must offer to do most of the child-rearing, or else men will not agree to have children. To these women I would argue that when women are willing to do the mothering, men do not have to cultivate their nurturing side. Jessica Benjamin argues that "ultimately, men do have a narcissistic drive to reproduce themselves— just like women do—but want someone else to do the work involved. Not only do they fear the feminine, but they feel that they cannot be present or they will fail in the market place."

Why should we force men to nurture if nurturing is so difficult for them? Quite simply because men must share parenting if women are to lead full lives. Also, when men finally do nurture, they usually agree with Pruett that "fatherhood is the single most creative, complicated, fulfilling, engrossing, enriching, depleting, endeavor of a man's adult life."

Since it is so difficult to imagine men who want children as much as most women do, I'll introduce Elliot and Paul, two men who took full responsibility for becoming parents and for nurturing. As we will see, when there are no women in the picture, men nurture with their full hearts, making absolutely certain their beloved child does not miss out on anything except breast milk.

ELLIOT ROTH AND PAUL VISCONTI*

What better proof of men's ability to nurture than fathers who parent—even infants—just fine without any help from women?

Six months ago Elliot and Paul's ardent wish for a child came true when the agency called to say a baby boy had been born for Elliot, who had been approved as an adoptive parent. When they first saw Gabe, Elliot said, "The emotion was so overwhelming, we couldn't speak. You can see our silence in the video. Yet we're both talkers. This was a new *kind* of emotion."

At the hotel where they stayed with Gabe for five days before they were permitted to take him back to New York, it took them a while to figure out how to make the Huggies stay on. But after all, it's not very hard, Paul says. "My sister's pregnant and worried that she won't know what to do. I tell her it's really intuitive if you're open. We read all the books, but it's in the doing." Elliot adds, "Parenting is about giving a child security and love and that comes effortlessly. It's about communication—figuring out what's making him happy, unhappy, whether he wants something new or familiar."

Of course *they* can nurture, someone is certainly thinking. *They're* gay men, and that means feminine, like the gay parents in the movie *The Birdcage*. Nothing could be further from the truth. Thirty-two-year-old Paul, a handsome, bespectacled intellectual, is articulate (not chatty) and very much the serious young professor. Elliot, ten years older, is warm and lanky. With his receding hairline, lazy, loose attire, and relaxed confidence, he might be a successful businessman on his Sunday off rather than a "downtown" painter. Yet when they met while working at the American Academy in Rome, one of the things that attracted them to one another was that they both love kids and, according to a mutual friend who got to know them there, both played with academy kids. They also clearly had worlds in common, Elliot being a painter and Paul an art historian.

Baby Gabe's stuffed animals, mobiles, play stations, and colorful blankets adorn their otherwise quietly comfortable artist's loft. Sharing a club chair with Elliot, six-month-old Gabe keeps turning his irresistible gummy smiles on me. But when I take him into my lap, he cranes his head around to find his dads and only grins again once he's back with one of them. Throughout our interview Gabe entertains himself bouncing on Elliot's thighs, sucking on his rattle, patting Elliot's cheeks, and periodically nuzzling against his chest in typical bursts of baby passion.

Gabe, they tell me, is just a very happy baby. But they also admit that they are *very* good parents, which, as everyone tells them, including me, they so clearly are. Not that they were immediately confident. It took about two months, they say. At the beginning they were going to hire a *doula*, a person (always a woman) who helps new parents to take care of their infants, but they realized they didn't *need* help, even though the timing wasn't perfect (naturally). Paul had a couple of months' work on his dissertation left to finish, so at the beginning Elliot did the lion's share. However, they had both planned well enough to be able to take nine months off from work. Says Elliot, "It's so amazing to have had the time to spend. I feel *so* connected to every stage. If I weren't, or if someone else had cared for him, I wouldn't have the confidence now."

Essentially Gabe has two parents who adore him, take care of him, and are with him most of the time. He also has two parents whose skills are complementary. Paul says, "People ask us, Who's the mom and who's the dad? We both mother and we both father. There's no difference." He explains that Elliot is faster to figure out what Gabe needs when he's crying, but he, Paul, has much more patience. Elliot, amused at the description, interjects, "So if we can't figure things out, Paul takes over." While both of them miss the downtime they used to have together, and both are amazed by the constancy of the managing, they love their new stage of life. Laughingly, they say they understand now about teenage mothers who throw the kid out the window. But they never really feel claustrophobic or smothered.

Elliot and Paul say they do feel more connected in a nonverbal way now. "We rely on each other concretely, and both of us feel such a deep connection to Gabe that we love each other for taking care of him. We know we can depend on one another. We feel more balanced, more secure with one another now." Not only do they divide things equally, Paul explains, but they don't have to think about it. It happens naturally. Whoever cooks, the other cleans up. Whoever's been "on," the other takes over.

But Elliot and Paul also get a lot of help from their large extended families. When I saw them, they had just returned from Florida where Elliot's mother and stepfather had thrown a baby shower for them. It's made him feel much closer to his parents, especially his stepfather, who had always been a bit of an outsider. "To Sy, this is the first time he's as connected as my mother. She doesn't have blood-tie privilege here. As it turns out, Sy is a natural with Gabe: he can talk to him, comfort him, just be with him for hours." Paul's large Italian family lives close by. When they brought Gabe home, twenty-five of their relatives and friends were in their loft to greet them. "His homecoming was a party," Elliot says. "That's what it's been like. Our friends have stayed close. Mostly they have kids too. And with the baby, our two families are connected." All of which gives Elliot and Paul a lot of pleasure, and a lot of support.

Where does such good fathering come from? In part, they tell me, they were both raised by traditional men who were also divorced and therefore less involved than they might otherwise have been. Elliot says, "My father couldn't do anything. When it was his turn to take care of us, we'd have to go to my aunt's."

Both Elliot and Paul are determined to supply Gabe with tremendous love and a sense that, as a man, he can be or do anything he wants. Ironically, their maleness has given them a certain advantage: neither is afraid of the overwhelming intensity of parental love largely because neither is afraid he will lose his sense of self in the process. Sure, Elliot wishes he could get his creativity back a little faster, but he is sure it will come. Paul says he's terribly distracted, but from his experience with finishing his doctoral thesis, he knows he can focus if he has to. Thinking it over, Paul says, "We both want careers and to be a part of Gabe's life.

And we're both comfortable enough in our work to take time off to parent. But maybe we're so confident because we're men."

Perhaps that's it. They are confident enough of their places in the world that, as Elliot relates, on the rare occasion when he's uptown at some meeting, he'll pull a diaper out of his pocket or one of Gabe's toys "and just feel *so* happy." They don't have to worry that the diaper means they are "chained forever," or that they will always be thought of as "just" homemakers. To them, having a child means they get to be in the world and come home to the miracle of Gabe. Not surprisingly, they plan to adopt another child.

WHY CAN'T CHILDREN BE MORE LIKE WORK?

Elliot and Paul are lucky. Perhaps being gay, they do not feel obliged to conform to traditional male standards. Certainly, being older, they are more confident in their work and willing to give up some ambition in order to raise children. But for most men, as Osherson says, "work is easier than relationships. It often calms us, serves as a means of reducing our anxiety and sense of loneliness." Remember Matt Soper asking the men in his congregation to admit that their worst day at work is easier than a day of child care.

Because men find intimate child care so difficult, they have to fight against their training to forgo intimacy and to father indirectly "by fostering, securing, protecting, guiding, etc." The usual secondary parenting, Pruett concludes, leads to an "empty fatherhood," the feeling that "I've blown it with my kids." Once men begin their fathering as "indirect" parents, it is exceedingly difficult to switch into an intimate mode. Osherson describes the typical father fiasco when a dad who has never really done daily child care tries to get close to his children:

> The father decides to take Friday afternoons off to be with his kids, then, after a couple of weeks, his plans fall apart. The father, trying to "play baby" and really wanting to sneak off and return a few calls, feels anxiety about not using his time competitively. Plus, the experience stimulates memories of his own father's absence from childhood. He doesn't know this, but just feels empty and restless at home. He feels, "the more I'm with

the kids, the lonelier I feel," but is ashamed to say it and doesn't
understand. He doesn't feel as good at parenting as his wife.

Work so deeply defines men that they are ill at ease when they are not
performing or relaxing from performing; hence, the falling into the arm-
chair with the paper, channel surfing, yelling for relief after twenty
minutes of playing with the baby after work.

For most men child care is not a complement to work; it is harder
than work. Unfortunately, their compromise—partial, often half-hearted
child care—rarely generates satisfaction. Unless you put in enough hours
to have your own rhythm, confidence, and relationship with the children,
it doesn't feel right to any of the participants. But in order for men to learn
how to do child care, they must understand (and withstand) the inner
voices telling them to flee.

Dave Casson, the Presbyterian minister who shares child care and the
ministry with his wife, says that he came to his decision out of a sense of
fairness, but also, "I wanted to see if I could be closer to my kids than my
dad was to us. I could say I was trying to grab some connectedness for
myself. And I did. I know my kids real well. They trust me. And my wife
and I really are partners. We share our dreams, experiences, and reality."
But he had to learn to accept hands-on fatherhood: "Fatherhood is all-
consuming. It's a warped universe. You can't get anything accomplished.
But it's impossible to father if you don't accept that reality. Still, my
impatience and frustration with it has been appalling."

For Dave, accepting the reality of fatherhood has paid off. "Ultimately, I'm really happy I do this. Sometimes I think I'm some kind of
martyr, but then I know that's lopsided. Even if parenting stinks in the
moment, as it can, I always know I'm doing what is right. I'm learning
how the moment can be less important than the whole. If you are going to
parent and work, you have to use an entirely different calculus.

"As a minister, I learn all the time about other men's feelings and know
how many traditional men are filled with regret. Mostly I see most men
longing for affirmation of their affective side. Perhaps because of that, I
wanted to live intentionally. I'm very glad I made this decision."

A lot of men are making the news today for committing themselves to
parenting, even giving up high status and income to do so. The *Wall
Street Journal* frequently runs such stories. One, "High Powered Fathers

Savor Their Decisions to Scale Back Careers," describes the forty-nine-year-old president of American Express, who became a consultant in order to devote 40 percent more of his time to his four kids. He says he feels "as productive and content as I ever felt. The conflict is gone."

Some very unorthodox fathers, like the ones in this book, seem to have known from the beginning what other men conclude only after regret leads to a radical life change. Yet none of the fathers portrayed thus far has actually had to dramatically alter his work life in order to father. Now I'd like to introduce a father who carefully designed the rest of his life—including his work life—to accommodate the intimate parenting that is usually done only by women.

JAMES RICHARDSON

If there were a pro category for fathering, Jim, a fifty-three-year-old African American denizen of Greenwich Village, New York, would definitely be in it. He's one of the few parents I know who does not feel he's missed out on his kids' childhoods, and indeed he hasn't.

This summer, while ten-year-old Cassie is in camp, thirty-two-year-old Jed, an actor and musician, is coming home to work alongside his dad. How does he feel about that? I ask. "Terrific," says Jim. "I love working with Jed. He's smart, he's polite, he's interesting." Of course, the same could be said of Jed's father. As for his fathering, in the morning I spent interviewing Jim and Cassie I learned as much about great parenting as I did about their lives.

Watching his daughter Cassie bounce from her own chair to his lap for a hug, as well as listen and contribute to our very candid, adult conversation, I saw as free and intimate a relationship as I ever dreamed of for a father and daughter.

How does a father get to have such an easy, satisfying relationship with his kids? "The key," says Jim, "is low rent, low overhead. *You can have so much fun with your kids if you just have enough time.*" As his own boss, Jim has chosen to work only twenty to thirty hours a week. The rest of his time is for pleasure—mostly the pleasure of his children and a documentary on electromagnetic fields, his special interest.

Jim works as an electrician, plumber, and carpenter. In fact, he was upgrading the circuitry in my apartment when I noticed him explaining the wiring to my entranced five-year-old with a patience surpassing Barney's. To most of her questions and mine, Jim would answer with an easy, trisyllabic "su-r-e," the first syllable dipping down in tone, the final note high, as in, "Why not? Everything's possible." "You must be a good father," I commented as he paused in his work to compliment my daughter's dancing. "Sure I am," he said frankly. "Tomorrow you can see for yourself. My daughter's coming to work with me before we go to her violin lesson. Whenever there's no school, she's my assistant." That settled it. Jim agreed to talk about fathering, and I was ready with my tape recorder when they arrived.

Cassie looks much like her dad—the same pecan skin and upturned nose. But where he has a paunch, she's lanky, just the girl side of young female elegance. Her dark brown hair, which she wears parted in the middle and hanging to her shoulders, is straight, whereas his copious curls are drawn back into a ponytail. Toting a violin case, Cassie seems especially excited about their morning practice and offers a demonstration of her latest melody, "Boogie Danse Blues." "*Dad*," she scolds when Jim gives her the wrong piece of music. "I'm sorry," he responds, then, with an obedient "Yes, dear"—required by such healthily assertive preteens—he holds up the correct page of music while she plays. Afterwards he pronounces the recital "cool," and they quickly discuss her rendition.

Although he wears flaring Bermuda shorts and a funny hat, his daughter isn't the least embarrassed. On the contrary, when I ask what Cassie likes best about her father, she says, "He's funny, energetic, understanding, and he teaches me, not academically, but for strength. I'm not really afraid of anyone, and if some kid teases me, I just walk away." Is there anything she'd change about him? "No, except maybe his singing. Sometimes, with my friends, he'll burst out singing and even skip down the street, and I have to go, 'Oh, no.' "

Singing, I learn, was always Jim's distraction of choice whenever Cassie is problematic, although, he adds, she really never is. "We just don't have discipline problems." I believe him. It is clear to me from Jim's pride at her violin playing, the "notes" he gives her afterwards, the respect with which he listens to what she has to say, that Cassie feels her great value to Jim. When I ask whether there are things she would discuss only with her mom, she seems puzzled. "I talk to my dad about everything," she says, and he too doesn't hesitate to talk about everything with her sitting close, including his younger sister dying of a drug overdose. Not even her parents' divorce troubled Cassie, she claims, since she didn't lose either of her parents when they separated.

When Jim and Cassie's mother divorced two years before, Jim made a point of getting an apartment near hers, and near to Cassie's school. "I've given up space and sun, which I love, to be close to her," he explains, making it perfectly clear he could not have been without her. They'd always been close. Jim explains that when Cassie was born, her mother fell ill with toxemia, and Cassie, who was jaundiced, stayed in intensive care. So every day for ten days he spent up to sixteen hours a day holding Cassie, feeding, and loving her. At home Cassie's mother, who worked when necessary, would express her milk so Jim could feed her.

Now, every morning, he walks the round trip of seventeen blocks to pick up Cassie, bring her home to make breakfast and practice the violin, then takes her to school. They speak on the phone every night he's not with her. They go bowling together, play pool, and work on her homework projects. He's never missed a class trip, including the three-day overnights to upstate New York. Once, they spent a day walking all the way downtown with Cassie balancing on the protected median separating the West Side Highway from the river walkway. "I just chatted with her while she concentrated. It was great for her self-esteem. That was really hard to do."

At Cassie's weekly swimming lesson, "a lot of parents just stand around at the swimming pool. Not me, I jump right in and play with the kids." Did it ever bother him that he is the only dad at the swimming pool or on a class trip or at the playground? "Never," he says. "I was just there for my kid."

Jim puts in more time than most parents I know, but he says, "I'd like to spend more time, not less, with Cassie." Would you like that? I ask her. "Yes," she says, "I would."

Of course, time alone isn't what makes for a great father. Jim says he thought he'd always been a nurturing sort of man and had never even imagined himself practicing traditionally male secondary parenting. As the eldest of eleven children, he'd taken care of his brothers and sisters.

Also, his own parents "did everything with TLC." His mother enjoyed mothering so much she never really gave it up. When she "retired," the kids chipped in and bought her a house in North Carolina, where Jim was born and lived before the family moved to Harlem, then Queens. "She has college girls living with her down there. Three doctors and four attorneys have passed through my mother's house. She nurtures them."

What kind of man was his father? "Well, the only altercation I remember having with him was when I was very little, five or six. I'd done something wrong, and he took off his belt. I cried and pleaded, and he said, 'Here, take this belt.' Then he pulled his pants down and told me to whip him because he hadn't taught me right." Jim says, "He was a sweetheart with us, and so proud of his brood." Although his father worked for a living—he was a maintenance man—he was a gambler by night, and he always won at cards. "He could charm the snakes out of the trees," Jim says, but Jim didn't follow in his footsteps. "He'd always take me to these male-bonding functions: card games, deep-sea fishing, booze, cigarettes. It embarrassed me. I knew there was more to life. As competitive as I am—and don't play tennis with me or you'll see it—I didn't want to live my life playing those games." Instead, he chose to cultivate his other, loving side.

It wasn't feminism that shaped Jim's fatherhood, though clearly feminism allowed it to flourish. "Taking care of children is just who I was. It was normal for me. I always had men friends who were similar: nurturing, giving, not condescending to children or anyone." Since his work was flexible, he usually took as much care of his children as their mothers did, and sometimes more. Jed's mother was the "aide-de-camp to the president of the Metropolitan Opera," so Jim was the one to stay home when Jed was sick; he planned the holiday festivities with him; he went to school activities. At home, says Jim, "we had every musical instrument, and we'd play music together all the time. Cassie found the one musical instrument I couldn't play—the violin! So I go with her to her lessons, and I listen to her practice every morning." Actually, he says "we practice" every morning, although he doesn't play. That's how involved Jim is.

For me, Cassie's violin is emblematic of the quality of their relationship: Jim's parental attunement, the seized opportunities, the rarity of it. Violin, after all, isn't the usual choice for a ten-year-old girl, nor is a Stradivarius the violin she'd normally play. How is it that she does?

One evening Cassie and her dad watched a public television show on which a young Asian girl played a violin "like gangbusters," Jim says. When he saw how excited Cassie was, Jim concurred, "I know what you mean." Cassie continues the story. "Then we found this violin on the street, and my friend's dad makes violins, so he repaired it for us." Jim makes me look at the Stradivarius label inside. Whether it's an ersatz version or that rarest of eighteenth-century instruments, I am still impressed. The two wait with pleasure for me to register my admiration, and I do.

For Jim, there's been no price to pay for paternal devotion. "A lot of men see me on my religious trek every morning to pick up Cassie. I think they admire that. I get awe from them, reverence and respect. I think they wish they could do it."

What do you get out of fathering? I ask Jim as we conclude the interview. He thinks for a moment and recalls that some twenty years earlier, he built the first adventure playground in New York City. It was on the Lower East Side. "My whole existence has been an adventure playground," he said. "Watching Cassie grow is an adventure. She's like a flower blooming. Seeing her learn and loving it, seeing how smart she is. I learn something about her every day, and she me. When I told her about this interview, she said, 'Sure,' just the way I do with things in her life. Just like that playground, my job with her is to facilitate a reasonable, loving environment, to help her learn and have fun. If I had to sum up the most important things I've done in my life, I'd say, my children. They are numero uno."

All the portraits in this book show men who father from the heart, but none more than this one. Jim illustrates the most important principle in modern fatherhood: if fathers spend the time, sacrificing some of their goals to make room for child care, they are surely good enough nurturers. But strategy here is vital. Given our upbringing, good enough fathering only happens when mothers allow fathers to share the parenting and respect their different approach. As we've seen, in situations where mothers cannot be the primary parent, fathers flourish. They can certainly flourish under typical circumstances as well.

Elliot, Paul, and Jim all demonstrate the benefits when men spend time alone with their children. Even Berry Brazelton needed that in order to form strong relationships with his own children. In *Working and Caring,* he writes:

> I found that I always depended on my wife to make the critical decisions when she was there. When she wasn't, I had to face a deeper sense of responsibility in myself. It was so different when she was away, to be really in charge. My own feelings about being a parent grew stronger, as did my relationship with my child.

If a pediatrician and eminent author of best-selling child-care books observes that he did not parent fully until he was alone with his child, if even he relied on his wife's expertise, then how can we expect ordinary men to take on their half of the parenting? The problem here, as Brazelton suggests, is that when a mother is nearby, the father rarely flexes his full nurturing muscles.

With newborns, it may seem there is nothing fathers can do. But as one new father said, "All I didn't do was breast-feed." That is surely the goal, though it takes perseverance. Since fathers rarely have experience babysitting or playing with dolls, most lack the familiarity with babies that their wives have. Few trust themselves to figure out what babies need. Most of the rest are self-conscious and feel as awkward doing infant care as they would pirouetting in a tutu. Ultimately, however, infant care is an acquirable skill.

Fathers who have some in-hospital instruction on infants are more sensitive to their newborns; those who handle them, dress and undress them, and feel their naked flesh on their own are more physically at ease parenting than fathers who keep their distance. If they can be in charge of keeping track of suggestions from the baby books, they will increase their expertise. For the bibliophobic, there are videos on infant care. Instruction is everywhere.

No matter how willing new mothers and fathers are, some resistance to hands-on fathering is inevitable. A father who does well with a contented infant may still hesitate to deal with a hysterical one. The best training for all parents is to be left alone with their children.

On the practical side, a supplementary bottle-feeding makes it a lot easier for men to participate in infant care. But even if the mother wants to nurse full-time, the father can still do the changing and bathing. Since each feeding may take up to an hour, this will just about divide the basic care, still leaving the comforting, the cleaning up of baby effluvia, and the shopping for daily essentials and accoutrements for the father to do.

Ron Taffel suggests that the father who has never taken care of his child should start anywhere, even with a simple task like making a Sunday breakfast alone. Mothers should stay out of the way. Don't monitor, don't comment, as he puts it. The child may not like her father's care the first or second time. By the third, though, she will count on it, or even insist on it.

And what, finally, does all our new information about fathers suggest? The most important message is that we should rely much more on men to parent than we presently do. Although ideally both parents can make equal commitments to work and family, if finances or workplace rigidity makes that impossible, there are even advantages to the father, rather than the mother, cutting back on work to be more available at home. On a personal level, fathers bring certain important male qualities, such as greater independence and an emphasis on mastery, into children's lives. Also, if the father is doing more of the parenting, the children get more of both parents since most women can be relied on to parent as fully as possible, even when they work full-time. On a cultural level, every father who takes the lion's share of responsibility for his children expands society's limited view of men.

As Taffel puts it, "It is simply patronizing to assume that men cannot nurture." They can, as all the fathers in this book so clearly demonstrate. Now both individual women and society have to tell men that they must.

CHAPTER 8

Freer Mothers, Stronger Marriages, Happier Children

One of the great benefits of sharing parenting is how much better it is for the couple. In two-parent families, the couple is always the most important part of the family constellation. It is the way the parenting adventure began, the basis for harmony in the home, and the children's model for friendship and love. As hard as it is for couples to resist their inclinations toward traditional motherhood and fatherhood, those who do are generally rewarded with marriages that continue to thrive after they have children.

I've recently coauthored a book on marriage with a family therapist whose years of clinical practice led her to conclude that the principal reason the divorce rate has risen to an unprecedented 50 percent is the tendency of partners to backslide into traditional roles when their children are born, thus destroying the equality and friendship they previously shared. As the spouses' roles diverge—the mother doing most of the child care while the father earns most of the money—they grow apart, blaming one another for their mutual resentments. The wife frequently feels burdened by all the child care, even when she agreed to it, and feels offended by her husband's freedom to go on with his life. The husband often grows lonely as his work carries him farther from the emotional center of family life. Like his comic counterpart in the sitcom *Married, with Children*, he may be constantly irritated by the sense that he has become the family worker bee, supporting the queen's pleasures with the sacrifice of his own.

Under favorable conditions, children do bring couples closer. Loving the same child can be a shared experience like no other. One divorced mother confided that although she had battled her ex-husband for exclusive custody and lost, once she accepted the idea of joint custody she found herself having the most gratifying conversations with her ex about her son. "No one else," she commented, "is as passionately involved in him as we are."

Only they have known him from birth, and only they share the guilt for what he suffered during their bitter divorce. So even though both of them are remarried to people who are deeply involved with the child, they still parent primarily with one another.

If both are involved, a child's parents know him or her well enough that every mundane detail can be meaningful and affecting. No one but the other parent is quite so thrilled when a child offers to comfort her grandmother with her favorite stuffed tiger, or as dismayed when she tells that same grandmother to go home. Though others along the way will be intimately involved, rarely is anyone else as identified or as invested in the child's future. This involvement creates an extraordinary bond.

For my husband and I, who had traveled the world together, helped with each other's work, and lived through a near-fatal health crisis together, our infant daughter was our greatest undertaking yet. The image that always captures the feeling is of the two of us conferring in hushed tones over our three-day-old daughter's diaper rash. Frequent washing was called for, but since an infant cannot be submerged in water until her umbilical cord falls off, we devised the following remedy. With him supporting her head and shoulders and me holding her thighs, we dipped her bottom in a sink full of lukewarm water before each diapering, a maneuver that required the concentration and coordination of a surgical team. Though we had many contented (childless) years behind us, we had never worked together so breathlessly. Neither of us can remember just why this process took four hands when she weighed less than seven pounds. Nonetheless, there we were, transfixed by our little charge, enveloped in her care. Like a honeymoon, tending her together in those first days felt so private that we didn't invite parents or friends to see her for a week after we brought her home.

Not only do two involved parents both love their children ardently, often helplessly, but the discussions they have about parenting cut to the depths of personality and philosophy. Whether they are about the proper way to respond to a toddler's tantrum, private versus public school, or religious training, parenting issues bring partners into closer focus, allowing them to know one another better—and differently than they had before.

If fathers and mothers are both nurturing the children, they are more likely to feel empathy than animosity during the roughest parenting trials. As one woman put it, "When I call him and say, 'Can you get back early? It's just one of those days,' he knows exactly what one of those days is like and is home in ten minutes." Also, they have each other's support and a precedent for cooperating to resolve problems.

Instead of driving a wedge between lovers, a child can expand and deepen that love. Moreover, the more involved fathers are in parenting, the more willing mothers are to separate from the child, leaving more room for the couple time that so many men miss after the children arrive.

I am not suggesting that shared parenting ensures marital bliss. No matter how partners parent, children introduce the kind of emotional strain that can shatter old harmonies and certainties. New parts of a person's character reveal themselves—overprotectiveness, impatience, selfishness, vulnerability, childishness, all the primitive emotions that surface with such a pervading novel experience—and they may not be to the partner's liking. Both partners, exhausted and unsettled in their own particular ways, are generally needier of understanding and physical relief. The "who's doing more" issues in the relationship rise to an all-time high.

Yet, if both parents care for the baby, they go through the awkward exploratory stage together and are therefore less prone to blaming themselves for problems. They experience similar, rather than conflicting, pressures. They both understand the phenomenon of "baby blitz." Like Maddy and Patrick or Elliot and Paul, each partner can contribute his or her strengths; like Angela and Matt or Jennifer and Mike, even if the responsibility isn't 50–50, partners still respect each other's "motherwork." However, sharing the parenting is only the first step in the process of modernizing motherhood and restructuring family life. The next step involves dispersing the mothering throughout a larger parenting network.

THE PARENTING NETWORK

The sociologist Jessie Bernard, reviewing the major anthropological research on motherhood, reported that the less solitary maternal care is, the more tender the mother is with her children: "These research teams found that women in cultures where they were given the heaviest load of childcare were more changeable in expressing warmth than those in other cultures and more likely to have hostilities not related to the behavior of their children."

The idea that maternal tenderness flows in inverse proportion to solitary care flies in the face of our conventional wisdom that mother should be the "ever-present, always-responsive" caretaker of her children. The intensity that the isolated mother-child duo can generate may not be characterized so much by tenderness as it is by the sheer electricity of such exclusivity, the strong current heating up the love, raising the probability of a systems blowout.

The image of the tribal mother with the baby affixed to her body is the half of the picture from nonindustrial cultures that we romanticize. But we block out the half in which others—grandparents, a community of women, older siblings—are in charge of the child while the mother works elsewhere. The success of such alternating rhythms of child care with purely adult enterprise—whether it be work, community ritual, caring for the sick, or painting clay pots—may be what's relevant about tribal motherhood for our transitional culture. After sharing parenting with a child's father, embedding motherhood in a network of supportive relationships is the second most important change we must make in today's family life.

The mother who works, who is involved in the community, sees her friends, and gets time alone with her husband can only do this if she steps back to become part of a parenting network. Ideally, it is a network of mother and father, grandparents, a trusted caregiver or day-care center, and friends or neighbors who love the child and can care for her on a regular basis. This is a hefty shift away from the traditional model of motherhood, but it generates enormous advantages.

This week my parents are visiting from out of state. Although we have only about four visits a year, my daughter is in heaven when we are together. Just as my husband and I feel the relief of being off the hook, she feels the relief of being part of a group. Instead of yelling for us when she wants something, she'll ask, "Can someone can read to me, please?" Often anyone in the group will do.

Of course, most children bask in a grandparent's doting attention. But there's another phenomenon at work: most children like being part of a tribe. They enjoy spending their time with one, then another of the people they love. Whether we are with her grandparents or our close friends, our daughter is fascinated by the web of connections among us, the ebb and flow of pairings, the different ways each member of the group relates to her. Even at age three she understood the depth of the commitment certain people have for her. Her joy in them is not simply their willingness to entertain her. She lavishes affection on them, is more concerned, and more interested, than she otherwise is—as they are with her. If there is a dispute about social dynamics, she does not hesitate to tell me. For example, she let me know that my friend Emma is her friend too, which is true. Hence the dispute about who gets to talk with Emma when she visits must be settled on that basis.

The parents I know who live within easy visiting distance of their own parents or who have created an extended family with their friends enjoy less pressured parenting than isolated parents. Like Maddy and Patrick, they can take time for themselves and also have the pleasure, not to speak of added security, of making their nuclear family part of their larger family group. Their children are not fazed when grandparents pick them up. Liam has a separate life with his grandparents, a room in their home, special things he does only with them, such as attending church. They are an extension of his nuclear family but also a discrete entity.

For parents who extend their families by building networks, parenting does not have the relentless quality it does for those who parent alone. Not only do they get more time with their spouses, they have the pleasure of knowing that their children are forming bonds with their own intimates, creating echoes of reflected love. If one family member is not in a loving mood, someone else probably is. When love doesn't come from just one or two sources, it can seem, to the child, to be everywhere. A parenting network can create a constancy of love one person cannot generate.

Although a parenting network disperses the mothering among several people, it does not lessen the importance of a child's mother or allow her to focus primarily on herself. Mothers and fathers are crucial to children, but they need not provide the exclusive parental attachment. Nor should they assume that they alone can give the child solace, security, and love.

Certainly, the mother alone need not feel this. When parents are part of a larger network, a kind of magic happens. A child doesn't lose her parents, she gains other loving parent figures. And because this makes parenting so much easier, the parents are much more likely to sustain their own loving connection than if they are completely on their own.

What may be unusual about both Maddy and Patrick and Angela and Matt is that while they have close supportive families, they have also extended their family networks beyond their biological borders. Because the church is so much a part of Angela and Matt's lives, they had full support when, arriving in Los Angeles, their four-year-old broke a toe and their infant was hospitalized with a breathing disorder. Other church members helped settle them in the community, provided vital information about everything from doctors to schools, and offered new friendships.

In addition to Maddy and Patrick's family, there is Momo, as Liam calls her, their baby-sitter, and both children's godparents, who visit frequently. There are also the other parents in the building, especially us, who know the children in a daily way and are always ready to fill in.

It sounds easy. Who wouldn't want a fleet of doting significant others for their children? In fact, creating a parenting network requires planning and emotional effort. Every one of the child's parent figures involves a relationship to the parent as well, and often it is a delicate, complex one. We have only to think of the usual mother-daughter altercations over how "my grandchild" is being raised. Or the baby-sitter uproars one hears about, rife with dissatisfactions and resentments on both sides. That is why it is so important to understand the incomparable benefits of dispersing mothering among several significant others, and the formidable obstacles to doing so.

OTHER MODELS, OTHER MOTHERS

As challenging in practical ways as creating such a parenting network can be, the greatest obstacles are cultural and psychological. The American nuclear family—an oddly narrow configuration—came into being as a matter of circumstance, the result of rapid economic and geographic mobility. Except for Native Americans, we are all descended from people who left or were forced to leave family and community behind. Following suit, we have moved with such frequency and over such a large country, we typically live beyond the scope of our childhood origins. Remarkable industry, innovation, and tolerance is a byproduct, but so too is rootlessness and disorientation. As much as we yearn for a sense of belonging, we distrust community and find it difficult to settle into one, especially to open our nuclear family to it. Yet that is what contemporary family life calls for.

The nuclear family, in which mother is the linchpin of family life and parents alone do child care, rarely works anymore. Jonathan Lampert, a director of the Ackerman Institute for Family Therapy, not only believes that auxiliary child care is a modern necessity, he goes as far as to say "our lives require that we redefine parental privilege and work collaboratively with caregivers, negotiating our powers instead of assuming them." As he describes it, the postmodern family is more reminiscent of the communal sixties than the nuclear nineties, but it is also more realistic. Unlike the hippie commune or utopian community, it respects the centripetal pull of family while relaxing the formerly rigid familial boundaries to include other parenting figures.

Most white, middle-class mothers have been unusually reluctant to share the care of their children. The maternal ideal obliges women to be everything to their children, and maternal guilt makes them fearful of relinquishing the management of their children's lives. Caught by such social and psychological forces, mothers find it terribly difficult to tolerate other caregivers, even the child's father, let alone to recognize that other caregivers can have their own, important relationships to the child. They are not mother stand-ins but truly "other mothers."

The sociologist Patricia Hill Collins coined the term "othermothers" to describe the network of "grandmothers, sisters, aunts, or cousins who help raise other people's children. And when needed temporary child care arrangements can turn into long term care or informal adoption." She refers to African American mothers, who not only have a history of communal child-rearing but whose community networks helped them to raise their children while they labored to put food on the table.

Collins believes this communal approach not only gives people a chance to survive but "helps to diffuse the emotional intensity of relationships between bloodmothers and daughters." Her analysis, like mine, posits the advantage in multiple attachments for the child too. In her words, "African American communities have also recognized that vesting one person with full responsibility for mothering a child may not be wise or possible."

This is also true, she notes, of Latina mothers, among whom a *co-madre*, or godmother, is responsible for certain aspects of child-rearing and has official baptismal functions. My own Latin baby-sitter thought nothing of spending $1,000 on a plane ticket to be at her goddaughter's baptism, although she had many pressing financial obligations. For her, the designation of godparent is a sacred trust.

A few decades ago Senator Daniel Patrick Moynihan's famous report on the problems in the black community blamed the matriarchal strengths of black women—and the absence of strong fathers—for the breakdown of the black family. However, a less sexist view might have congratulated black women on a winning strategy that saved countless children despite poverty, racism, and danger: namely, shared parenting. The black family is also characterized by the open and flexible boundaries necessary for parent networks to function. According to Kenneth Hardy, chairman of the Department of Child and Family at Syracuse University, it is precisely this kind of family flexibility that allows "for informal adoptions, surrogacy, and para-parenting."

The sociologist Pepper Schwartz finds that "para-parenting" is now becoming a universal American phenomenon because one-quarter of American children live with one parent and one-quarter of the adult population lives alone. She describes a sort of committed, nonblood "othermother" relationship that is becoming more common in this time of fragmented families. In other words, of necessity—as in the black community—the white community is finally learning the advantage of opening the family to community support, dispersing the mothering, and sharing parenting with others.

Just as African American motherhood can serve as a model for integrating motherwork with other work, it can also serve as a model for dispersing the mothering among "othermothers." Of course, the two mothering modifications are inextricably linked. The mother who knows others take responsibility for her child can pursue her other work with far less guilt or anxiety than the mother who is her child's exclusive nurturer.

DISPERSING MOTHERING BENEFITS CHILDREN

The greatest emotional obstacle to creating a parenting network is a mother's guilt for preferring work to being her children's exclusive nurturer. However, the benefits of a mother's employment are not only hers, as conservatives believe. The real surprise is how much the children benefit when mothers pursue their independent lives and let others do some of the motherwork. The psychologist Sandra Scarr wrote an award-winning book in 1984 based on her extensive research showing that children benefit by learning to trust several adults rather than one. She concluded, like Hill Collins, that "in fact, it is probably better for them not to be at the emotional mercy of just one mother." Given all the fiction and memoirs written about the hellish intensity and overwhelming influence of mothers, dispersing the mothering should seem quite sensible to more of us.

Kathy Weingarten, another psychologist, approaches the subject with the question, "Do children really need a mother at their disposal? Are they better off with a mother whose life revolves around serving theirs?" Having herself grown up with such a mother, one whom she loved and found loving, her answer is still a resounding no.

Consider how the family feels to a child. When a mother is the exclusive parent, she may well be emotionally exhausted, overinvolved, or resentfully distant. In such families, because the father is all too often viewed as a foreign dignitary visiting the home, the mother may compensate for the paternal void by giving more than children need —overparenting—thereby interfering with the development of self-reliance.

A colleague of mine, one of the rare female professionals in the suburb where she lives, describes daily incidents that characterize this problem. Once, for example, when she was driving her nine-year-old daughter and a classmate to school, they arrived only to discover that her daughter had misplaced the lunch she had prepared. My colleague said, "Oh, that's too bad," and left her daughter to solve the problem. But the schoolmate wondered, "Why don't you just go home and make her another lunch? That's what my mother does."

Her daughter, exasperated by such a reaction, snapped, "My mother has to go to work. Can't you see she's dressed for *work*?" My colleague has concluded that when all the attention of these smart, educated women goes down one narcissistic hole—their children—the result is self-centered, demanding dependents.

Simply put, it may just be too charged to be reared by one person for whom motherhood is a vocation, at least when there are only one or two children. I remember how my friends with stay-at-home mothers—a rarity in the modest neighborhood where I grew up—felt scrutinized and pressured. They seemed more resentful than grateful, either because they had to worry constantly about their mothers' feelings or because they never had to consider them at all. Either response impairs a child's development. As Jessica Benjamin explains, "Mutual recognition, including the child's ability to recognize the mother as a person in her own right, is as significant a developmental goal as separation."

When motherhood is a vocation, the mother is not in a position to teach her child to cultivate independence, and the child, especially a daughter, may resent that fact. Joyce Maynard, literary wunderkind of the sixties, was raised by a mother with a Harvard Ph.D. who nonetheless did only occasional odd jobs. At forty, as a divorced mother of three, Maynard speculates that "one of the things that I came to recognize was that the root of my anger and resentment of her was her own self-sacrifice and the fact that she had failed to provide any kind of model of a woman who takes care of herself."

Candace Falk, feminist theorist and director of the Emma Goldman Archives, acknowledges this problem in relation to her own teenage daughter, Mara. She points out that even when a mother has been successful at work, as she has, she can still be too self-sacrificing. She explains: "I never really marked off a place for myself within the family. As much as I've accomplished, I lose track of it when someone needs me. The problem is that, like many women, I realize I rely on others to provide the part of me that is missing. That is, I have been primarily a reactive person. On the surface, I'm a professional woman, but as my seventeen-year-old daughter Mara well knows, I lose my own center easily. She wishes I were more able to assert myself and admires women who are self-contained, able to hold their own." The painful empty-nest feelings Candace is experiencing now that Mara is about to leave for college have given her a new perspective. She believes she relied too much on Mara's energy and need for her. Now, just beginning to seek out the pleasures and supports for herself that she neglected before, she ruefully observes, "I shouldn't have had to wait for Mara to leave before I could find my center again."

Children want mothers who take care of their own needs and who remain a part of the world. Though a mother's employment does not ensure either, it does help. What's more, children identify with their mother's work; it is important to them. Nearly half of the grade-schoolers in one large survey said they wanted to do the same work as their mothers when they grow up. The psychologist conducting the survey concluded that one reason mothers' work is so impressive to children is because they understand it better than they do their father's work and are more likely to have visited their mother's workplace. That is, mothers communicate more about their work than fathers do. They tell stories about work and express their feelings about their workday.

If, in turn, a child expresses resentment that her mother works, a mother can take some comfort in understanding that her children are naturally ambivalent. One part wants all mother's attention, another wants her to be in the world. Diane Gottlieb suggests that if some days the child seems to resent a mother's working, the mother can just say, "I'm sorry. I love my work, and I love you. I have to do this. It's part of who I am and what I value"—thereby teaching the child to value that part of herself as well. On another day the child will probably tell her she is pleased that her mother works.

Not only do children often like to have a mother who works, but they are generally interested in the work. The writer Rosellen Brown said she always put her work away when she heard the school bus, but one day she just had to finish a paragraph. Her little daughter, still in her snowsuit, stared so hard that Brown told her to just go into the kitchen and wait a minute. "But Mommy, I want to see what you're doing. I want to see what your work looks like." Today her daughter is also a writer.

I'm not proposing the simplistic notion that if we have work we feel good about doing, whether for money or love, our daughters will too. Far more important is the reality that if our children perceive us as having selves it gives them permission to have selves too, and to do what is right for them. Not what *we* want for them, as many children feel. If they feel our joy in pursuits apart from them, they learn that they too can enjoy life apart from us.

Nina, the literary agent, was on her way to London on business. For the first time, perhaps because her youngest was then four, she realized that while she was traveling for work, she was having a wonderful time just being by herself on the plane. As she told me, she finally grasped, "I'm allowed to have fun even though I'm not with my family. I told the kids on the phone, 'I'm having the time of my life.' " What surprised her was that they stopped whining at once. Their usual complaints about what was going wrong and when was she coming back simply ceased.

Nina sent an invaluable message to her children: I'm a mother who loves being with you, but I also love my life apart from you. It clearly relieved and heartened them. Nina freed them by setting limits, delineating her boundaries, saying, This is *my* time. The guilt that deprived her of her solitary pleasures had not been helpful to her children. Guilt can keep mothers home, but it cannot make them enjoy being there—a difference children feel.

It is only common sense that children thrive when their parents are happy within themselves, within their marriages, and in their roles as parents. The acknowledged experts are beginning to encourage mothers to pursue their own lives, apart from their children. The coauthors of *Child Care/Parent Care*, Marilyn Heins and Anne M. Seiden, write that "children are very vulnerable when their parents' needs are unfilled, either as persons, partners, parents or members of the general community." Also, they remind us, parents need time off from parenting just as all workers need time off from their jobs. Finally, throughout their book they emphasize the very practical need for multiple caregivers by asking mothers to consider what would happen to their children if they needed to be hospitalized or were called away because of an emergency. "Children are emotionally safer if they have had the opportunity to master mild degrees of 'separation anxiety,' " they say, "than if they meet it for the first time in an overwhelming dose."

Even if couples are convinced that parenting networks benefit the whole family, they may be rightly apprehensive about setting them up, particularly if they do not have parents nearby to form traditional extended families. In this next portrait, we'll meet a couple who not only share their parenting but did all the hard work of creating an extended family network with a well-chosen day-care center. By doing so, they were able to meet the demands of corporate life and parent at the same time.

LOCHLIN AND SANDY REIDY

For Lochlin and Sandy Reidy, corporate life and family life make a perfectly fine blend, and they should know. Both are employees at Southern New England Telephone, SNET, where they have worked for more than twenty years. They have also been together for about the same time, raising their second families.

Although Lochlin has to work on the Sunday scheduled for our interview, they are so in sync, I tease, that he pulls into my driveway less than a minute after his wife arrives with four-year-old Ashley from their home just up the road. Lochlin oversees emergency repairs on phone lines, which have been in a constant state of emergency with the summer's incessant rains. But in his neatly pressed jeans and bright pink knit shirt with its monogram from a hotel in Bermuda, you couldn't tell Lochlin has been working two weeks straight—especially with his handsome five o'clock shadow and short salt-and-pepper bangs helter-skelter on his forehead. Only the beeper that goes off three times in three hours steals his attention. Well, not quite. Once Ashley, who is playing in the yard with our daughter, "serves tea" to her parents. Another time, she climbs up her father's thighs to do a back flip.

Sandy is a staff specialist, part of a team of four that designs and implements quality control measurements for employees. Though she is off this Sunday, she is dressed formally in a cream-colored crepe blouse and coordinated knit vest, pearls at her neck and pretty gold button earrings, her nails polished a berry red to match her lipstick. Yet she seems as relaxed as Lochlin. It may be her Connecticut Yankee breeding: Sandy, with her ruddy cheeks, an open forthright face softened by her feathery blond hair, grew up not ten miles away on her parents' dairy farm (though it's actually city-bred Lochlin who can trace his ancestors back to John Quincy Adams). How relaxed both Sandy and Lochlin seem may reflect how they feel about their lives—the combination, perhaps, of the wisdom of age (they are both in their forties) and seniority at work.

Corporate life can be grueling, Lochlin explains—as any life can be if you let it.

"In my first marriage," he says, "I was working six days a week and, it felt like, twenty-four hours a day. The urgency then was to achieve, to collect money, to get the next car, to move up in status." Looking back, he realizes he wouldn't have had to work so hard if his wife had been earning too. But as it was, "I was so exhausted when I was home, I didn't spend much time with my sons and eventually lost contact with them when my ex-wife moved away. I wasn't going to allow that to happen with Ashley. And even before Ashley, with Denise—who was two when Sandy and I got together—I felt I had a second opportunity to see what children were. It became important to me to think I guided this person. I got so much satisfaction from really watching her grow up in front of me."

Because his second marriage was different, Lochlin could be different as well. Sandy shared Denise's upbringing with Lochlin, and since she also worked outside the home, Lochlin was often in charge. Also, in the process of becoming a family themselves, they consciously thought through what kind they wanted. Sandy, who had been primarily a house-wife in her former marriage, wanted an equal partnership and full-time work. In fact, she seems to have applied her professional expertise in quality control to her own life.

"When I got pregnant with Ashley, there were certain facts we began with: one, we lived in New Milford, a rural area we both love, and I worked almost an hour away in New Haven. Lochlin worked closer, about twenty minutes away in the Danbury facility. Two, I wouldn't stay home. I know I need to get up and get going. I have a drive to accomplish things and make money, be with people. I thrive on change. I *definitely* was going to continue to work. So I took a five-month maternity leave, then Lochlin stayed home with Ashley for almost another month, then Denise took care of her during her summer vacation from college. At nine months Ashley went into day care."

It may be Lochlin who changed most during that time. "I discovered I loved staying home. I loved taking care of Ashley—feeding her, changing her, playing with her. I loved planting a garden."

With a smile, Sandy pipes in, "Perennials 360 degrees around the house. It was a whole new hobby for Loch. On weekends we'd drive around, looking at gardens, go to garden stores."

Lochlin looks for a moment like a kid who's been found out. "I never had a chance to live like that," he says. "It's so different from going into work, sticking to a schedule, attending to crises. I loved getting the housework done during the week and then playing on the weekend, all the vacuuming done. I *felt* better."

He also discovered he was a better father. "My whole temperament is different with Ashley. I can do what *she* wants to do and have the gratification of helping her accomplish things. I wasn't a patient enough person before to realize her needs and requirements are greater than mine. One Saturday, for example, we made a rhubarb pie. The kitchen was a mess afterwards, but seeing her eyes when that pie came out of the oven was easily worth it. Or, in the car, driving to and from day care, we select a route together, watch the construction of the houses going up, talk about the calves getting bigger, the seasons. I'd never notice the world in that way without her."

Both Lochlin and Sandy believe Country Kids Play Farm, Ashley's day-care center, has enriched her life, and theirs as well. Far from being merely a convenience, they see it as an extension of their family life. "We're partners with them," Sandy explains. Every week we discuss what's going on with Ashley, anything new at home or at day care. We know all the other parents." Plus, as Sandy is quick to admit, "they give her things I could never give her if we were home alone together. As part of a group, Ashley's learning social skills. They provide structure, rules. She sees other children being disciplined; it's not just her. She knows other kinds of children from other cultures. They learn songs in French, in sign language; they learn swimming, dancing; they take trips to the theater and local farms. Their teachers are experts in child development. I couldn't offer Ashley all that. She adores it. She knows all the kids and all the caregivers, though every year they move to a new group. And everyone knows her."

Finding the right day care wasn't simple. As soon as Sandy knew she was pregnant, she began her search. She visited day-care centers and family care, made surprise visits, asked pediatricians and other parents, eliminated places where the children didn't seem motivated; at her midday visit to one, for example, she found that the toys were all put away while the children sat around bored. She and Lochlin thought about the baby-sitter alternative but felt Ashley would be stifled by the isolation.

Country Kids was the most expensive care they found, but it offers the most: in-ground pools, different playgrounds for each age group with appropriate equipment, hot meals prepared in its own kitchen, even heating under the carpeted floors to keep crawlers warm. The center provides everything from diapers to formula, and also launders the children's clothes, Sandy adds enthusiastically. And the caregivers send home the details of the day—everything from how long Ashley slept to what she ate and when she went potty. And if that's not enough feedback, Lochlin's mother who lives nearby drops in so often that all the staff and children call her Mana, as Ashley does.

Far from disturbing their connection as a family, Sandy believes Country Kids has made their time together better. Ashley is in a different environment all day and "brings that home with her. We have a daily reunion. She tells me who she talked to or brings me the flag she made. She has a good day *and* a good home life where we value and support and teach her. Ashley doesn't feel deprived. She loves the other kids and the caregivers."

For herself, Sandy says, "it's a healthier combination for me to be working in a challenging job and come home to a little one. I think it's good for her to know Mommy and Daddy are also working people. She will be able to do so many things at the same time, like we do, and set priorities."

Lochlin clearly agrees. "Sandy has that drive to work. It's important to her. I know how good she is too. The only thing is, I wish they rewarded her more for what she's accomplished there. She should be at a higher level. But I'm so proud of her. And I think it makes us closer. We're equal partners with where we're going and who we are. We can talk about what's going on at the company. We understand each other's work. As for child care, it's not woman's work. It's just not fair that any one person, that Sandy, should have to be saddled with all that."

All the Reidys seem to thrive with their lives set in a reliable routine: Lochlin drops Ashley off at day care about 7:00 A.M., goes to the office, then picks her up by 5:30 P.M. Sandy gets into work about 8:00 A.M. and is home about a half-hour after them. If Ashley's sick, Lochlin usually stays home with her, or, if the illness lasts several days, they alternate. They spend their evenings together and all their free time. Last year Lochlin, Sandy, Denise, and Ashley went to Bermuda for two weeks. They also took Ashley to California to visit friends and went on ski weekends to Vermont. They both get more than a month's vacation time now, and as Sandy says, "I also take 'Sandy' days. I just voice-message my manager, send everyone out the door, and rest for the day—no rushing, no commitments, no goals."

Lochlin wakes with Ashley on weekends and reads with her or does puzzles until Sandy gets up, then he gardens or plays golf. If they go out socially, they just take Ashley. Lochlin explains that they've been able to do that because Sandy is so good at figuring out how to occupy her or redirect her when frustrated. "I'm more, 'Stop it, do it my way,' which generally doesn't work." He adds, "Ashley's always included in what we do. We want to include her."

Sandy recalls that when she got pregnant, people said, What, are you crazy? With your older daughter nineteen, you're finally free! "But we didn't change. We just took Ashley along with us in our lives. Now friends our age, who don't have small children anymore, envy us." "Particularly the men," Lochlin says. "They didn't get a chance to participate the way I do now."

Both Lochlin and Sandy feel that SNET makes family life possible. No one at the company is penalized for taking a day off for child care. Although people expect corporations to run on strict and impersonal rules, at SNET everything is done at the discretion of an employee's immediate manager. What counts is completing the work. Also, anyone can take up to six months off with the guarantee of the same job back, or a year with a guarantee of a job at the same pay level. There's no problem with emergency leave or telecommuting, if someone requests it.

The great advantage, they think, is that everyone is in touch. Managers and employees alike are local. Company-sponsored events are held in Connecticut, and everyone attends. "It's like a family," Sandy says. In fact, Denise, now a college graduate, has started work for SNET in human resources and is simultaneously getting her master's degree in the subject. She often doesn't get home until nine or ten at night—hours that Lochlin and Sandy used to keep. But later on, they explain, she will be able to put in a 45–55-hour week, as they do. "No one counts the hours; there's no overtime. We just have to get our work done, and we do."

They don't allow the office to overwhelm their lives. Sandy has learned to compress her hours by not taking lunch and taking work home if she has to. She's also more creative about getting things done, and more willing to ask for help.

At the end of our talk, when Ashley and my daughter are making it clear they now want our attention, I ask my last question: what problems are caused by working full-time for a corporation and raising a child?

Without hesitation, Lochlin sums up what he and Sandy have been telling me for the better part of an afternoon: "It doesn't cause any problems at all. None at all."

With that, he sweeps a jubilant Ashley up for another back flip, nuzzles her, and heads back to finish Sunday's troubleshooting while Ashley and her mom go home.

As the Reidys' lives clearly show, sharing parenting helps to maintain mutual respect and closeness in a marriage. But if couples are going to work and also have time for themselves, they do have to extend parenting beyond the limits of nuclear family. When parents have full responsibility for a child, they are too vulnerable to stress and resentment; their children are too vulnerable to them. Creating a parenting network is different from just hiring help. It involves a new way of thinking based on the model of "othermothers"—whether grandparents, baby-sitters, or day-care providers—who are, as Sandy says, partners in parenting a child.

Such an attitude requires mothers to acknowledge that they have their own separate lives, and so do their children. As hard as it may be for mothers to leave small children, even when they have arranged to frame the night with their presence, it gets easier. "When I dropped my son off at the day-care center, he was happy and I felt a hallelujah chorus," one mother told Jessica Benjamin. By the time a child reaches twenty-one months, says Benjamin, three or four hours a day with her is really enough. Most of the time spent away will be daytime, so it's useful to consider those hours from the baby's point of view.

After the early morning activities, the day is generally a lazier time for babies, who nap after you go off to work and again in the afternoon. They may very well sleep a third of a mother's work time and spend the other two thirds getting to know their nonparental world.

Another consideration for the guilty parent is the difference between being there for a child and being ever-present. Says Susan Geffin, the music teacher who raised three children, "I feel our kids have always had our presence, even if we're not there all the time. We're there when they need us most. When they come home late at night and want to talk, I listen. Especially when they're saying something I don't want to hear. Then you really have to listen, and I do."

It is the attitude, the sense of entitlement that allows for relaxing maternal management. If a mother is comfortable with having time apart from mothering, the child will quickly grow to respect that time. For example, parents who wait until a child is asleep to have a quiet restorative dinner can often keep that time even if the child wakes up. Parents can explain that this is *their time together*, and if the child would like to sit quietly and munch on some bread while they have dinner, that's fine. The child not only learns that parents have the right to their time but usually grows bored without parental attention and returns swiftly to sleep.

Of course, children, being children, can be relied on to protest vigorously at least some of the time. But those times can be occasions for parents to teach respect for the needs of others. For example, most preschoolers have a hard time getting dressed and leaving the house in the morning, a transition made all the more difficult by working parents' impatience. However, instead of wrestling a child into her clothes every morning—as my husband and I had grown accustomed to doing at one point—Pamela Sicher suggests an entirely different approach. We should simply tell her that if she does not dress, we cannot go to work and proceed with our day. Therefore, we will have to sit on the couch and do as much work as possible from home, and she will have to occupy herself. When we tried this approach, we sat gravely, briefcases on our laps, and waited. In under two minutes she came running in with her clothes. That's how impressive a parent's priorities can be to a small child.

The basic formula is always the same: the more a child has of his parents at their best, the more they can give him and teach him about wholeness. To take time for oneself, one's marriage and one's work is not to selfishly abandon a child. It is an acknowledgment of having more than one role and valuing them all.

CHAPTER 9

Extending Family

Americans' inclination to isolate themselves is a ticket to nuclear family hell. Our tradition of leaving the nest at eighteen may build independence, but in doing so we miss out on one of extended family's greatest resources: the built-in "othermothers": grandparents, siblings, nieces and nephews, aunts and uncles, and cousins. Because most couples do not have such extended families nearby, most must plan to replace them as soon as they consider having a child. But Americans are also peculiarly fatalistic in this department. It may seem unromantic or inauthentic or even un-American to create an extended family in the absence of a biological one. Yet extending family is such a decisive factor in the success of working parents, they really cannot afford their reluctance. All of the parents I describe in this book extended their families in some manner.

Grandparents are not the only way to extend family, but they are the most obvious one, both because of their bond to their children and the mutual benefit of their involvement. Currently grandparents are raising 3.4 million children; 6 million families depend on grandparents for primary child care.

Indeed, grandparents are so valuable to raising children these days that, unless they live in a dangerous or professionally untenable place, it is well worth making their proximity one of the priorities in choosing where to live. Working parents can also try to entice grandparents to move nearby.

Only two of the ten couples I interviewed made such a choice, and both feel eternally grateful. The guiltless freedom and profound family security that Maddy and Patrick enjoy speak eloquently for extended family. Not only do the Reidys live close to her parents, but his mother lives near their daughter's day-care center and visits often, offering the kind of participation employed parents cannot.

I interviewed one couple from New York who moved to southern California just before her parents were about to retire. Then, instead of moving to a retirement community in Florida as they had planned, her parents decided to follow them west. The children investigated planned communities with them and found a good one an hour away. Now the grandparents baby-sit frequently, celebrate holidays with their grand-children, and attend all their rites of passage. Their daughter says that she has become closer to them since the move: "We respect each other. It's almost like friends." Her mother told me that they have made many new friends through community activities, and that while it might have been nice to settle where their old friends retired, they are doing fine.

In some areas of the country the "mother-in-law house" is a popular feature of older properties, a miniature of the big house built a couple of hundred yards away. Having spent two of the best weeks my parents and I ever shared in just such a rental arrangement, I know how much I would give up to have them near me while my daughter is young.

Short of importing one's parents or migrating to their locale, parents can amplify contact with supplementary visits, offering plane tickets as Christmas gifts and taking family vacations together. When families cannot afford this approach, they sometimes substitute less frequent, longer stays. My neighbor's mother comes from Australia to visit once a year, staying for a month. She lives with the family, albeit in the living room of their small apartment. During her stay she takes care of her grandchildren, giving the parents time off. As a result, this wise grand-parent, though far away, is still a part of her grandchildren's lives.

Of course, grandparents can be problematic. Diane Gottlieb cautions that they sometimes interfere with parenting, creating family power struggles. Such friction is most common when three generations live together. However, she also believes that conflict can be avoided if each family has a private living space and the new parents lovingly but firmly spell out the details of authority and acceptable behavior.

In Gottlieb's view, the long grandparent visits may be too much strain on everyone. Instead, she suggests a less volatile arrangement—grandparents coming to give parents vacation time or sending the child to visit the grandparents alone (when they are old enough). Between visits, grandparents might make and send audiotapes for the child, perhaps reading a story they have read together. Parents might ask children to send a weekly drawing and schedule phone calls to grandparents.

We made a game of our daughter memorizing her grandparents' phone number and dialing it herself. I have suggested to her that when she is particularly sad or happy she might like to call them, and she often does. The evidence of how much comfort they are to her is their gift of a now thread-bare blue nightgown, which she has insisted on sleeping in every night for almost a year. From age four, she selected gifts for their birthdays and made cards for them. We've drawn maps from our house to theirs. We mark off the day of their next visit on a calendar. The result of their dedication to her and our strategies to keep them connected is that although they live in a distant city, our daughter is thrilled when they come, even though their visit sometimes means that we, her parents, go away for a few days.

Unfortunately, grandparents are not always conveniently available when their grandchildren are small. They may have many other grandchildren, or they may have died. Perhaps they do not get along with their children. Or as one woman told me, after a lifetime of parenting, her own mother preferred to spend her time doing the things she didn't have time for before.

If grandparents cannot be part of a parenting network, parents can often think of other family members or friends of family to impress into service. Being needed, trusted, and valued is a powerful inducement to becoming a part of a young family's life. Julia, a single mother I interviewed, invited her aging aunt to move from Boston to New York to help raise her son. My husband and I cultivated a relationship with our elderly childless neighbors, exchanging dinners and visits. Though only one of the two remain, and a stroke has landed her in a nursing home, our daughter still eagerly visits her and considers her a significant person in her life.

Some preschools and day-care facilities today take advantage of senior citizens who want but don't have children in their lives. In fact, some

day-care centers are purposely built adjacent to senior facilities to encourage the connection. When there is no obvious surrogate grandparent
available, parents can try to find a nearby senior who might like to
"adopt" a new grandchild and/or earn some extra money caring for a new
baby.

Extending family feels quite natural to new parents. Having a newborn inspires one to reach out—for information, if nothing else. It is
awkward to call the pediatrician every time the baby has a new blemish
on her cheek. Next best to family—and sometimes better—are friends
who are willing to be godparents.

In my twenties, and not yet a parent myself, my first husband and I
were "othermothers" to Diane and Charles Gottlieb's baby girl. Although
we lived twenty miles away on snowy Vermont roads, we saw their baby
frequently enough—and were sufficiently enthusiastic—that she happily
stayed with us for occasional weekends. Since I wasn't ready for a child
myself, I was able to experience some of the pleasures by taking on the
role of "aunt," her actual aunts living far away.

A recent *New York Times* article on "para-parenting" makes exactly
this point. With so many people living far from their own families and
without children, many are happy to have a parent or mentor relationship
with their friends' children. If you have close friends who are not ready
for children themselves, asking them to be godparents to your children is
a way to keep the friendship close in the face of what can be a divisive
turning point.

In addition, new parents benefit from forming friendships with other
new parents they meet at a birthing class, a pediatrician's office, or a
community center. Creating some ongoing activities to bring these new
acquaintances together on a regular basis—whether a monthly potluck
dinner or Sunday morning coffee—can bring about opportunities to
swap child care or combine it. From some relationships come helpful
information and support, and often abiding friendships.

Having age-mate children is a powerful incentive to form friendships—not only because of the similar experience, but because the parents are all doing the same things at the same times. One mother told me
she and her husband spent every weekend morning from dawn until
naptime with another couple whose baby was about the same age. "Who
else was up at those hours? What else was there to do, particularly in

winter? We all loved it." It's not only nice to have the company, it is helpful in parenting well.

There is unquestionably an advantage in being mindful of the social component of parenting, planning in advance to surround yourself with a warm, helpful, like-minded group. Children, even infants, are great socializers. It's not that they love people—although they almost all do—but that they attract people. Having a child, like going to college or starting a new job, is a socially expansive experience. After new parents settle into a routine, they find it easy to bring others into their lives, often in a closer way than ever before. Whether it is an aunt who comes to help, grandparents, neighbors, friends, or a church group, they all become a part of a now-extended family. The other crucial part is formalized child care.

GETTING HELP: DAY CARE, BABY-SITTERS, NANNIES, AU PAIRS

Most employed parents of newborns are back at work in less than six months. The majority have relatives who look after their children. But others must pay to create a parenting network, and like the Reidys, most of them use day care—either at a center or a family provider's home. Only 3 percent report using baby-sitters in their homes, a tiny percentage of which are live-in nannies. The widespread assumption that in-home baby-sitters are the best, if most costly, choice is groundless. Each arrangement has its strengths and weaknesses.

It is also important to have a second source of nonparental care, such as a baby-sitter or relative, for weekly evenings out. Not only is the parents' dependence on one person or place reduced, but the baby gets to know two different othermothers. The arrangement encourages flexibility and the potential for future changes in the parenting network.

However, finding even one caregiver can be far more difficult than parents assume, particularly in our country, where child-care workers are paid so poorly and have little or no training. If an aunt or older sister has not volunteered, then parents usually require a couple of months and a surprising amount of fortitude to find the right care. Maddy and Patrick placed an ad in the neighborhood paper, screened approximately one hundred calls, interviewed a dozen people, checked references, and settled on the sitter they have now used for five years. Sandy Reidy inspected day-care centers, made surprise visits, called pediatricians, and interviewed parents who used the centers she was considering.

Were these finicky parents? Not at all. Some parents do have the luck to settle on their first choice, as we did. But most are not that lucky. According to Marilyn Glen, the director of northwestern Connecticut's Child Care Connections, a child-care center and family day-care referral service, many parents are willing to pay its $35 fee because its services can reduce the average ten- to sixteen-hour search by half. Services that locate baby-sitters and nannies usually charge upwards of four times that amount.

The paradox of child care is that while no work is more important than caring for children, individual parents and the culture in general have thus far been unwilling to invest in it. Our country is shockingly unprepared for this new family need. American day care runs the gamut from excellent to deplorable. Barbara Hamlin, an expert on the subject who researched part of the Connecticut portion of a recent four-state study, says that the woefully inadequate day care they reported was found largely in states, like North Carolina, that have little regulation. The free market doesn't work so well in child care, she believes, because parents are not necessarily aware of what good quality means. Also, they have a strong need to believe that the care they have chosen is good, whether that is true or not.

Many parents resent paying high fees, despite the intensive labor that child care requires. They see it as woman's work, and therefore unskilled. When family finances are tight, child care is considered expendable, even when the mother's present and future earning potential is sacrificed—not to speak of her personal need to work—so that she can stay home with the children.

Our child-care problems are mostly a result of our economy not having caught up with our new lives, but they also stem from our deep ambivalence about supplemental child care. We are not sure we want to establish ourselves as a country that offers fine child care—like France or Sweden—because, like birth control, it would truly change the nature of family life and of women's lives. So we nurse our suspicions. Even Penelope Leach looks askance at child care, warning women that, "if you are going to take a job that, even if it is officially part time, keeps you out of the house from nine to five every weekday . . . you have to accept that you will be sharing your child's upbringing. His attitudes, discipline and education will be as much in his caretaker's hands as yours." Well, yes. And perhaps that's a good thing. Heins and Seiden, no less qualified than Leach, write that "consistency has been much overrated in childcare advice." They feel that children can adjust very well to mood changes and people changes. In fact, they clearly believe that good child care complements parent care and suggest that parents provide caregivers who offer an approach different from their own: "A parent who is warm but disorganized might actually benefit the children by finding a sitter who is more disciplined. Parents who are strong on discipline often correct the balance by leaving their children with more permissive people." Clearly the challenge for today's parents is to overcome their prejudices and preconceptions about child care with solid information on the prevalent options.

Day Care

Both family and center care have advantages that many people, even those who use them, do not always realize. Unfortunately, many Americans associate day-care centers with poverty, probably because they were originally created by settlement houses to help poor women. Angela Soper referred to them as "unsanitary" places where children are "raised like cattle." That is probably how an earlier generation of parents felt about nursery schools before they were fully accepted.

Good day-care centers, like good nursery schools, are small, personal, and a lot cleaner than most homes or individual baby-sitters—who may have idiosyncratic ideas about cleanliness and disease prevention. Some are absolutely luxurious and cost more than individual care. Witness Country Kids Farm, where the Reidys' daughter goes: infant care costs $210/week for nine-hour days; children under three, $189/week; children over three, $160/week. One adult cares for three babies or four older children. That may seem like a high ratio if one is reminded of a mother of triplets, who definitely needs help. However, a mother also has all the other work of maintaining a home and herself. A professional caregiver only tends the babies. She also has set hours and time off. And if all three babies cry at once, then one of them has to wait. Few babies at home escape the same fate, especially if there are one or two older siblings.

Not all good day care is so costly. Subsidized day care for low-income families costs considerably less. At the Children's Center in the same neighborhood as Country Kids Farm, for example, care for children over three costs parents at most $125/week. However, they also offer a sliding scale of $8–$95/week for parents of two earning less than $44,000. While the facilities are not luxurious, they are homey and charming—an old Tudor house whose fireplaces have been carpeted over, making cozy nooks for kids, and whose built-in bookshelves are piled with toys.

Most communities offer choices in all child-care categories, from the private $260/week to the subsidized sliding scale centers and family day care running $60–120/week. The large day-care chains like Bright Horizons often offer supplementary services, such as picking up parents' dry-cleaning. Private or subsidized, however, the day-care center should be accredited by the National Association for the Education of Young Children to ensure quality.

Mary Burnham, the director of the Children's Center and a former kindergarten teacher, advises parents to choose a center or a home where there's plenty of laughter. Look for interactive care, she says, and ask how they discipline children. If they say they use time-outs, then ask what that means and how often the technique is used. Make sure caregivers are supervised. Burnham herself was part of a satellite program that supervised nine family care providers, offering training, inspection, and a hub where they could discuss their work. In her estimation, these are better indicators of good care than "glitzy paraphernalia."

Megan Yenter, a New Milford, Connecticut family care provider for four years, tells parents to be wary when a place is too tidy. If you take care of children, she says, you have to tolerate mess; kids make messes. A lot of family care providers have all the toys back on the shelves halfway through the day. The most important thing to note is whether the family care provider talks to children in a loving way. Megan also believes the caregiver and the parent must be partners with a close enough relationship so that they can tell each other what a child has been up to at home and in day care.

While it may be hard to locate an accredited, supervised, joyful center, the often suspect publicness of such centers gives them specific advantages over individual care. The Reidys stressed the reliability, the training of the staff, and the supervision at Country Kids Farm. Salaries are generally low. For example, at the Children's Center, a college graduate might begin at a paltry $12,000 with benefits. However, with job security, fair work guidelines, and camaraderie, child-care center workers often have higher morale than nannies, who are usually better paid. Also, because they care for groups of children, centers offer children conviviality and social training.

Baby-sitters and Nannies

Although day-care centers may initially seem scarier and less convenient for parents than hiring a baby-sitter, once everyone gets used to them there may be less actual risk and stress.

It is difficult to ensure that a private baby-sitter is adequate. Every parent seems to know the story about the nanny who (so it comes out years later) took her little charge to the cemetery every day to show him what happens to sinful children. Baby-sitting is among the lowest-paying professions; there are no set rules, and a lot of the employers are not experienced supervisors. Furthermore, there is no management consultant to call if things go awry.

The advantage is that a child continues to get the full attention of an adult, stays in familiar surroundings, and is cared for by someone the parent hopefully gets to know very well. Indeed, a lot of parents, including me, are crazy about their baby-sitters.

A nanny provides the most intimate care for a baby and offers parents complete freedom to come and go as they wish. However, having a live-in nanny generally entails a considerable loss of privacy for parents— specifically, the privacy with their child. A nanny may interfere with a parent's effort to establish his or her own parenting rhythms and intimacies. It is hard to develop parent confidence if there is always a professional standing nearby, especially one who often does not have many other gratifications in life.

Heins and Seiden point out that live-in baby-sitters can often feel just as isolated, bored, and discouraged as many parents who are home alone with a child—even more so when they live far from their own family and friends. The sociologist Julia Wrigley, who made a study of nannies, found that while parents often think of their nannies as "part of the family," even those nannies who liked their jobs felt isolated and insecure, being keenly aware that they held their jobs at the whim of their employers.

Given class and cultural differences, few understood or approved of their employer's views on child-rearing.

From the parents' point of view, a caregiver can be another emotional presence, someone else to deal with at the end of the day. The vagaries of her life and moods can intrude on the household or affect the child. The child too can become terribly dependent on that one caregiver, falling apart if someone else must fill in—as happened the day the bridal magazine editor came to do a feature on Amsale. Moreover, it may take extra will to do the necessary parenting if someone else is there to do it when you come in tired from work.

Since a baby-sitter can also provide incomparable care, dependability, and convenience—as in our case—it is worth spending the money and time to ensure success. On the simplest level, that means offering a fair wage, even if someone will accept less. Like any employee, the less a baby-sitter feels exploited, the happier and more reliable she will be. Parents must also make the job description clear because the sitter will invariably have different ideas of how to fill in the gray areas. For example, if parents do not want the child to watch TV during the day, they must say so; if the only discipline they approve of is the use of time-outs, they must let her know.

However, once parents have specified the nanny's duties, it is to everyone's advantage to let her control her work. She will feel far less stress knowing that she can work at her own pace and do as she likes during the baby's nap time. Just as employers everywhere are learning the importance of letting workers set their own schedules, so too should parents who employ caregivers. But unlike employees who work with others, the nanny faces the additional problem of isolation. A parent can help by encouraging her to take the baby to the local library, the park, the community center, or the home of a baby whose caregiver she likes.

According to one nanny, it is essential for parents and sitter to have a weekly meeting. This is a time to discuss the child, go over what the parent would like her to be doing with the child, and air grievances. If the sitter has to stay overtime to have a meeting when the child will not be vying for her attention or the parents', it is well worth the extra pay.

In hiring a baby-sitter, parents have to think about attitude. Is this a cheerful, joyful presence for a child? You should ask about her background, avoiding the darkly complicated childhoods that might make for emotional impairment. You can ask how she would handle stressful situations: if the baby won't stop crying, if he starts to choke, if the child hits her in anger, if she cannot reach you by phone. What would she do in an emergency? Ask how she would work if her own children fell ill, how often she is away, and what her other obligations are. The answers will not only reveal her competence but give you an idea of how easy she is to communicate with.

Above all, parents must check references. A candid former employer should give a full picture, including the limitations they found. In a trial week, spend a day or two at home with a new sitter just seeing how things go. Or make a surprise visit home. After the first week or two, if a child is not pleased to see the sitter in the morning, you might want to consider whether this is the right sitter for your child.

Au pairs are young women, often from Europe, who want to spend a year living in America. Recently some agencies have begun to specialize in young American women from small towns in the Midwest who would like to sample life in a big city. They take care of the children and live in the home but are generally not expected to do housekeeping. Some parents prefer au pairs because they are well educated, speak fluent English, and cost considerably less than other baby-sitters, typically $100/week. However, others find that the one-year turnover of au pairs, who are allowed only short-term work permits or who have their own plans, is too disruptive for children. Some parents have also discovered that supervising a young person can feel like having another child.

Because the au pair lives with a family, takes meals with them, and brings her friends home, this can be a very complex relationship. The au pair may have a different view of her status in the household than her employers do. As a college student, I became close friends with the French au pair of acquaintances of mine. She was only a couple of years younger than the parents she worked for, yet they regarded her strictly as an employee. Our friendship had to be conducted outside of their home. When I was their invited guest, I was asked not to visit with her. Although they were neither formal nor unfriendly people, they felt the need to draw rigid lines around their family, their social life, and her employment. Many au pair situations turn out quite happily for both parties; however, they do require the right chemistry and a lot of social skill on both sides.

LIFE ON THE PARENTING NETWORK

Just as sharing parenting with a father is emotionally complicated for most women, so too is sharing parenting with another woman, whether one's own mother, a baby-sitter, or a worker at a day-care center. It is often very painful to find that a child, having spent more hours a day with a hired caregiver than with either mother or father, appears to love the caregiver best.

My friend with a housekeeper named Alberta has a child who called her parents "Almommy" and "Aldaddy," as if they were all members of the Alberta family. Many children howl when their baby-sitter leaves and push themselves out of their parent's arms to follow her. Many do not want to leave their day-care center, or they are so thrilled to see their caregivers in the morning that the parents, particularly the mother, grow insecure. The major issues that confront parents with caregivers are rivalries and maintaining the primacy of the family.

All of these are new parenting issues for middle-class families, which only relatively recently have routinely come to include two employed parents. The child-care handbooks generally ignore the problem, and indeed, they do not take the new reality of employed mothers very seriously in any context. Yet a child's caregiver, at least in the preschool years, will be the parents' and the child's most intimate other, and that is why a rivalrous love triangle can form with mother, caregiver, and child. The mother rather than the father more often forms this rivalry because she and the caregiver are both women, thus tending toward maternal domination.

The mother triangle may be the most challenging problem on the parenting network. No one warns a mother about how hard it is to stand by and watch her child place the baby-sitter in the romantic lead while she is cast in a supporting role. No one even warns her that it happens. But it is so common that, according to Clifford Greenhouse, the director of the Pavilion Agency in New York City, "mothers' jealousy is right up there with incompetence as the reason why nannies are dismissed." Having been in the nanny business for fifteen years, Greenhouse assures mothers that most nannies are not trying to take over their child. Parents have to know how to structure the relationship to avoid rivalry. He suggests that baby-sitters, even live-ins, withdraw as soon as parents return home, even if it's inconvenient and even if the child cries. That way the child will not be torn between the two. Also, the parent subtly asserts primacy.

Whatever parents do, they should not discourage love between the baby-sitter and the child. Many mothers are tempted to fire a baby-sitter whom the child adores, simply because she feels her own relationship is threatened by their love. However, as Arietta Slade, a professor of clinical psychology at the City University of New York, puts it, "The right caregiver—and that includes a counselor at a good day-care center—will feel emotionally connected to the child. If the child weren't attached to her, he'd be lonely and bereft whenever his mother was gone."

To help them accept their child's attachment to a caregiver, Diane Gottlieb continually reminds apprehensive patients that the caregiver is helping them to be more effective mothers, just as an associate or assistant at work helps them to do the job. Instead of assuming, as the father usually does, that the child is preoccupied with his sitter and will pay attention to his parent later, a mother may take a child's temporary preference as an either-or choice, "fearing that she will lose the relationship forever." The child is really just having difficulties with the transition, as young children often do.

Gottlieb assures mothers that "a child unconsciously understands that her relationship to her mother may be more conflicted than her easier relationship to her baby-sitter, but it is also richer and therefore more deeply engaging." Children respond to the complexity of the parent-child bond, taking the parents' praise and blame more to heart, letting themselves fully express their feelings with a parent, not a sitter. If there are three major parent figures, the child learns to develop distinct, appropriate relationships with each one, according to their unique emotional possibilities.

NYU's Linda Carter offers the most important idea underlying the parenting network: a child's love is not a matter of competition. She says, "The more love there is, the more the child's capacity for love grows. A child's loving relationship with a caregiver will mean more love—not less—for everyone." Nonetheless, she also counsels parents to maintain the primacy of the family by explaining to the child that while the baby-sitter is someone they all care about, she has her own family. Carter suggests that parents define times for family activities, such as snuggling in bed in the mornings or visiting relatives.

No matter how trusted the caregiver, parents should always make sure one of them is with the child at crucial times like visits to the dentist or doctor. Although the nuclear family need not provide the only parenting a child gets, it can still be the smallest, most intimate of the child's concentric circles of care. Whatever the management, the child must feel the intimate love of both parents as primary. Whether the child does may sometimes be difficult to determine, as the following story about our own caregiver shows.

THE STORY OF ROSA

When our caregiver, Rosa, left for a two-month vacation to visit her family in Puerto Rico, our usually sunny, nonviolent three-year-old sobbed constantly, ran and hid under the bed if we tried to comfort her, and hit and rejected the replacement sitter and her beloved grandmother. In her sleep she cried out Rosa's name, repeating it like a Greek lament, in a widow's soul.

We knew she would be bereft and angry. Rosa had taken care of our daughter since she was three months old, living in for the first two years. But we had prepared, having Rosa talk with her about the trip, making a video of Rosa and our daughter, scheduling weekly telephone calls. Nothing helped. Seeing the video, she tried to crawl into the television set, then dove, hysterical, under the bed. After the first phone call, I counted five tear bursts. And believe me, I have no wish to keep score. I merely want to describe the blow that a child can feel on losing a beloved baby-sitter. This is a major grief that no battery of preparations or extra dose of TLC will dispel.

If a child is attached to a caregiver, even her temporary loss can register an eight on a child's stress scale, right behind death and divorce. One little boy "Windexed" his new sitter when his own went back to El Salvador; another began to insist on sleeping in her parents' room; and a third refused to return to her day-care center. Susanna Neumann, a consulting psychologist to two New York City nursery schools, warns that "even when children say 'I don't care,' they're usually just trying to convince themselves because they are so afraid of being flooded by feelings." Also, some children believe they have to protect parents who now seem (or might be) unhinged because they have just lost a mainstay of their family organization.

On the other hand, Neumann adds, "no matter how operatic a child's grief, the loss of a babysitter is not comparable to the loss of a parent. Parents have a significance no one else has. Not that their grief for the babysitter isn't real. It's just amplified by all the other anxieties of their age." That's why children often save their most contrary behavior for parents, testing the full range of their emotions, and are such lambs with their baby-sitters.

Neumann suggests that parents respond to a child's unspoken fears: Was it my fault? Will everyone leave me? Will I be alone? Did you make her leave? Keep talking about those feelings so the child knows he is not alone. Parents also need to be prepared to tolerate their children's need to act out their anguish and seek comfort in regression. They should accept a child's anger at her "omnipotent" parents for "allowing" the baby-sitter to leave. Let her zone out on television or divert her with a family vacation, she suggests, adding that, "as ineffectual as parents might feel, they have to remain stable so the child can have his or her feelings. Then, slowly, over a month or two, they will integrate the loss." She reminds parents, too, that a child's life does not have to be perfect. The point is that parents can help a child heal.

Moreover, mastering this loss can turn out to be a meaningful growth experience for children and parents. For one thing, progress isn't linear. Children oscillate between regression and progression. At the nadir of my daughter's misery two weeks into the ordeal, when she realized Rosa was really gone and would sob off and on when she was at home, she nevertheless rallied at bedtime. "I'm very brave," she repeatedly told us as we discussed the monsters in her room. Unprompted, she announced that she was a big girl and didn't need her diaper at night. And she was right.

Challenges can catapult a child into new maturity. However, if a baby-sitter's departure feels like a crisis, parents may have to consider whether they have played a central enough role in the child's life. Perhaps they have allowed the child to become too dependent on the baby-sitter.

Parents who did not have enough nurturing themselves may actually let a baby-sitter take their emotional place, explains Pamela Sicher. They probably want to be the central parents but fear they will fail or prove unworthy of their child's love. In that case, a confident, in-charge baby-sitter can relieve the parents of feelings they might not want to face. For her part, the caregiver, who may have chosen a nurturing profession to make up for nurturing she herself did not get, may encourage a child's dependence and insist on her own mothering importance. Then, says Sicher, the caregiver can be like an addictive drug to the child. When she leaves, the child suffers not only loss but "withdrawal."

If this is the case, Sicher advises parents to step in and take over, working through the fears that may have kept them more distant before. During those two months of our daughter's "nervous breakdown," as we called it, my husband and I hardly saw our friends. I rushed home from work early every day. When I got there, my daughter greeted me with trembling excitement. Each day, it seemed, there were a hundred issues we had to talk over, agree on, spar about. It was exhausting, but as my husband said on the eve of Rosa's return, "I'm almost sorry she's coming back. I've sort of gotten used to doing all the work."

Somehow our daughter had maneuvered her formerly reserved dad into spending hours lying with her on the floor doodling and jabbering, the kinds of things she used to do with Rosa. But she would also cup his face with her palms, whispering, "My daddy," the way she used to whisper, "My Rosa."

Rosa did come back. But for all of us, I think, her return was anticlimactic. Yes, we were happy to have our friend, helper, baby-sitter back. Yet so much had changed in the time she was gone—not the least of which was our daughter, who now knew she could survive loss, even the loss of her Rosa.

Looking back, I can see how our family life would have been easier if our baby-sitter had not lived with us but had nightly returned to her home, leaving us to reconnect as a family. We also could have further dispersed the mothering among two different caregivers. With a parenting network of several loving othermothers, no one loss, whether of a baby-sitter or a family care provider, would be devastating.

Extending family, whether it entails bringing godparents into intimate contact with a child, finding the right child care, or sustaining healthy relationships with a child's other caregivers, is a contemporary adaptation of a successful old model of child-rearing. However, our modern version entails so many new concepts for parents that it often requires an emotional reorientation, particularly with regard to trusting "strangers" with one's children, overcoming prejudices against group care, and respecting a child's relationship with other caregivers. As our experience with Rosa suggests, it also requires a new and careful attunement to parent-child relationships. There are new skills involved as well, such as getting along with caregivers, defining family boundaries, and creating clear work guidelines.

If parents, particularly mothers, are not going to be ever-responsive and always available, then they must find new ways to nourish a maternal bond; if parents cannot rely simply on being the only one the child will love, they have to be more mindful of the quality of that love. Raising children with a parenting network is not as private an undertaking as child-rearing has been in the past, but it can provide a larger safety net for parents and children both, and a richer soil in which they can all grow.

In these times when family life is so subject to change, a parenting network provides a new stability, although it also requires that parents envision a different family life. As hard as that is for parents, family life that is adapted to reality is better for children.

A child will adapt to whatever life a parent leads, whether it is spending weekdays in day care, at his parents' store, or even months in a Brazilian jungle for a parent's anthropological research. Whatever patterns parents adopt will seem normal to a child, and each will have its strengths and problems. Too often parents miss the forest for the trees. They center their lives on their children, forgoing their own satisfying lives that children could participate in.

All the parents in this book gave up a lot to parent well: Amsale and Neil do not live in their neighborhood of choice; Jim sacrificed a television career to be his own boss at a less pressured job; Angela and Matt don't have "a lot of things." All of them gave up sleep, many evenings out, and some degree of ambition so that their children would always know how loved they are. They may all "chase their tails" during the week, but all of them know their children's schools and friends; they give their children a sufficient amount of their undivided attention to know them well. They also provide them with models of fulfilled lives so that they too will be able to raise children and follow their dreams. And just maybe, by then, our world will make it a little bit easier to do.

CHAPTER 10

When There Is Only One: The Single Mother

No one faces a greater challenge in developing an extended family than the single mother. But why discuss mothering alone in a book about redefining motherhood? Because at one time or another 58 percent of American children live solely with their mothers. More than one-quarter of American children are born to unmarried mothers, and one-quarter below the age of three live with a single mother.

More significant than the fact that almost as many women mother without partners as with them is that for most single mothers, the economic, emotional, and social problems of parenting are magnified tenfold by poverty. The facts are harsh and startling: of the eight million single mothers in America, only half are employed, and that half earns on average $18,600—a figure barely above the poverty line for a family of three. Unemployed mothers now have a median income of $6,000 a year, with child support contributing an average of $2,600. That, notes the historian Robert Griswold in his book *Fatherhood in America* is less than many men pay for their car insurance.

Although single mothers are so numerous, they have few social supports to alleviate their appalling fiscal distress. Even with day-care subsidies for the working poor, a woman may not be able to afford the supplementary baby-sitting to enable her to take courses or train for a better job. Furthermore, as Hillary Clinton has pointed out in *It Takes a Village*, poorer mothers often work nights or on rotating shifts, thus missing out on conventional (and therefore subsidized) day care entirely.

167

The glamorous pay of broadcast journalists, like TV's *Murphy Brown*, is not the norm for single mothers. As for *Grace under Fire*, earning fourteen dollars an hour in an oil refinery is great, but few women actually get such jobs.

Even when a single mother is financially secure, she is still apt to feel far greater maternal guilt than her married counterpart, believing that she has deprived her children of a "normal" family. If that single mother also happens to be a woman of color, then her problems are compounded, as Maya Angelou adroitly describes in an autobiographical narrative:

> Her singleness indicates she has rejected, or has been rejected by her mate. Yet she is raising children who will become mates. Beyond her door, all authority is in the hands of people who do not look or think or act like her and her children. Teachers, doctors, sales clerks, librarians, policemen, welfare workers are white and exert control over her family's moods, conditions and personality; yet within the home, she must display a right to rule which at any moment, by a knock at the door, or a ring of the telephone can be exposed as false. In the face of these contradictions, she must provide a blanket of stability, which warms but does not suffocate.

And yet, as Angelou's own life testifies, despite financial duress, anxiety, and contradictions that do defeat a lot of single mothers, it is still possible to mother well and to cultivate one's life. If single motherhood magnifies the problems of contemporary motherhood, it can also underscore the rewards of mothering while pursuing independent goals.

Because the single mother is rarely privileged to play the traditional stay-at-home role, she is also more likely to have independent goals. Put another way, the single mother falls so short of the maternal ideal, she is often more motivated than the married woman to create her own mothering rules and therefore is often freer to live her life. And she can do so even without Angelou's multimillion-dollar talent. More often than not, she resembles one of the two single mothers presented in this chapter. Even if she is a professional, like Kierra Foster Ba, the subject of our next portrait, economic austerity alone will have called for enormous emotional strength while destructive family models will have compounded the burden. However, she will also be an original, and mistress of her life.

KIERRA FOSTER BA

Kierra, a thirty-five-year-old single mother of a twelve-year-old son, is a tribute to the healing powers of parenthood. Although her motherhood, coming unexpectedly at the age of twenty-three, demanded great sacrifice, she was wise enough to invest in herself along with her child. A high school English teacher now, she glows with the dual pleasure of being a mother and an educator.

Kierra is a strikingly handsome woman—with two braids framing a sculpted face and a wonderful gap-toothed smile—and strikingly centered, to borrow a New Age neologism. Her son Cherif is at camp when I visit, yet he is very much present in his mother's conversation and in the family snapshots on the mantel. Although Kierra lives in what she describes as "a tenement on a drug-infested block," her small railroad flat is very much a home: well ordered, with lovingly placed flowers and her framed degrees hanging on the wall. "An autobiographical self-portrait" she did when she was teaching fifth grade captures her impressive resolve in the dead front Frieda Kahlo stare. On its border are small pictures clipped from magazines, each representing parts of her essential self, she explains: water for her Piscean nature; flowers, which she loves; and a drum for her drummer father.

Kierra's story is dramatic. She gave birth to her son seven months after beginning a master's program in African American literature at Yale. Knowing how inopportune a time it was, she intended to terminate the pregnancy until a dream convinced her that her son's birth was destined. Her then-husband, panicked by the impending responsibility, left his medical school studies in Senegal, where they had met, to join her. But Kierra ended up having to mother her husband as well as their infant son. In addition, she did all the housework, her graduate studies, *and* held down two part-time jobs. The marriage lasted only another year.

As successful as Kierra was, both as a mother and as a student, she hardly recommends parenthood before one can support a child financially and psychologically. "His birth was devastating. You can't be at Yale and be pregnant; I couldn't drink or socialize and I wasn't in scholar mode. In addition, most of the students at Yale, including the students of color, were second- and third-generation college-educated. I was the first in my family, and insecure. Pregnant or not, I was learning that I wasn't a study jock. But being pregnant, I was terribly confused and my self-esteem was low."

Although Kierra believed then, and still does, that "you really have to be middle-class to raise a child, otherwise you're looking at bills you can't pay instead of parenting with a free heart," she plunged in. She also paid a price: as a result of the emotional pain, she gained sixty pounds during her son's first year. Motherhood was her one joy. Even nursing her son made her feel powerful and purposeful. Most important, perhaps, Kierra was also convinced she could be a good mother and make her son feel valuable: "I wanted to notice my child, praise him, include him, and allow him his feelings." She would give Cherif what she had longed for as a child.

Her own teenage mother left when Kierra was seven years old, unable to win custody of her children or endure more of her husband's abuse. As the oldest child, Kierra had to take care of three younger siblings, including an eighteen-month-old baby. That first year after her mother left, she remembers, she missed fifty-four days of school—days her father could not hire sitters or do the child care himself. By the age of ten she was doing most of the parenting, including registering the children at school and buying their birthday gifts. Between having to perform tasks far too difficult for a child and being beaten for falling short, Kierra, in her words, was "out of it" most of the time. Nor did she develop the self-esteem she was determined her son would have.

When I ask Kierra how she, who had so little mothering herself, could be such a good mother, she had specific answers: her self-reflective nature, abundant affection from her sisters and her volatile father, and good counseling when she left home at age fourteen. Her explanation seems accurate; however, I am struck by one other: by having to cook, clean, and take care of a baby while trying to attend school, Kierra replicated and mastered her childhood situation. That is, Kierra's own motherhood was a chance to do well, as an adult, what she had done as an "out of it" child. It was an opportunity to experience good mothering through the blossoming of her own child. Nonetheless, mothering with no partner, money, or time is cruelly difficult.

At Yale, Kierra did not have an apartment big enough to offer room and board to another student in exchange for child care. She couldn't afford the best child care. Once she came home to find her son ill because an irresponsible teenage sitter had given him food she was warned would produce an allergic reaction. The best Kierra could do was put Cherif in child care three days a week while she attended classes and went to work. Only once, when her father took care of Cherif for a week so she could finish her master's thesis, did Kierra have sufficient study time to rediscover what she had come to Yale for.

Throughout it all, however, motherhood remained a joy for her. As a graduate student, she formed a mothers' cooperative to exchange child care, help, and friendship. After she moved to New York the pressures eased somewhat. Kierra and Cherif spent an hour on the bus together morning and night on the way to work and child care. During that "free time," they would read, look at the sights, and talk to the passengers who came to know and like the intelligent, friendly child. "Saturday was our day. I joined the Museum of Natural History, we'd go to puppet shows, have picnics in the park with other single mothers I purposely cultivated. My social world was built around Cherif. We had a lot of fun."

Although the pressure abated after she graduated and could work full-time, a master's degree didn't solve Kierra's financial problems. While she is far from poor, Kierra's domestic economy says more about a single mother's challenge than any of my opening statistics. College and graduate school left her thousands of dollars in debt, living in New York City requires spending thousands more for the private school she believes is necessary for Cherif, and even her inadequate housing costs $700 a month in rent.

Why live in a place as expensive as Manhattan? "If I lived in an outer borough," she explains, "housing would have been cheaper or better, but then my son would have had to commute over an hour by train to school. Also, I grew up in Manhattan, and this is where I feel at home."

I had always assumed teachers' salaries were generous, but Kierra corrects my impression. The $38,000 she earns annually—including summer school teaching—is typical. Yes, the hours afford more family time, but with class preparation and meetings, a teacher's workday is longer than most people imagine. Rent, loan payments, and private school leave Kierra with about $11,000 a year for all her other expenses.

In everyday terms, that doesn't leave much for child-care costs; for example, by the time Cherif was six, Kierra occasionally had to leave him alone when she attended class or a meeting because she didn't have baby-sitting money.

For Kierra, however, the most important thing is that neither she nor Cherif has felt deprived. They have the essentials and, after that, what Kierra values most: their relationship, Cherif's education, and her independent life. She has no regrets about working while she raises Cherif. "I knew I didn't want to stay home and take care of him, even if I had the money. He wouldn't have liked me if I had been home all the time!"

As it is, Cherif has a mother who delights in him when they are together yet continues to develop her independent life. "I hate when people say mothers must put family first. No, put yourself first. When a mother is too self-sacrificing, the child becomes the keeper of her hopes and dreams. That's too much pressure on the child."

She finds it unfortunate that in our society mothers are held totally responsible for children—even for things they cannot control. And working-class mothers are held particularly responsible. She points out that if a poor woman's baby is crying, it is always *her* fault. Furthermore, Kierra's experience as a teacher and a mother leads her to conclude that when there's mischief in a class, it's perceived as the black child's fault. If a black or poor child has a problem, teachers assume there's something wrong at home.

Often that's not the case. If it is, we blame the mother rather than the pressures on her. "As a society, we hate the woman who left her children alone, especially if she's left them to go to a nightclub, let's say. But that mother may very much need the release she gets from going out, the time alone. The more she gets for herself, the more she will give to her children. Mothers have to have their lives too."

While Kierra would prefer that children are never left home alone, she feels society has to help mothers so that they are not driven to such extremes. "I'd like to have the support so I don't have to feel so guilty if I have to go to a workshop on Saturday. Our culture could provide child care and places kids can go on weekends if parents have to work. We also need parenting classes, support groups, and help, especially for single parents. I wish we had a *society* that put children first so that mothers didn't bear such a tremendous responsibility alone."

For Kierra, societal support isn't a substitute for parental responsibility but a way to help parents be more effective. She believes that taking personal responsibility for a child is an opportunity for growth. "Motherhood—parenthood—is kind of divine," she says. "If you raise a child who is happy, you've done a great thing in life. What children bring in return is their hope, their aliveness, and their excitement about the world."

THE PSYCHOLOGICAL CHALLENGE OF SINGLE PARENTHOOD

The portrait of Kierra not only illustrates the economic straits of the single mother but shows how much she feels society's disapproval: *her* child is singled out if there's trouble in a class; *she* is assumed to be the problem; society does not accommodate her family's needs. Her success in parenting is purely a product of her own formidable determination, as is her success in the world. Kierra's experience is probably typical: having a child impairs the single mother's potential for success at the same time as it motivates. Kierra felt her self-esteem drop, and she, we must remember, had the enormous validation of her education and acceptance at Yale.

Not all the single mothers I interviewed were as worldly and professional as Kierra; however, all were successful in their mothering and making their way in the world. Even so, they all felt they had paid a high personal price. Again and again I heard how hard it was to create sufficient private space and distance from the child. For example, few of the single mothers had sufficient energy to form new love relationships.

Renee, who had five-year-old Sterling when she was thirty-five and who currently attends graduate school, describes the sheer exhaustion of solo parenting: "You put the baby to bed, you get up if she has a bad dream, then you pop out of bed at dawn when she wakes. Everything I do, like cleaning the house, takes hours instead of minutes because it's always, 'Mommy, come look at my picture.' As for when I have the flu, or my daughter does, it's mommy-hell." While she chose to have a child on her own and has some help from her mother, she feels she doesn't have five minutes to breathe. Like Kierra, she hardly goes out because, as she explains, "a movie, that's thirty dollars once you pay the baby-sitter. Dating will just have to wait until I'm out of graduate school."

Money does not solve the problem. Julie, who chose single motherhood and had ample money for help, believes it is not mere chance that her son was five before she married: "Before that I dated a few times, but I couldn't have stayed awake long enough for a relationship, or even an affair." Yet Julie, like most of the single mothers I spoke with, missed having adult companionship, if not partnership.

Diane Gottlieb says that "your greatest challenge as a single mother, outside of sheer economic survival, is to balance your parenting life and your social life." Even couples can lose themselves when they become new parents, she reminds us, but one partner will usually coax the other into a dinner out or a night away. The single mother, however, must create her own social life, even while working and parenting. Often, too, Gottlieb points out, the children, who have become her protectors during a painful divorce, discourage their mother's new love relationships, either out of simple jealousy or a fear that she will be hurt again. How many single mothers have heard even their very small children say of the rival for her attention, "Mommy, I don't like him. Tell him to go away."

The single parent who feels especially wounded by a former partner or fears being abandoned again may also come to depend on the child as an "abandonment-proof" relationship. Pamela Sicher cautions that the mother who denies herself her own life is likely to burden her child with feeling responsible for her. And when a child begins to form peer relationships, this kind of mother may make the child feel that separateness is not permitted.

Of all the impediments to a single mother's social life, however, guilt may be the greatest. The single mother may try to compensate for the lack of a father at home by parenting that much more. Blaming herself for what she perceives as her child's deprivation, she may simply feel that much less deserving of her own time and pleasure than the partnered mother. But from their own perspective, children of single mothers are not disadvantaged. Sicher tries to dispel such unnecessary guilt by explaining that "the mother who feels guilty over not providing a father may define her child as a have-not, even when, in fact, children don't compare their lot in life until adolescence. How they live is normal to them, so mothers should take that attitude too." The children themselves, she continues, can be entirely satisfied. They have a mom, friends, school—all the things they need. They do not spend much time on mourning a father they never had or an involved father who no longer lives with them. If their needs are met, their "tanks can be full."

The question is whether there is a perceived loss by the child. Certainly if a father dies or abandons a child, the child will understandably mourn. In these cases, a child needs extra support, and Sicher suggests the single mother look for outside help, particularly if she is grieving herself. She may not be able to give even as much as she otherwise would, or perhaps she needs her own outside support. In the case of divorce, the child also mourns the loss of his original family constellation. However, if the child still has the other parent or has never had him, then he will probably not feel deprived.

A recent *Wall Street Journal* article made this very point in covering a single mother who raised her twenty-one-year-old quadruplets on her own and whose "story shows how successful such families can be when a strong parental example of resiliency is present." Not only did she rise from receptionist to the head of the Washington State Film Office, but her children, who are all in college, loved their family life. As one said, "I would want it just the way we had it."

Not only is it unnecessary for the single mother to feel guilty, says Sicher, but it is unwise to burden children with the guilt that underlies overparenting. "The mother who thinks that because she made a mistake in love or marriage, she must give 150 percent to her child, will exaggerate a youngster's natural (and frightening) feelings of omnipotence." When a mother does not feel the right to say no, it means that she is unwilling to admit that sometimes she does not have enough to give. A child who never hears no eventually gets the idea that his demands are "royal"; that is, so important that they *must* be met. On a more subtle level, the parent is giving the child the message that she or he is too weak to handle a no. Omnipotence and fragility, she points out, are two sides of the same coin.

Far better for a single mother's own life and the child's if she can focus on the advantages her family offers her child and the disadvantages to children of overindulgence. "But if a single mother's pain is acute," Sicher acknowledges, "that may be impossible to do, at least completely." Sicher knows firsthand. When her son was three, she separated from his father.

And although she soon began to date the man she would marry three years later, "it was a long time before I could meld my separate relationships with my son and my new partner."

As Kierra's story—and Kathy's, which follows—clearly illustrate, "Single mothers don't have to come up with perfect solutions for their children: the kids just need to know they aren't alone with their feelings." That is true even when the children express a sense of deprivation.

Julie, who did not marry until her son was five, faced one of the hardest moments of her single mothering when her son, at age two, began to call the man next door "Daddy." Because she is not guilty, she was able to resist the usual impulses to supply him with a daddy, distract him from his desire by showering him with toys and entertainment, or respond with disapproval. Sicher's counsel to single mothers is to acknowledge the child's desire for a father with an affirmation such as, "It must feel good to be able to say that word to someone." She explains that the mother does not need to view the child's longing as a reflection of her insufficient nurturance. Her attitude should be positive even facing the practical ramifications. So if the child, perhaps a slightly older one, tells his mother he called the neighbor "Daddy," she might simply ask him, "Well, what did he say?" implying that it is all right with her to do that and thereby giving the child the approval he is seeking. The very suggestion that the child and the neighbor can settle the question themselves means that the mother accepts that the child has this need.

Similarly, the child of a single parent needs to know he won't be punished for having a relationship with his other parent or stepparent. In her own life, Sicher felt she had succeeded in making sure her son felt supported in loving his stepmother when, as a teenager, he asked her, "Do you think Mommy Ar" (as he calls his father's wife) "is a good stepmother?" implicitly suggesting what they both well knew, that she very much was.

Even when single mothers cannot provide a good model for marriage, they need not feel guilty. Allison Anders, a single mother as well as an award-winning film director whose movies *Mi Vida Loca* and *Grace of My Heart* are about single mothers, offers this advice: "Know your strengths and admit your weaknesses to your kids. That's what keeps you from being burdened with guilt and feeling like a failure." Because she pursued a goal and achieved it, Anders says, her own daughters—now teenagers—take for granted that they can do what they want in life. As for what she herself hasn't been able to do—have a lasting relationship with a man—"I just tell them, use me as a model for careers, not relationships. I'm not good at those."

The Social Challenge of Single Motherhood

Single mothers may need more than average ingenuity to avoid the isolation of nuclear family life. Because they rarely have sufficient income, they are often unable to buy help and to thus create a parenting network with child care. If a single mother's own family is not close or supportive, it may not be possible to create a network with extended family. Kierra's mother disappeared when she was seven, and her father was often unavailable; however, when she first moved to New York, it helped enormously to settle herself and her son in her father's home. Allison Anders became a single mother at nineteen and had a second daughter three years later. Her mother, also a single parent, had just had another child herself and could not help her, so Anders lived on welfare. "Survived" is actually her word, because, she says, "welfare isn't living."

Whatever the lack of funds or immediate family, though, some sort of parenting network is always possible, if only a single mothers' exchange like the one Kierra set up at Yale. But more is better, particularly for single mothers, because the ease of parenting is directly proportional to the breadth of the parenting network. How much more is possible? Often, more than is apparent.

Julie lost her own mother around the time her son was born. Her father had died long before, leaving behind a childless aunt who had lived with her parents. A seventy-seven-year-old is not the obvious candidate for coparenting, but Aunt Clara turned out to be an excellent one. Not only did the baby bring a new meaning to her life, she gave Julie's son another parent figure. Julie eventually expanded the boundaries of her family by inviting Clara to move from Boston and live close to her and her infant son in New York City. Although Aunt Clara was nearly eighty by that time, she was (and still is) so vigorous and loving that she provided a fine complement to Julie's limited parenting time. Her proximity meant that Julie could continue with her social life as well as her work. Clara not only helped with the daily child care but took care of many of the household chores, like the financial accounting (her former specialty).

The first time Julie had to be away overnight for business, she learned how important Clara was to her son. He responded to her anxious solicitation by saying, simply, "It's okay, Aunt Clara will be here, won't she?" When they spent a year in France for Julie's work, Clara lived with the family. At eighty, she also studied French to prepare for the trip. And while Julie has since married, Clara continues to live with them in a roomy nineteenth-century brownstone built to accommodate the kind of extended family we rarely see today.

It is no accident that among the single mothers I interviewed, none was isolated or resentful, no less defeated. They all had lives, and as they all made clear, they adored their children. Mothering, after all, isn't just drudgery; it's a delicious, wildly intense passion and closeness. As the portrait of Kathy Meetz shows, the single mother can avoid almost all the usual hardships when she trades some of her privacy for community and defines family for herself.

KATHY MEETZ

At forty-one, Kathy, who cleans houses for a living, has never regretted not marrying the fathers of her teenage daughters, Erin and Emma—even though staying single prevented them from ever having "one of those perfect families with perfect matching outfits."

"I think of us as an artistic family. We're free," she says. And so they are: free, close, full of fun, and, as far as I can tell, happy with their lives. My friend, whose house Kathy cleans, said, "She's an incredible mother, always taking her daughters to the city for museums and poetry readings."

"Yeah," says Kathy when I ask her about that. "I plug them into everything I can: theater, piano lessons, reggae festivals, town hall meetings, Quaker meetings. This summer a friend of mine is teaching Erin to make pottery. I want them to know the sky's the limit."

Kathy and I sit on my screened porch while a storm thunders around us. She is undisturbed. Wisconsin-bred, her speech is broad and plain, but she talks rapidly, sitting forward in her chair; time is tight since she has another house to clean that afternoon. She wears the accoutrements of her hippie past: Birkenstocks and a corduroy shirt over jeans, granny glasses, yin-yang earrings dangling below a gamine haircut with long bangs and shirred ends. Her face glows with exuberance. Then and now, she lives as she likes—and she likes her life.

Marriage just wasn't for her, Kathy says. Her own mother was a "servant to her husband. She even gave up her religion for him, which took away her spirit. Now she's an angry, married-to-the-same-man-for-fifty-years woman who's killing herself with alcohol."

Although her father was an excellent provider, he rarely talked to her or her siblings. Their mother interpreted his feelings for them, or else they had to figure him out through his body language. "He was either a mystery or a threat, as in, 'When your father gets home. . . .'" Kathy couldn't imagine how men fit into family life since her own father never did.

"Erin was a love child," Kathy reflects. She and Erin's father were political activists together. "I was just caught up in the spirit of changing the world, and having a child seemed a part of that." Emma's father, on the other hand, pressed Kathy to marry him. But she felt that he wanted to take over. He thought she should get a "real job," while she preferred sporadic, unstructured work like typing term papers for college students. Finally, she left him and continued with the spontaneous, nomadic life she had always lived, sometimes organizing on Native American reservations or living with friends. Only when it was time for the girls to go to school did Kathy settle in the town of Torrington, Connecticut, where her sister lived.

What's so unusual—and instructive—about Kathy's experience is that she never felt like a single mother because she didn't mother alone. "I always sought out and lived with other women with small children," Kathy tells me. "I've been more of a communal mother than a single one." Kathy has always been in charge of her kids. But other women—her first midwife, her sisters, her friends—have helped take care of them. For Kathy, that's been a better choice than parenting with a partner. "If I had to deal with another adult, getting him to have an alliance about what we're doing with this child, I'd be distracted all the time. I've tried once or twice, but it didn't work. On the other hand, I haven't missed it."

That communal spirit has served Kathy well. "I'm an excellent networker," she says. "I know all my kids' friends and their parents.

Whenever there's a problem—or before there's a problem—we talk. I'm the listening, available mom, and the kids talk to me. That's what *I* can do." Even though she has sometimes had to leave the kids home alone since they were little, she feels they too have a network. And they always know where to reach her.

Kathy not only uses people resources, she uses clinics, guidance counselors, and books to help her children navigate their uncertain, sometimes menacing world. For example, anticipating the difficulties of teenage girls confronting sexual harassment, prejudice, and the beauty imperative, she and her older daughter are both reading *Reviving Ophelia*, a sophisticated analysis of those problems.

Does she get time for her own life? I wonder. She responds emphatically. She's cleaned out the attic for her private space where she can be alone, read, do her beadwork. She's active in several political organizations, including the United Farm Workers. "I have to have my own life, a way I can stay myself," she explains. "Especially now that my kids are growing up, I have to start a new stage of my life. I can't lose myself in theirs. When they're out of the house, I'll go visiting again, travel, picking up work wherever I go. That's the benefit of my life."

I ask her whether she isn't resentful about house cleaning or the low income it provides. No, she likes cleaning houses, she tells me. "I get off my fantasies of having a beautiful home. My mind goes wherever it wants to go. It's personal work, like folding laundry and caretaking, which I like." The people she works for are wonderful, she feels. If they weren't, she'd move on.

Her family has no health coverage, and she has neither sick leave nor paid vacations, but luckily they've never been seriously ill. On the other hand, she works only four days a week, has flexible hours, and is home by 5:00 P.M. Money isn't a problem. They simply live within their means. "I've saved, and I manage. I earn $12 an hour, plus what I can sell from my beadwork: my rent is only $500. Erin's father pays $291 in child support and has sometimes paid for extras, such as summer camp. We don't have a lot of material possessions, but we go everywhere. I took them to Cancun last winter. We had a ball.

"Every so often," she admits, "I get into worrying that we don't have a real home, a yard and garden. But you can't have everything. I had that growing up—the three-course dinners, a stay-at-home mom. But we weren't very happy. That may be why, although my mother chose to stay at home, she always encouraged me to do whatever I wanted, even having my children without that traditional family. It's just been different for us, that's all."

It's pouring when Kathy has to leave, the rain a blur of falling water. I offer an umbrella. But Kathy, her smile radiant, says, "No thanks, I'm fine," and skips down my front steps to her car.

Different is what single-mother families are. Different from one another, because mothers have had to come up with such individual solutions to their parenting problems. And different from the maternal ideal. It may even be that because they break all the rules of traditional motherhood just by being single mothers, like Kierra they are more comfortable in their nonconformity than mothers who have the opportunity to be traditional and reject it. Or it may be that, as with Kathy, their nonconformity helped them to create the family life that was right for them. They have to create some worldly success in order to live, and they do so by their own determination, rarely supported or validated by our society.

Although single mothers are more vulnerable to maternal guilt than partnered mothers, they are also motivated—by the sheer exhaustion of total parental responsibility—to acknowledge their own needs, if only for rest and time off. But often guilt and circumstances keep them from acting on their social needs. For the single mother, not only does a parenting network provide a crucial safety net in what can be a dangerously isolating situation, but it may be what finally allows her the time and emotional freedom to pursue her own adult relationships.

Because single mothers are affected so much more by the vulnerabilities of most women's lives, they must address them head on. According to the experts and the single mothers I have interviewed, the most important tasks for women raising children alone are to establish financial viability, set up a parenting network, and cultivate peer relations.

Nothing makes a stronger case for a mother's continuing to work than the poverty of single mothers. When women sacrifice their earning power to raise children, they not only put themselves in jeopardy but endanger their children's lives. Most people today are economically at risk. For-merly secure professions are no longer so. Even the doctors I interviewed feared that if they lose their positions, they might not easily find another.

Quite simply, when both parents work, the children have that extra financial security. Furthermore, should the father leave, become ill, or even die, at least the mother will not face the financial crisis so many single mothers discuss. If a woman who has been out of the workforce for years suddenly finds herself raising her children alone—and without adequate financial support—the first plan she must make is how to support herself, immediately and in the future. Making such a plan is, of course, often terribly difficult. But even if work and/or training require using more child care than a mother wants to, she may improve the time she does spend with her child by gaining the emotional confidence to parent well.

Once a mother has an adequate job, she can begin to cultivate her social life along with creating a parenting network. Most people do understand the pressures single mothers face and are willing to lend a hand. One single mother who is also disabled and in a wheelchair got help from her friends when they signed up for certain blocks of time to relieve her. Belonging to a church or synagogue, a community organization, or a parent organization can often break the single mother's isolation. Al-though she may have to invest more time initially than she feels she has, she may find more help and support for the future. Some women, like Kierra, start their own single mothers' group. Often I see inquiries for such groups on the pediatrician's bulletin board. That way mothers on their own can join forces to create social lives for themselves and safety nets for their children.

Ironically, what often stops a single mother from creating a better life for herself is maternal guilt, which persuades her to focus all her energy on her child. However, looking at the picture in another way entirely, a single mother can alleviate guilt by recognizing the strengths of her situation. While she does not have a partner, she also, as Kathy reminds us, doesn't face the problems that parenting with partners can bring. And whether her child still has relations with the other parent or not, most children adapt and believe that their family, no matter what the configu-ration, is just as it should be. The child will also feel a special closeness to his mother and pride in her survival skills. These children often help much more in the home because the mother truly needs that help, and they are often more empathic toward their parent.

As much as we have heard lately about the distress that children of divorce suffer, it seems to me that much of it is attributable to the extreme financial distress of a single mother's situation and the animosity between divorcing parents. While single mothers certainly have more family fissures to repair than they may have counted on, their own growth is, if not inevitable, then probable, and with it their children's.

To whatever extent she finds her own fulfillment, the single mother does have one distinct advantage that all mothers can learn from. Because she must of necessity thwart the maternal ideal and define mothering for herself, she becomes a model of independent motherhood, balancing work and family, creating family life according to her own ideas. However, as much as she demonstrates new attitudes and family structures, the appalling economic conditions she confronts also raise the final issue in modernizing parenthood to fit the lives we now live: society's unmet responsibility for children.

CHAPTER 11

Solving the Mother Puzzle

Study Says Society Fails 19 Million Youths
NEW YORK TIMES, OCTOBER 12, 1995

Every day, it seems, headlines like this one highlight American society's neglect of its young, though in the past decade this particular far-reaching study may have been the most startling of its kind. It was based on the Carnegie Corporation's conclusions after determining that one-third of America's thirteen-year-olds use drugs, that educational achievement has stagnated, that the teen suicide rate has doubled in the last decade, and that one in five teenagers lives in poverty. The study called for smaller, better schools, counseling, and health centers.

But the government is not likely to create this infrastructure of schools and support centers without a strong public outcry, which in turn would require a dramatic change in popular attitudes. Unfortunately, our status quo is based on our belief that child welfare is the province of parents, not society. We do not really expect society to protect the young.

In August another headline pointed to "Low Ranking for Poor American Children: U.S. Youth among the Worst Off in 18 Industrialized Nations." This study, done by a public policy research institute in Luxembourg, reported that poor children in the United States are poorer than the children of all other industrialized nations except Israel and Ireland. Why? While the United States had the second-highest living standard, it also had the least generous social programs and little subsidized child care.

What can such facts possibly have to do with solving the mother puzzle?

In a culture that blames mothers for the ills of their children, children's misery can lead to a dangerous misogyny. Although the Carnegie Corporation study does not conclude that mothers should return full-time to the home to better raise their children, the conservative sectors of our society, and even some liberal ones (such as most child-care experts), do. And while the Luxembourg study does not blame American mothers for their children's poverty, our social policies often do. Why else would we dismantle welfare for the avowed purpose of "helping" people— mostly women with children—take personal responsibility for their fiscal lives?

While most studies conclude that *the government* must assume greater responsibility for children, political and business leaders, who are by and large wealthy men with stay-at-home wives, have increasingly shifted the burden of responsibility for children back onto the individual family. The 1996 welfare reform abandoned guaranteed cash subsidies for the poor while declining to guarantee their training, health care, employment, or child care. It cuts future budgets for public assistance by $15 billion, leaving states to make up the difference—or not. Senator Daniel Moynihan has predicted that a lot more children will be sleeping on grates.

Washington has also reduced support for Head Start as well as after-school programs. Nor has it allotted the $200 billion needed just to bring American school buildings up to safety standards. In neglected inner cities and rural communities, schools have deteriorated to the point where ceilings are falling in, antiquated heating systems produce noxious soot, and fifty-five students are jammed into classrooms designed to hold thirty. Poor neighborhoods may have as little as $3,000 to spend per pupil, compared to the $12,000 per pupil spent in the best public schools. American education is in shambles. Yet children spend almost half their waking hours in school, and for most, education is their primary means of bettering themselves.

We cannot blame mothers for the failure of American education, nor can we continue to depend on them to compensate for that failure by volunteering in classrooms, fund-raising to supplement school budgets, or running their own after-school programs. Employed mothers simply do not have the time to save public education—unless, of course, they are career educators or politicians.

Solving the mother puzzle will require mothers to relinquish some of their personal responsibility for nurturing the young and to demand that others—fathers, extended family, caregivers, the American workplace, and the government—take on more. As we enter the new millennium, however, the most conspicuously missing "other" is the government, whose policies currently hinder children's growth more than it helps. Inadequate schools can destroy a child's love of learning; unsafe streets can kill or corrupt a child; childhood poverty all too often results in a failure to thrive. Business is a close second in its neglect of children, leaving workers without sufficient family time. Just as important as breaking the rules of traditional motherhood is altering American business and politics as usual.

BENEVOLENT BUSINESS

The individual's relationship to society and business has recently changed in dramatic ways. We seem to have reverted to the model of an earlier era when Americans did not expect society to guarantee the essentials of survival, let alone the opportunity to thrive. Workers routinely logged twelve-hour days, and are doing so once again.

As I suggested earlier, the dolorous consequences of spreading mothers' time so thin has led to calls for mothers to return home. To many, the obvious solution is the division of labor in which Dad works a twelve-hour day while Mom is home to protect children from ever-increasing social dangers and to help run our inadequate schools through their volunteer work. But why should an economy so rich and so versatile turn its back on a century's progress?

In a major federal survey, one-third of the men and women interviewed said they would work part-time if possible. The study concluded that we are suffering from a "time famine." Jobs demand nearly all our waking time, and we feel obliged to give it.

Remember the Reidys? They "cut back" to a 45–55 hour week after Ashley was born, while their older daughter, starting out in the same company, routinely put in twelve-hour days. Remember Matt, who had to warn his church elders that he would work only a forty-five-hour week rather than the expected sixty to seventy hours. Or Melanie, who dropped out of the work world because she could not imagine a job in her field that required less than a sixty-hour week.

Fewer than 5 percent of senior executives at major corporations are women. But those that are, such as the women leading half of Kraft's operating units, work a ten- to twelve-hour day, seven days a week, and travel 30 percent of the time! This is the American concept of work. This twelve-hour-day work world explains why the Princeton students listening to Shirley Tilghman did not believe that she could have been a mother and a prominent scientist in our present era. "You did it back then," they said, "but now the labs are much more competitive, more cut-throat, more labor-intensive." And they are right. Ironically, just as women entered the workplace in full force, competition in a lean economy increased the workload for achievers to the breaking point.

Another recent study by the Public Policy Institute at Radcliffe College concluded that, for all the talk of changes, the American workplace has not become more family-friendly. Reporting the widespread American wish for more flexible, less demanding work, they point out that one out of four of the workers interviewed voluntarily reduced their earnings in exchange for a better quality of life. The study recommends that the care of young and old be "critical elements of our economic structure" and that the workplace offer benefits for part-time workers. Instead of the fixed-time model of work, they suggest other models in which teams of people decide for themselves how they will meet production goals.

In lean times some parents have no choice but to work more than they planned. However, *some* work is discretionary, taken on to fulfill ambitions or to purchase unnecessary luxuries. In her book *The Overworked American*, the Harvard economist Juliet Schor argues that, on average, Americans work two months more a year than the French or the Germans. Yet, she writes, Americans could choose to work a four-hour day or for only six months out of the year and maintain a decent living standard. In countries with better social services, individual families do not have the household space, appliances, or multiple cars that American families insist on. They do not expect the material advantages; on the other hand, they can count on reliable public education, far more generous unemployment benefits, and excellent subsidized child care—all of which makes for stronger family in ways that a second car, fourth television, or paneled rec room cannot.

The choice between overwork and time does not exist at the individual level alone. While people need more congenial working conditions, the right kind of jobs are not always available, even when someone is willing to take a cut in pay and to give up luxuries. Yet parents above all need those congenial working conditions if they are to parent well.

The *Wall Street Journal* recently reported two studies showing that parents who control how, where, and when their work gets done are more effective parents. Focusing on women—because the work-family conflict is always seen as a woman's problem—one study suggested that the greater a mother's authority in decision-making on the job, the fewer behavior problems in her children. Obviously, the less stress parents have, the better they feel, and hence the better they parent. The more discretion they have over how they spend their time, the more they can be with their children when they think it is most important.

We saw in the Reidys' case that although they worked long hours, they controlled those hours, took time when they needed it, and refused to work at the expense of spending time with their daughters.

The choice between overwork and family time is the public face of modernizing motherhood, and it is as important as a woman's ability to mother in the style that preserves her sense of self. But the choices must be made on an individual and collective level simultaneously. Couples planning careers help their futures immeasurably by examining what kinds of work will allow for a better quality of life and avoiding jobs that will "own" them. The succubus professions—whether trial law, investment banking, or certain corporate jobs—will eventually modify their demands in order to attract the young. And as the Reidys said, finding a family-friendly company is half the battle. The one they work for, Southern New England Telephone, has made their parenting possible by accommodating their needs.

Jim Richardson's advice for balancing work and family was low rent: keep expenses down so overwork isn't necessary. Matt, the Church of Christ minister, essentially agrees. He counsels his congregation to do without the extras in order to have more family time. But that advice may not work for parents who do not have flexible jobs with reasonable hours and cannot pare down expenses.

Until many more battles are won on the family front, many parents will have no choice but to muddle through with makeshift situations and to make more sacrifices than they wish. We all see them around us every day: the receptionist at the dentist's office who has her baby with her because a slight fever ruled out her usual day-care arrangement; the economist who leaves word on my husband's line that he'll call back after he's picked up his son at school; the small-town newspaper calling for a fund drive to help defray medical expenses for a seriously ill child whose parents have no health care. In my own life, I often rise between 2:00 and 4:00 A.M. in order to meet work demands I just cannot fit into a day requiring extra child care. Miraculously, as many parents today know, the sacrifice of sleep is a dependable (though hardly desirable) solution when there are no others.

There are hopeful indicators of real solutions. Americans have begun to celebrate, even award family-friendly businesses that offer flextime, leaves of absence without penalty or loss of benefits, maximum personal control over time, and on-site day care. We have certainly begun to recognize that many workers want these policies and that it pays off for businesses to provide them. According to the Bureau of National Affairs, employers lose $2–12 billion annually in employee absences related to caring for sick children alone. More generally, family policies help by creating less stressed and more effective employees, and thus lower turnover.

When First Tennessee National Corporation trained one thousand of its managers in family support, allowing employees to create their own schedules, it retained employees twice as long. What's more, happier employees meant happier customers; profits increased by over $100 million. By extending maternity leave to six months, Aetna Insurance cut resignations in half, saving $1 million annually in hiring and training.

Working Mother magazine and *Business Week* both do an annual review of the most family-supportive companies, which also receive government awards for their leadership. Among the most effective innovations they report are IBM's option of part-time work for up to three years and personal leave with health benefits; Xerox Corporation's life cycle assistance of $10,000 in benefits to be used for family improvements such as child care or college tuition; and Microsoft's elimination of set work hours and flexibility in telecommuting. When Lotus Development Corporation offered four weeks' paid leave to new mothers *and fathers*, one-third of the applicants were men.

Forbes recently ran a cover article about companies that offer more enticing, "stress-easing" benefits to employees, such as on-site drop-off laundry service, handymen who fix what's broken at home, weekly massages, and, at Xerox, one-year paid sabbaticals to do volunteer work at a charitable institution. But perhaps the most important innovations—given our current crisis—are those at companies like Hewlett-Packard and American Bankers Insurance Company, which have sponsored nearby or on-site public schools for their employees' children. Why this sudden generosity? According to the *Forbes* reporter, Kerry A. Dolan, demographically the United States is aging; skilled labor is more valuable than ever. Therefore, "giving their workers more ease and freedom is enlightened self-interest." Companies that sponsor public schools, for example, can expect to recoup their investment in ten years. In fact, most of the companies described in the article have virtually no turnover whatsoever.

Although these companies are exceptions in a world where employees are expected to give their life over to work, they do serve as alternative models. If we are lucky, attentive, and willing to demand change, they will help reshape American business. News that such investment brings a high rate of return will spread, particularly if the best and the brightest migrate to family-friendly companies.

According to the *Wall Street Journal* columnist Sue Shellenbarger, many of the best and the brightest today are asking recruiters, Is there a life after work? Often, she says, they are not even married. One such twenty-two-year-old chemical engineering graduate had six job offers. Another, who hardly saw his own hardworking father, was determined that he would be a part of his children's lives. Corporations like Intel, which interviews about twenty-five hundred undergraduates a year, is asked that question by half of them—as opposed to just one-fifth five years ago. According to the same article, recruiters believe such demands usually come from "on the ball people" who can "set their own priorities within time limits." Companies are trying to attract them with promises of a livable work life.

"Benevolent business" may seem like a contradiction in terms. Business, after all, exists to maximize profits. However, business also has a long history of support for sports, education, and culture, typically with an eye on buffing its public image. Think of Mobile Corporation and *Masterpiece Theater.* More directly, providing old-fashioned charity is an American corporate tradition, whether in the form of giving to the American Red Cross or lending corporate jets to transport cancer patients. Family support may be the twenty-first-century form of enlightened self-interest. And it may even pay better, both in promoting a positive public image and in attracting employees.

A NURTURING SOCIETY

Changing society may be harder than changing the workplace, which, after all, is driven by the bottom line. Society, as reflected in social policy, legal decisions, educational trends, and the media, is a far more complex entity. Because collective change is so hard, a society—like an individual—often responds to great stress or resists cultural shifts by lashing out at perceived scapegoats.

The profound distress of today's children has created just such national stress. American society, including but by no means limited to "angry white men," has responded by blaming individuals: the employed mother, the welfare mother, the teen mother. It does not look, for example, at what alternatives the teen mother has for self-fulfillment, or at how society can encourage a young woman to choose independence. Seeing ourselves as generous to a fault, we assume that our benefits to the destitute have corrupted and infantilized them, preventing them from pulling themselves up by their own bootstraps. We look everywhere but at our values for explanations of the failures to educate children or protect them from abuse.

It is no coincidence that this social resistance to change has occurred at a time of such profound change in women's lives. In a sense, the taking one step back is the subject of this book; however, it is just as important to focus on our giant steps forward. For all the problems that have surfaced, women's new status has also put family and child welfare onto the American agenda. And in the end, I am convinced that Americans as a whole will respond positively.

The very fact that our society in theory now accepts women as the equal of men gives individual women a sense of entitlement they did not have until the mid-1960s. Until relatively recently, women with demanding careers simply didn't have children. Now women have started to refuse to make that dreadful choice. Every time they refuse, they are tacitly asserting that women alone cannot be responsible for America's children. The more women participate in the business and political spheres, the more they give public voice to women's needs and the needs of their families. The more education, financial independence, and political power women have, the more they influence society.

Take, for example, the issue of child care in America. Our child care is a national disgrace. The four-state study referred to earlier was conducted by four universities looking into four hundred family and child-care centers. They found that care was poor in 40 percent of the centers, and that only one in seven offered warm relationships or intellectual stimulation. Day-care workers are paid on average five dollars an hour, which is less than what they would earn at McDonald's. As a result, day-care centers suffer a 42 percent annual turnover rate compared to 18 percent for other employees. Most are untrained and unsupervised. The reason for this crisis is that our culture does not regard child care as serious work.

Full-time care at a day-care center costs parents on average about $5,000 a year; family day care is about two-thirds that much. It's not surprising that families earning less than $18,000 a year spend 25 percent of their income on child care. And day care is what most Americans who buy child care depend on; only 3 percent, remember, can afford in-home baby-sitters. Lower-middle-class and poor families cannot even afford adequate child-care centers, typically relying on informal arrangements with friends, neighbors, and relations.

Deplorable as our child care is, those who make the laws are largely unaffected. Most of them are wealthy men whose wives raise their children. Child care is not high on *their* agenda. As one sociologist investigating the child-care problem in America has pointed out, many of the women in powerful positions still accept male prerogative at home even when equality is spoken there. The result is that they coparent with their nannies:

By delegating child care, they are able to put in the long hours required by rigid workplaces. Mothers have less reason to

> press fathers for equal participation if someone else is doing the
> work. By buying other people's labor, dual-career parents can
> individually exempt themselves from larger social problems.
> Their private solutions ... limit pressure for broader changes.

Only when women insist on men's responsibility for child-rearing do men
concern themselves with the problems.

Fortunately, women have changed sufficiently to make child care an
issue. Whether they are applying for the post of attorney general, like Zoe
Baird, or moving from welfare to work, child care is a visible issue in their
lives. As more employed women balk at trading their jobs for full-time
motherhood, subsidized quality child care will become one of their primary political demands.

Once women stop blaming themselves for the national crisis in child
welfare, they are more likely to ask that others take their part in raising
American children. Listen to the words of one mother whose situation
and analysis typifies today's American middle class.

EUGENIA WILTSHIRE

Eugenia never planned her life around being a mother. What
motivated her to have a child wasn't so much biological impulse, she says,
as the desire to respond to the crisis in the black family by nurturing a
black child. However, that proved harder than she thought. Her capacity
to nurture was there, but she soon found herself without support from
others.

Eugenia and her husband had met in Africa where both were working
at the time. It was such an artificially carefree environment, she reflected
later, that it didn't teach them a lot about each other. "He knew I was a
feminist, but that got lost when we got home."

Like millions of other women, Eugenia felt that parenting was primarily her responsibility since her husband had not signed on to coparent. "I
let myself fall into this hole I had always blamed other women for,"
Eugenia says—taking on the traditional mother role. The result: resentment and a sense that she has lost herself. Just the week before, she tells
me, after fourteen years of marriage, "I made two announcements: one,
that I am getting a musical instrument; I *have* to have music in my life. If

we can't afford a piano, I'll get a flute. And two, I'm not going to cook this week. I'm not even going into the kitchen. It was my first attempt to get myself back."

It took so long to get herself back because both her professional and personal independence were jeopardized by motherhood. As Eugenia explains, another blow after returning from Africa was finding that the staff jobs in broadcasting she had previously found were no longer available. "Overnight, it seemed, they were only hiring freelance." While she tried working this way, the hours were long and variable. She had to quit when her son Andri was two.

For the next seven years she and her husband worked at the business he started, often bringing Andri with them to the office. Then, like most small businesses, theirs failed. "It was an awful experience. We'd put everything into it."

Thereafter, they both took a series of jobs they didn't like. Together, they now make about $90,000, which would seem like a princely sum, particularly since they send their son to public school. But it's just not enough: "Every time we get a little ahead, it's braces or summer camp." Eugenia says they have never been able to afford the extras that would have made parenting easier.

Eugenia certainly might have found herself more satisfied had she been able to structure her family life to support her independent life, as the couples in this book have. However, Eugenia's experience is typical of many women. She rightly feels she did model her life according to suggested 1970s guidelines for women: she got an education, worked hard, and nurtured her child. As she well knows, hers is not a situation of personal failure. That is why her conclusion is so devastating, and so relevant for this discussion.

"I could never recommend having a child because our society isn't conducive to parenting. Children and families aren't a priority in America. Good care for children should be a given. Children should be learning from the beginning. If we had great day care, by the time kids got to school the schools would be different. Also, it would change the whole character of family life.

"Things go wrong so quickly. Children develop bad habits or they don't develop learning or social skills. Some families can't teach these things because the parents were never taught. There's no alternative for so many people. If the family can't provide a nurturing, learning environment, the children are doomed in America.

"Parenting is too damn hard, and the elements subverting parenting are growing: television, video games, violence, drugs, greed, AIDS. There's a lawlessness that's taking over, a menace waiting to gobble up our children. The influence from the outside is so great, it's frightening. There are no guarantees, no matter how much you nurture your children. I'm terrified for my son, I really am."

Upper-middle-class parents can buy their way out of America's problems. They pay for nannies, nursery schools, private schools, summer camps, lessons—and psychologists when there's a problem. They generally have the connections to give their children a good start and the financial fallback to help them while they build their careers. They can afford safe neighborhoods and security systems that keep danger out.

But those a step down the economic ladder can no longer count on buying their way out of America's social problems, particularly if, like Eugenia and her husband, they must deal with racism as well as tight budgets. They cannot always protect their families, and they often come from families that could not protect them. The middle-class perspective, then, is radically different from that of America's wealthy. It is different from the perspective of the poor boy who has worked his way up and believes everyone can do the same. The successful in America may be personally deserving, but they are also statistically lucky. When large numbers of children are self-destructing with drugs, gangs, crime, and suicide, they cannot all be personally at fault.

Eugenia remembers coming upon the idea of the Israeli kibbutz in college. "I thought that was great. Maybe not in that extreme form, but some kind of cooperative learning and caregiving *would* be better for children. Even then it seemed to me that the family isn't the best place for nurturing children. We have all of these institutions that fix things after they've gone wrong with children. Why not have these institutions in place from the time a child gets out of the hospital?"

Prevention is just common sense—investing in youth rather than prisons, in education rather than welfare, in family supports rather than foster care. Recently President Bill Clinton argued for a $30 million program to prevent teen pregnancy, citing a study showing that the present cost in medical care, welfare, lost productivity, and foster care is $7 billion. Indeed, why not create an infrastructure of subsidized day care, good schools, and counseling and health centers to prevent childhood poverty, pregnancy, drug abuse, and illiteracy? A majority of Americans, it seems, would rather blame mothers. However, while the voice of reason is presently peripheral, its steady hum may well be heard.

DROP BY DROP

During the sixties and seventies, the new economic conditions, attitudes, and needs of American youth changed American society, ultimately helping to stop a war, end sanctioned racism and sexism, legalize abortion, and support the environment. Now the new economic conditions, attitudes, and needs of families must change American society. And I believe they will.

Every parent I interviewed for this book is aware of how society might make family life better. Jennifer, for example, wishes she had a four-day work week and Kierra calls for a culture that "provides child care, places kids can go on weekends, and parenting classes." Like Eugenia, Kierra says, "I wish we had a society that put children first so that mothers didn't bear such a tremendous responsibility alone." That is the consciousness she brings to the voting booth and to the classrooms in which she teaches American teens. Matt and Angela, Dave and Debbie, all integral members of their churches, bring their sense of fairness to women and respect for motherwork to their ministries.

Every woman who replaces traditional motherhood with self-nourishing motherhood creates ripple effects in our communities and our places of work. It may begin with her assumption that her husband will take time off when the baby is born, so that he, in turn, requests parental leave from his employer. It may be simply that her family and friends show no dismay when she travels for work, leaving her husband in charge of the household. It may be that her husband stands on line to register the children for school, picks them up at the day-care center, and attends PTA meetings. Because both women and men must now be involved in their children's schools, they will inevitably press for budgets and legislation that support education.

One neighbor, a mother of two whose husband works for the New York City Parks Department, helped to raise money to refurbish the local playground, pay for a guard, and get the most unwieldy of cities to clean and maintain it. Last spring ten parents of preschoolers got together and raised corporate and private money to pay for a French immersion program in two of the six kindergartens in our local public school, a program that will extend schoolwide by the time these kindergartners are in sixth grade. In some public schools in New York City the PTA raises as much as $150,000 to compensate for recent budget cuts. We now have MADD (Mothers Against Drunk Driving) and MAD DADS, fathers who became their community's youth leaders. Certainly there have always been involved parents who lead Scout troups, teach swimming, and create playgrounds. But never have parents been required to do so much.

Children are where the individual and the political world meet, for they are affected as much by us as by our society. Individuals must demand livable working conditions and viable communities if their children are to thrive. The greatest changes to date may have come from what is called "maternalist politics," which, in the early part of this century, created the settlement houses, free child care, and even the Children's Bureau of the federal government. However effective these changes were, they did not restructure society, and that is what our present family lives demand.

As Jessica Benjamin says,

> Women can't win on the individual level alone. The real battle is with the cultural representation of maleness and femaleness that boys and girls are exposed to. You have to change the culture to counteract the market model that defines such ferocious ambitions for young people. The site of the struggle is not just the family. It is as much—more—in the public culture and the regulation of work.

Benjamin's insistence on political along with individual change is all the more significant because, as a psychoanalyst, her expertise is effecting individual change. Yet it has made her all the more aware of the power of the public world in the lives of individuals. As the mother of two, she is also personally aware of having to work more than she would choose. "Most people don't want to work all day," she has observed. "But at the same time most people find the expression of their individuality through work. We should not have to choose. None of the extremes are good. However, if we are all to have both work and family life, we will have to reorganize the social structure."

That reorganization must progress on the micro and the macro levels simultaneously. At home, both women and men must plan, care, and pay for their children. In the public sphere, women must assume sufficient power to change the cultural imagery and the political landscape. Men must change sufficiently so that their representation of life and their political expression uphold humane values.

If women alone demand benevolence from business, they might get it, but they will also continue to be tracked separately. More systemic change will come about as men take on their fair share of domestic responsibility and therefore feel the same pressure that women do to find humane work. They will refuse to put in the extra four hours a day or travel six months a year or spend Sundays at the office. They will not penalize their employees for leaving to take a child to the doctor. They will press for on-site child care. As men change, so does the society.

The good news is that men *are* changing. Many now do some (rather than no) child care. They admire devoted family men such as Dave Casson, who sees in his congregation and among men in general a "longing for affirmation of their affective side." From the pulpit, Dave encourages men to use their real, not pseudo, masculine strength: "Power, raw robust power from the Author of power himself—power greater and different than any we've seen on ESPN: power not to dominate or destroy or oppress, but power to liberate and create and love."

As women change, men change as well. Every one of these changes has reverberations in the lives of those around us, in the schools, in our businesses, communities, and the larger culture. When I went to school, the literature curriculum was made up largely of Dead White Males and Jane Austen; now there are courses on women's literature, African American studies, the Asian American experience, and the voices of new Americans. I recently noticed an article about a Wharton School of Business symposium on work and family, which will become part of the standard curriculum. The goal is to teach students to plan their careers according to their values. Now the novelty of such a course makes news. In a decade it may be the norm. The *Wall Street Journal*'s weekly column on work and family might one day be a daily column in every newspaper.

We no longer have a problem that has no name. Most women know exactly what the problem is: men have to do half the child care, and schools should be better, work more humane, and child care subsidized. Also, women are no longer isolated. They are working with other mothers who share these problems. They are reading books and articles that prove, again and again, that society—not women—is responsible for the crisis in the American family. In fact, most of the articles quoted in this chapter were reports by women journalists on the front pages of the country's major newspapers. Three decades ago there were far fewer women journalists, and fewer still whose ideas about important news counted.

These advances might seem small given America's social and economic distress. But as someone who was part of the women's movement of the 1970s, I know firsthand how droplets of change add up, and how quickly. Feminists back then fought for equal education, equal access to jobs, equal pay for equal work, and anti–sex discrimination and abuse measures; by and large, these battles have been won. Feminists then made women the equal citizens they are now. And despite recent claims to the contrary, 1970s feminists also put motherhood, motherwork, and child care in the forefront of women's issues. Not only did every feminist event routinely provide child care, but in women's groups everyone participated in child care. Not only did feminist workplaces have children's play corners, but feminists pressed for parity in parenting. All of these innovations laid the groundwork for the very concepts I have set forth here: dispersing parenting, helping mothers to participate socially and politically, and creating a society that takes more public responsibility for children.

WAITING FOR THE GOLDEN AGE

Of course, while most parents would love to see the changes enumerated in this chapter, many may be left wondering how to manage their own family lives without them. The answer is to work for change and to choose work as sensibly as possible, given the realities of the job market.

Obviously, if we are to live in a nation where family life is strong, parents have to make their political clout felt, both in the polling place and the workplace. In addition to supporting candidates who propose family supports, they need to form their own lobbying groups, as retired people have. One such group, the National Parenting Association, was formed to poll parents on important issues as a means of showing politicians what parents want. There is room for many more.

Parents also have to figure out how to survive until those presently nonexistent supports come to be, an effort that takes an entirely different kind of ingenuity and courage. Couples who decide to have children owe them workdays that usually end in time for family dinner and children's bedtime; they need to avoid the sixty-hour work-immersed weeks that many ambitious people take for granted. Parents who walk around with cellular phones at their ears and beepers primed to go off in the middle of story time will have a very hard time convincing their children that they are cherished.

The couples in this book all found creative alternatives to the family-nullifying lives that awaited nearly every one of them. None initially chose careers that guaranteed sufficient personal time, but they made the necessary adjustments and sacrifices. Jim Richardson, for example, gave up a successful television career for less glamorous and less remunerative work as an electrical contractor. But he bought himself family time and independence. How do others make these choices, and what prices do they pay?

Shirley Tilghman, the prominent scientist at the cutting edge of DNA research, managed to work sane hours by selecting experiments that would yield more results, by setting them up so they would not need her attention at night, and by avoiding the "macho" labs that demand long days. The extra hours on the job, she explained, are mostly spent socializing. However, her lawyer husband suffered professionally for leaving the office early. While her career flourished, his floundered—a probable factor in his decision to leave the marriage when their second child was young. Society may well have been more demanding of his hours, but he did not anticipate this by avoiding traditional high-pressure offices the way she avoided traditional high-pressure labs. If men and women both calculate well, they may be able to find the right work environment to allow for time with their children.

I interviewed two surgeons, the parents of a three-year-old, who explained that they decided to take academic and hospital positions to gain more control over their work hours and to have other physicians to fill in. The wife, a trauma–critical care specialist, is on the academic faculty of a university hospital. She now has to work as many as eighty hours a week, with one thirty-six-hour shift, only because she has recently been made director of surgical intensive care. Previously she was able to work fewer hours. She points out that certain kinds of surgical specialization, such as ophthalmology, ear, nose, and throat, or plastic surgery, offer steadier hours and fewer emergencies than, for example, cardiothoracic surgery. Her husband, a gastrointestinal surgeon, says that working for HMOs or hospitals is far less well paid, but it does offer parents more controllable hours than private practice generally does. For him, being a full-time attending surgeon in a hospital gives him greater flexibility because he has surgical residents to complete twenty-four-hour coverage. Thus far he has been able to be home with their son when his wife is on duty during their baby-sitter's time off, and vice versa. Though they would both prefer working shorter hours, they are managing well enough to plan for a second child.

Law is generally as demanding as medicine, but even there, the kind of law one practices can make all the difference for parents. Mark Waite of Sugarlands, Texas, does commercial litigation, which is the most grueling and unpredictable legal work. However, wanting time for his two children, he specifically chose a small firm instead of a large one where lawyers are expected to clock a minimum number of billable hours. His company only expects him to prepare his cases; *he* mostly controls his time. If he wants to take his child to the doctor, he does; when one of his children is ill, he and his wife each take half a day off. Although he may have to bring work home with him, he usually gets home by 6:30 P.M. And there are ways to lower the stress even more, he says. Lawyers who work for a government agency or a corporation often get home at 5:00 P.M. Lawyers can also work part-time by doing contract research to prepare cases for litigators.

Mark's wife Tracy, a CPA, switched from public accounting (seventy hours a week) to corporate accounting in order to have more family time.

She took a $10,000 pay cut but can pick up her children at day care by five-thirty. Both Mark and Tracy sacrificed professional status and money for time; neither regrets it.

Dave and Debbie Casson decided to share a ministry, offering themselves as a team to fill one job. They gave up two salaries; on the other hand, their work is more effective. As Dave notes, they both work more than half-time and supply the input of two creative people. This arrangement might not feel as ego-gratifying as being *the* one and only minister (art director, head of surgery, correspondent in China, and so forth), but it comes with a lot more personal gratification for people with families; it also keeps partners equal.

Self-employment is another option, whether freelancing, consulting, or running a grocery store. Mike Laser's consulting gives him freer time to be with his daughter. Amsale, who sometimes works seven days a week running her dress factory, still controls her hours. A couple may also opt to start their own business, like Maddy's parents did, although this route might involve some trial and error. Maddy and Patrick originally thought they would run an inn together, a perfect venue for the family-centered. But after a summer of working at someone else's inn, they realized they hated it. The mom-and-pop business is also a gamble. While sometimes it can lead to more control, it also involves great risk and therefore stress. Eugenia and her husband were able to take their son to their office when they started up their own business. But after seven years they were devastated by the failure of their business.

In some professions putting in a few years of sixteen-hour days earns sufficient leverage so that later on, like the Reidys, you can cut back to normal hours. It's a trade-off many young people might be willing to make if they are sure that fewer hours are in the future. The Reidys' choice also demonstrates the advantage of partners working for the same company. Not only do they understand each other's work and pressures, but they have an easier time arranging for alternating days off to stay with a sick child or staggered hours so they can divide up the daily chores.

Realistically, planning a career compatible with raising children sometimes requires the kind of sacrifice we almost never expect of men, particularly if they are passionate about their work. But that sacrifice does not have to be heartbreaking. The musician Susan Geffin says that "music chooses you, but I chose the aspect." Working 20–35 hours a week teaching piano, she was able to raise three children in Plano, Texas, and support the family during periods when her husband was unemployed. Teaching music fit family life better than performing; however, she also loved to teach, so the prospect was attractive. With this career choice, she had her family and she had music, a far better alternative, she believes, than giving up music to raise her children. Had she done that, she said, she would not have been as good a mother: "Without music, who would I have been? I'd have been gone."

On the other hand, many men now feel that without family they are "gone," so much so that some have made comparable sacrifices. Secretary of Labor Robert Reich wrote an op-ed piece for the *New York Times* in which he explained his resignation from the Clinton administration: "I have the best job I've ever had and probably ever will. No topping it. Can't get enough of it. I also have the best family I'll ever have, and I can't get enough of them. Finding a better balance? I've been kidding myself into thinking there is one. The metaphor doesn't fit. I had to choose." That is the cruel truth. No one can have it all, but if men and women plan for reasonable, flexible careers, they can both have enough.

Few of the choices available to working parents today are ideal. Until we actually have a four-day week or six-hour workdays, most parents will feel they do not have enough time. They will have to choose work that allows for family life. In today's climate this is an increasingly possible option—particularly for those who are willing to make *some* career trade-offs, as the examples in law, medicine, and business show. Our two-paycheck family is still quite new. Our government policies and workplace mores have not yet accommodated the unprecedented demands it has created. However, with political pressure and a continuing public outcry, that might well happen—if not for us, then for our children.

CHAPTER 12

Mothering, Growth of Self and Soul: A Philosophical Conclusion

Any book enumerating the psychically destructive traps of contemporary mothering runs the risk of minimizing the profound fulfillment it offers. A book that proposes replacing self-sacrificing motherhood with the self-nourishing variety may appear to diminish the importance of children in our lives. This I do not wish to do. Having children is not obligatory, but our desire for children is the engine driving us to solve the mother puzzle. Hence, this conclusion returns to my basic premise: when mothers work—at least, when they work under humane conditions—not only do they help themselves and their families to live more balanced lives, but they more fully experience how much children enrich life.

It is one thing to say that children ought not to be the sole purpose of a parent's life. It is quite another to say they do not deepen that purpose. They do, if only because their own purpose is so abundantly clear: to love, to explore, to enjoy, to accomplish. Caring for them can imbue your life, and life itself, with an immediate importance. Their pace, intensity, and need for you leave no room for the existential questions that dog many people's footsteps in all but the most exhilarating moments. Indeed, for me, becoming a mother brought me into more total engagement with humankind, a complete embrace rather than a skeptical withholding. It also added another dimension to an already full life, one that spans the territory from wonder to the numinous.

Of course, having children is not the only way to encounter this feeling. Countless people find it elsewhere: in creativity, in religion, in helping others. The very fortunate find it in a grateful apprehension of their ordinary days. Still, children may be the most common vehicle. Remember Lochlin talking about his daily commute with his small daughter, during which he noticed the changing landscape and the growing calves. "I would have never seen the world that way without her," he said. Remember his pleasure in her excitement when their pie came out of the oven. "Carnal plenitude" is what Simone de Beauvoir so aptly called it, wisely perceiving the essence of an experience she herself never had.

This is not to say that parents automatically feel carnal plenitude. With his first two children, Lochlin had neither the circumstances nor the perspective to reach such fulfillment. And as we well know, there are mothers and fathers who, although they love their children, still feel so much pain that they take their own lives. Think of the poet Sylvia Plath setting out two cups of cocoa for her sleeping preschoolers before asphyxiating herself in the kitchen below; think of Ernest Hemingway blowing out his brains.

Some parents are emotionally incapable of taking delight in their children, like Penelope Leach's father, who thought that children were an "expensive bore," or the immature or brutalized parent who is too needy himself to nurture adequately. Other parents may be too burdened, resentful, or deprived. However, under the right conditions, parenthood does engender an unprecedented plenitude, both carnal and spiritual.

For the devout, children can deepen faith. Angela Soper, a minister's wife and practicing therapist, said, "I never felt a greater understanding of God's love before I had kids. I never knew selflessness. There's something bigger than me. I think that the sacrifice involved makes you a better person. Now I have a greater capacity to love, I'm more accepting, less judgmental than before." With tears filling her eyes, she added that she now understands the significance of God sacrificing His only child.

While Angela's sentiments may stem in part from her religion, which considers having children a sacred obligation of matrimony, parenting works a kind of metaphysical alchemy on the secular as well. Kierra said it straightforwardly: "For me, mothering is divine, like being a part of a sacred order. With a child, you're handed such a tremendous responsibility; you are developing a human creature. If you can raise a child who is happy and likes himself, you've done a great thing." Great, I would add, like Nobel Prize great: something that takes a supreme human effort and advances humanity.

Most parents would understand Kierra's feeling, and so does anyone who has observed parents choking down sobs at a child's wedding, graduation, or piano recital. Yet children are a metaphysical experience in ordinary time as well as in extraordinary moments.

I recall, for example, that after our daughter was born, my husband and I fell into a pattern of "devoting" our weekends to just being with her: we set no goals, did no work, fulfilled no obligations. This time was different from the hours we spent with her during the week, which were always embedded in the details of our social-practical-productive days. Saturday and Sunday existed for enjoying her. Friends and relatives may have joined us, but our daughter was the center of our weekends; our togetherness was its main event. Toward the end of our first year of this rhythm I realized that nothing better described these weekends than the word *sabbath*; that is, a time, not of worship, for I am not a religious person, but of rest and of savoring the richness of life.

We still have our family weekends, though since our daughter is older and her own pleasures—from swimming in summer to reading by the fire in wintertime—often coincide with ours, I am less acutely aware of weekends as dedicated time. However, as our more independent lives have joined in a more complex psychological way, I also have acquired a greater sense of what in all honesty I would call holy, at least as the dictionary defines it: "perfect and transcendent, commanding absolute adoration and reverence."

I do not mean that my child has the status of a god for me, nor that I think either of us is perfect. But in our abiding connection and her daily development, I often perceive a perfection and transcendence that commands my reverence. And, yes, I absolutely adore her.

Some of this so-called transcendence, of course, is just the love affair that never ends, as a clever mother once described it to me. But the sheer extent of parental love can itself lead into spiritual terrain. Listen to what Elliot says of his six-month-old son Gabe: "It's a new kind of love in your life. It's different from the love for parents, work, friends, or a pet. It's all-encompassing. You're always thinking about him. It's a huge love. A wonderful feeling. I can enjoy him so much as an individual because I see his specialness. I see his personality from the beginning, a kind of karma he's always had. And then, his particular alertness has developed in terms of what we've given him. For me, that's a bit of immortality. He will carry a bit of us through his life. I imagine him as an old man, living on after us. We have so much to give him, to teach him, about what it is to be a part of the world."

Elliot describes feeling not only "immortality" in parenthood but also a heightened sense of connection, continuity, and belonging: "My life before was so much about loss. My father died of cancer, then my brother died. I took care of him for a year. There was so much loss it was hard to see the beauty of life, its continuation and renewal. . . . Gabe was born close to my brother's birthday. My mother immediately connected the two. For her, Gabe was a renewal of my brother, a new energy. My mother and I were never so close." Because children galvanize others in a parent's immediate sphere, a parent may simply feel closer to people, especially would-be intimates. But a parent may also feel more connected in general—to people past and future, and to the past and the future itself.

Maddy goes directly to the soul in her rumination on the metaphysics of parenting: "In some huge way, seeing life through my children's eyes is a rediscovery for me as a parent. Instead of paying bills and getting things done, I'm reminded of what a miraculous, spiritual world this is: seeds becoming plants, a bubble rising in the air. I ask Liam about things spiritual. He's sensitive to what we would call magic, angels, spirits. When my aunt died, he saw her in a castle made of flowers, he told me. He talks freely about the next life, as in, 'Maybe Mommy will be my baby.'

"His comfort with death and afterlife reconnects me with how free these ideas are. It's strengthened my own belief, even in the simplest ways. For example, my grandfather, whom I loved dearly, pops into my head three times a day. I think about the joy he would have from seeing my family. I feel the continuity of family so deeply now, there doesn't seem to be much separation between my children and my grand- or great-grandparents. Being a mother is spiritual for me. I find peace and satisfaction in that. As a composer, I have an intense need to voice my musical spirit. I love my work. But it's not the same soul satisfaction as children."

"Soul satisfaction"—so different from the terms I heard attached to mothering when I was growing up. Typically people used to say of mothers like my Great-aunt Paulie, "Her children were her life." Like

Maddy, Aunt Paulie surely derived enormous gratification from her children, and from their achievements and happiness. Even now I remember her in her sixties, having just learned to read, heaving with tears and holding her palms to her heart as she haltingly pieced together the letters of her son's name in a scholarly tome. Yet to me, Aunt Paulie's maternal gratification always seemed freighted with the pathos of dependency and the constant worry that accompanies such single-minded devotion. I was frightened by the vulnerability of a mother love that is the sole love of a life. Unlike Maddy, Aunt Paulie had no work she loved, no soulmate husband, not even an extended family close to her. How poignant it was to me that in death she chose to be buried not next to her husband but alongside her midwife, whom she rarely saw after her children were born.

My Aunt Paulie's self-sacrificing motherhood—in combination with the deprivations of the life she was born to—seemed to preclude the lighthearted jubilance of Maddy's soul satisfaction. Maddy's freer, less exclusive mother love will not leave her someday in permanent grief for her empty nest. It may even be that the psychological and social wealth of a woman's life contributes rather than detracts from the jubilance of mothering. To be fair, given the density and speed of our postmodern lives, we are more likely to lose the second sight or sense of wonder than my deeply religious Aunt Paulie was; therefore, parenthood may now bring an added jubilance she did not need. However, my own impression is that Maddy's soul satisfaction is the result of having both: the heart-stopping miracle of parenting *and* the complexity of our multifaceted lives.

As I write this, Elliot is leaving for Bogota, Colombia, where there will be an exhibition of his work. Since he's been away from work for so long, he expects that seeing this retrospective will reunite him with his art, so the trip is terribly important. At the same time he has never been away from Gabe overnight, and he is staying away a week. But while he is torn, he also feels doubly blessed, or so I interpreted his excitement.

After talking with Elliot, I found myself thinking of Chagall's depiction of a man flying through space while rooted to the earth by a lover's kiss. To me, the image is not only about a man's spirit soaring with love; it also suggests that he is soaring with the thrill of his own artistic creation—an expression of his individuality—while staying connected to his love. That,

I believe, is the essence of mothering and having a life. As Maddy explains it, from this richness flows the soul satisfaction of mothering.

TRANSFORMATION

That said, I would distinguish my position from the currently fashionable view that motherwork transforms by making a person good, by engendering a desire for cooperation and peace. This is, as I understand it, the argument of Sara Ruddick's *Maternal Thinking*. Rather than theorizing, as some so-called difference feminists do, that women are by nature more peace-loving and cooperative than men, she argues that the work of mothering creates goodness in the women or men who do it.

I wish that were true. But, in fact, some of the most hawkish attitudes arise in traditionalist circles where mothers are "ever-present" and "always-responsive" and motherhood is sacred. Consider the highly sentimental maternal ideal in Nazi Germany, to mention an extreme case. Suffice it to say that a mother is as likely to protect children and other living things by demanding an armed defense against a perceived enemy as by marching for peace. Some mothers have even left their babies behind to join that armed defense. Gioconda Belli, the Nicaraguan poet we met in chapter 2, did this because she believed that if she did not join the fight to bring down the brutal tyrant Anastasio Somoza, her children would have to do it.

Attributing goodness, cooperation, and pacifism to mothers, even when feminists do it, further idealizes motherhood. The most fundamental maternal tenderness often exists in inverse proportion to the amount of motherwork a mother must do. Certain kinds of mothering can even reduce maternal tenderness. And different cultures create very different kinds of motherhood.

Women (or men) mother according to their cultural values. Tenderness for one's child need not extend to saving his life or saving the world. With her heart bent on greater glory, a mother may lovingly await the day her son goes off to battle. With her eye on salvation, she may refuse medicine that could cure a child's otherwise fatal illness. Bowing to social rectitude, she may cut off her small daughter's genitals, force an older daughter into a hated marriage, or sell her children into prostitution, believing they or the family will be better off as a result. She may treat a child who marries outside his religion as if he had died.

Unlike Ruddick, I do not believe that maternal thinking is necessarily different from the thinking of the culture at large. People oppressed by a dehumanizing culture or economy will generally mother accordingly. Hence, impoverished mothers in the slums of Brazil withdraw love from a child who is not hearty enough to survive, allowing themselves to love only the strongest ones. While there are always heroic exceptions, people generally treat their children as they were treated and as their culture dictates. Many years ago the anthropologist Ruth Benedict argued that primitive people living under cruel natural conditions parent cruelly; those living in abundance treat their young tenderly.

We mother as we live. In extreme cases, rigid people become rigid mothers, angry people are angry mothers, disconnected people parent in a disconnected way. But these are extremes. Most of us only lean toward rigidity, anger, overinvolvement or disconnection. Life's experiences, including motherhood, can encourage or discourage them. If a woman must mother in a self-depriving way, her mothering may yield bitterness and intensify her defenses. However, a self-nourishing kind of mothering can bring soul satisfaction that diminishes her defenses and engenders tenderness. It is the way we mother and under what conditions—not mothering in and of itself—that can enrich us and make us better people.

Mary-Joan Gerson, a clinical associate professor and supervisor of psychoanalysis at New York University, studied the motivation for having children among female college students. Most wanted to experience "the honesty and freshness of children" or knew that raising children was something they could do well. However, Gerson found that in slightly older women, women in their late twenties, self-esteem correlated negatively with the desire for a child: the more urgent the desire, the less self-esteem. As she explains, "If you don't feel that good about yourself, having a child would be the area of self-actualization that you hope will compensate for the areas of deficits."

Having a child as a primary means of self-actualization is a very tricky endeavor. Low self-esteem, combined with a paucity of life alternatives, may create exactly the negative conditions that increase your defenses. Moreover, having to take care of children can make it harder to succeed in other areas. As Gerson points out, however, parenthood *is* compensatory.

While there's a terrible fear that you will repeat your own losses, part of a wish for a child is a wish to make up for what you didn't get, to finally get it right, psychoanalytically speaking. Kierra, for example, mothered successfully under conditions very similar to the seemingly impossible conditions she had faced while mothering her younger siblings at age seven.

My point is this: though Kierra herself wouldn't recommend it, even under adverse conditions motherhood can be transformative. Pamela Sicher explains that parenting can be the ultimate healing of self: "If there were no other help, no psychologists, support groups or psychopharmacologists, raising a child would offer the most complete potential for healing the wounds of childhood. In seeing your child flourish, you flourish with him or her; in giving your child security, reassurance, empathy, and understanding, you experience the fullness of yourself beneath whatever wounds and defenses you have accumulated."

As some of the portraits have shown, for some very young or anguished mothers, having a child cures the ills of the spirit in precisely the way Sicher outlines. Allison Anders, the award-winning filmmaker who had been a welfare mother in her early twenties, says, "The kids motivated me. I'd been such a party girl I would have just rocked on, probably to death. But I wanted to be a role model to them. I quit drinking, began to write, then went to school." Although she claims her motivation was to be a role model to her children, she was clearly fulfilled enough by them to give up drinking. That is, she was flourishing along with them. What fulfilled her is what she tried to show in her movie *Mi Vida Loca*, about teenage Latina gang members in Los Angeles. As she explains, no matter how squalid their lives, these teen mothers "are just as crazy about their kids as any yuppie mom. And in some cases having kids saves a girl's life." Anders believes her children saved hers. And in spite of having two teenage daughters of her own, she did not hesitate to adopt the three-year-old son of a teen mother who died during the making of her film.

My friend Janet had two children right after graduating from high school and a third several years later. Sometimes she lived in such poverty that, with no money for milk, she had to feed her babies sugar water. And though her husband left her without support for periods of up to six months, she recently described having her small children as "making life so rich."

I do not believe this is nostalgia speaking. Back then, while she was mothering, I was attending a nearby college and lived next door to her. Sometimes I baby-sat; often I just spent time with them, loving the joy in their home. Whether Janet, her husband, and children were dancing to music that played on a stereo in an otherwise unfurnished living room or she was giving the children their dinner at their tiny table, I saw the pleasure on her face. I never felt that she didn't have time for her own fun, which we often shared.

Against the social odds, they all flourished: Janet went to college and then to graduate school; her oldest daughter is a doctor now; her son just graduated from business school; her youngest daughter is planning a career in law. Although Janet certainly faced other problems in life, mothering wasn't one of them, despite the fact that her own mother died when she was young and her father was rarely there. Sitting around her kitchen table, her grown children home from their various pursuits and telling us about their adventures, I admire all three of them and the mothering that created their loving spirits.

Kierra, Allison, and Janet mothered with astonishing success under risky conditions for both parent and child. But to say it is possible is not to predict success. For every such mother who is transformed by mothering there is surely another who is overwhelmed by it. The fact that mothering can be transforming in such adverse situations, however, does suggest its potential power.

PSYCHOLOGICAL GROWTH

In the best-case scenario, motherhood is a freely chosen addition to an already fulfilling and economically stable life, and children are a primer for connection, for love, and for emotional growth. Their neediness, their will, the frustrations inherent in caring for them, and the love you feel for them, all demand that you become more flexible. Not that you necessarily will. But if, like Kierra, Jennifer, and Janet, you manage it, you must confront parts of your character you wish you could change. Children invariably raise a person's most fundamental issues of identity. If you have trouble with boundaries, with anger, depression, guilt, or intimacy, you will have it more so with a child in your life. Whatever your problems, you face them far more vividly than ever before.

Candace and her now-teenage daughter talked to me about the difficulties Candace's "issues" caused in their life together. While Mara was small, Candace supervised a dozen academic researchers in an archiving project. "I had a flexible job," she said, "but I wasn't emotionally flexible enough. I was the boss. I could have picked my child up before the absolute end of the day-care day. I could have made sure she wasn't the last child there." ("By an hour!" Mara adds, still resentful.) "But I was the overresponsible type, accountable to everyone. I couldn't say no. And the people I worked with were younger. They didn't have children and didn't understand my needs."

As a result, she felt trapped by her frantic work ethic and guilty about her daughter. But she learned, if slowly. As Mara grew, her mother developed more flexibility and backbone, and more economic security. By the time her second child was born, she had become a stronger person, able to control her work, set boundaries better, and respond to her children's needs. She was also able to buy child care that better suited her family's needs.

However painful, responding to children engages your deepest self. For one thing, children "get to you" more than anything else, even a close friendship or an important job. With them, you relive your own childhood dramas, and often the very ones you thought you resolved. When a problem arises, there it is, smack in the middle of dinner, sleep, your visit with your in-laws. There is no getting away. If your husband is angry with you, you can table a discussion until the next day or leave and go for a walk. You cannot do that when a small child is angry; she cannot control her feelings sufficiently to postpone them. Nor, if you want to parent well, can you rely on the kinds of defenses most of us use in conflicts with other adults, such as getting angrier in return, winning the argument, or acting hurt. The parent has to be the grown-up.

One summer morning my husband was dressing our four-year-old daughter for camp. She protested that her T-shirt, which he'd just managed to get on, was too small. "Wear it today, then we'll give it away," he said. No, she wanted a bigger one. NOW.

"You're a spoiled brat," he yelled.

"I am not a rat," she replied.

"Spoiled brat," he thundered.

"*You're* a rat," she parried.

Finally, he got her a larger shirt. Not only did he give up his anger but later, when I went outside to drive her to camp, I found them curled up together reading her favorite book. Since then, I would say, he has set the example in our household for firm but gentle responses to her upsets.

Yet, the other evening, he said to me, "The more I'm engaged by her, the harder it is to modulate my response." Where parenting is concerned, engagement does not make the work easier, because an important component of parenting is the enormity of the emotions demanded. If parents are unwilling to do that work, they usually grow more rigid emotionally, digging in their heels, insisting, or using force. If they cannot bear to hear what a child is saying or are too afraid to find out, they will fill the air between them with their own needs, the way Pamela Sicher's client Elena did when she was unable to accompany her daughter to camp.

If narcissistic parenthood stifles intimacy, parenthood that nourishes the parents as well as the child can become a model for intimacy throughout a person's life. In myself I have noticed, for example, a patience and ability to listen that I did not formerly have. As a young adult, I had learned to propel myself through my life (and away from my childhood circumstances) by a continual series of self-assertions. Whether talking my way into jobs or into recognition in school, I emphasized the performance I felt so obliged to give. If you feel constantly judged, you do not listen to others; you present your case. With a child, the tables are turned. So much of your function is to watch, appreciate, encourage, and listen carefully enough to know who your child is. There are certainly times to teach, but teaching is easy for me. I had to learn to let my daughter take center stage.

When my daughter was old enough for stories, I made them up for her, populating them with characters from her life, her fantasies, and her toy collection. I congratulated myself on having such a useful talent as the stories turned into one, endless saga.

Then she began to act out the stories as I told them, making additions and rejecting certain turns of plot, as in, "No, the tiger doesn't growl, she's friendly," or, "The children don't get lost. I show them the path." Frustrated by the flattening effect of her editing, I protested: "But you're not letting me tell my story." "It's not *your* story," she replied. "It's *my* story." And so it was. Or, I should say, so it is. Each morning starts with her decision about which of the characters will be active that day. Then, under her careful direction, I begin. The result is rarely to my liking aesthetically, but I have learned much about her concerns and thoroughly enjoyed becoming a tool in her explorations.

Now when she sometimes tells me, "You didn't listen to me," I realize she's not necessarily wishing to have her way. In fact, her complaint often comes after we have agreed that she really must clean up her mess or accompany me to the store. It may mean, simply, that I haven't been attentive enough to her feelings. As a result, I have vowed to be a better listener and think I may have become one—even to my friends. But my daughter's love has made it easier for me to listen.

Like a parent's, a child's love is unconditional. Children love you and take delight in your presence whether you look a fright, just failed your driving test, overcooked the pasta, or reduced them to tears with some idiotic outburst. Until they are teenagers and become, for a time, hyper-critical, they accept you, warts and all. No need to recite Hamlet's solilo-quy or to remember the names of all fifteen former Soviet republics. Unless provoked beyond endurance, children never fire you. That reas-surance in itself is restorative.

While parenting can be quite painful intermittently, overall it is soul-enhancing. If you teach children self-acceptance, you learn it yourself. If you teach them to care about others, you become more altruistic. In seeing their flaws, you are forced to reflect on your own.

In an open atmosphere, children call you on every false move, every insincere response, and every insipidity. And they honor you in becoming ever more themselves.

MOTHERHOOD WITH A HUMAN FACE

Once I asked the twenty-year-old daughter of dear friends what child-rearing advice she would give me. I asked her because she and her parents have an enviable relationship, and because she was so much herself and so comfortable in the world. "Break all the rules," she said unhesitatingly. Even before she explained, I knew what she meant.

When she was six, her parents took her out of school and together they traveled for several months through Mexico in a van. When she was seven, they left her with close friends for a month so they could each travel alone and rediscover their separate selves, as they put it. For several years she lived in a commune where all the adults, including her parents, shared parenting.

Were they good parents? The best I've ever known well. They were entirely themselves, yet responsible to their daughter. Their relationship with her was intimate, honest, and full of mutual delight—and still is. Not long ago they stopped to see us after spending a month with their daughter in Uruguay, where she studies political science at the university. She served as their translator when they lectured there at a professional gathering. Rather than stay in a hotel, they put up with sleeping bags on the floor of her unheated apartment in order to get to know her daily life, her roommate, and her friends. Midway through their stay, they took her and a friend skiing for a week. On the eve of their departure, their daughter's friends threw a party for them and each brought a small gift. That, we all agreed, was a parent's dream.

Breaking all the rules means living in your own skin in the life you want—with your child. Being exactly who you are and helping your children to be themselves is the kind of mothering that lends itself to the growth of self and soul for both parents and child.

The novelist Kate Braverman says of her daughter: "She's not like me—addicted to the brutal, dark night skies—she's a sunny, amiable child. I find it curious how she's turned out. I've raised her so unconventionally. This child has literally grown up at poetry readings. We lived in the jungle without electricity for a year in Maui. I've raised her as the daughter of a poet, and I must say she's flourished."

Notice that Braverman never tried to be the sunny, amiable mother of the myth. But she was always a nurturing mother. A self-described maniacally driven writer, she also knows "that there are times when I am going to lose a scene or a story because I choose to let my daughter have that moment. I recognize that there are moments when motherhood will take precedence over sitting at my computer." This is not the cold careerist or the distracted genius who neglects her daughter. Braverman values having a child but did not turn into someone else when she became a mother.

The same is true of Angela Soper, who says, "I know myself. I couldn't be a stay-at-home mom." So she plans her professional life, works as much as she can, and feels she's a better mother, more patient and available, because she does. Sandy Reidy isn't guilty about working; she has a drive to achieve and finds it's healthier for herself and her daughter if she does work. "We didn't change our lives when Ashley was born," she said. "She's part of it." Maddy says, "It's not my goal for my kids that they only do mothering or fathering when they grow up. So I too have my dreams." The mothers and fathers profiled in this book began with a strong sense of self that their children later enhanced. Of all the women I interviewed, only Melanie, who "didn't invest in herself," feels lost.

Maintaining self while nurturing involves more than simply cultivating your independent life and living the way you want. It also takes a kind of honesty that the American maternal ideal does not encourage. The psychologist Kathy Weingarten says that we don't tell our children the truth about ourselves because we are afraid of that dangerous nonmaternal self—the one that puts herself first, that, on occasion, feels sad, angry, ambivalent. We censor constantly to project the image of the ideal mother. When Weingarten discovered that she had cancer and decided she had no choice but to put herself first, her mothering changed forever. Once she told her children the truth about her illness and her feelings, she decided never to go back to living the mother myth because she has "a better life now, one in which more of the time, I do more of what I want, and believe I am a good mother for it."

Can we really talk to children? Can we tell them about our day, truly? Are we too sanitized, Disneyized, and dominated by our own parents' belief in the separation of child and adult spheres? Growing up, no one I knew had any idea about their parents' incomes, illnesses, or emotional lives. We guessed, but we were almost always wrong, misconstruing their frustrations as anger at us, their personal disappointments as indifference.

Mary Gordon wrote a novella about an incident at the beach when, for a split second, thinking she and her daughter had been pulled too far out by the undertow, she saw that she was about to save herself first. Is this the awful truth mothers spare their children? Would children be horrified to know that even mothers have an instinct for self-preservation? Or would telling the truth perhaps simply make mothers more human, and children more accepting of their own frailties?

When parents do not violate their true selves after they have children, they are more available and more authentic with their children. In this regard, children of even flawed parents who break the rules have an advantage over children raised in homes where people parent according to the flawed ideal of self-sacrificing motherhood. The latter may often look perfect but be emotionally tense with resentments. How could it not be so if women violate their training, their ambitions, and themselves when they become mothers?

Mothering has proved a disaster for most career women, who compromise, veer off track, cut back, and scale down, ending up far below the level their credentials suggest they could have achieved.

The Harvard economist Claudia Goldin recently published the appalling results of her long-term survey: *only one in six "baby boomer" college-educated women can claim career success* if success is defined as earning more than the lowest 25 percent of college-educated men. "Equality of opportunity," Goldin argues, "is not sufficient to generate equality of result. The goal will remain elusive until offices before more friendly to mothers. And most of the accommodation will have to be by men."

We must face the uncomfortable fact that most women do not live up to their potential because they have succumbed to the maternal ideal. That is, they do not continue on in their true character—ambitions included—once they have children because they are afraid to demand accommodation from their male partners and from society. This is an issue of identity—and of the soul.

Making motherhood more human and ensuring that mothers have lives of their own seems nearly impossible unless we're lucky enough to have just the right flexible job, a husband with a flexible job who likes parenting, enough money for help, children without disabilities, a devoted extended family—in other words, the moon and the stars. Yet however much the realities of our lives have to be changed, I believe that changing how we mother—in our hearts and our homes—is the most profound change it is in our power to make.

No matter what our circumstances, we can plan our parenthood so that our child's father has half the responsibility for nurturing. We can divide the child-care tasks from the beginning. We can embrace extended care, whether that includes friends, grandparents, godparents, or paid child-care workers. We can live our mothering lives honestly, revealing to our children the light and dark of who we are. We can cultivate intimacy with our children as well as our own independence.

Everything I have learned from experts who are mothers, and from mothers who are experts, has led me to believe that if we humanize and disperse our mothering, the result will be far more nurturing for everyone in the family, parents and children alike.

Margaret Mead, the pioneering anthropologist whose words open this book, embodies the spirit of new mothering in many ways. Although her work often took her thousands of miles from home—once for six months when her daughter was three, and a decade later for an entire year—Mead's daughter, Catherine Bateson, never felt abandoned. In her loving memoir, she writes that when her mother was with her, she gave her full attention and thoughtfully planned their private time. Also, they lived communally with dear friends of Mead's and near several biological and adopted aunts. Young as she was when her parents divorced, Catherine maintained an equally deep relationship with her father, who lived three thousand miles away. She speculates that her mother's exposure to different cultures strengthened her belief that it was "preferable that children feel a part of several households and have several caretakers to avoid the tightness of bonding to a single caretaker that so often provides the ground of an entire neurotic system."

Bateson, herself an anthropologist, did not rebel against her careerist mother by taking up motherhood as a profession. In fact, she measures the quality of Mead's motherhood by her own "deep pleasure in mothering" and feels her life was enriched by "the diversity of . . . arrangements and the different kinds of people with whom my life was linked." Her mother, wishing very much that her daughter have all the independence she herself enjoyed, wrote in a poem entitled "To Cathy":

> That I not be a restless ghost
> Who haunts your footsteps as they pass
> Beyond the point where you have left
> Me standing in the newsprung grass,

You must be free to take a path
Whose end I feel no need to know,
No irking fever to be sure
You went where I would have you go. . . .

So you can go without regret
Away from this familiar land
Leaving your kiss upon my hair
And all the future in your hands.

If motherhood is neither sainthood nor slavery, if mothers can guilt-lessly enjoy the independence that women have fought for these last decades, we will nourish our children along with ourselves.

Talking a year later to the men and women I interviewed, one theme stands out: parents who raise children while living their own lives must continually adapt—to new job and child-care situations, and to partners' changing needs. It takes effort, but these parents glow with the joy of continuing growth.

Although Gioconda had to be away from her daughter Adriana for a three-week publicity tour last year, Adriana was fine and the trip paid off: Gioconda's book did very well in Europe. This year, while working for one month on the 1996 electoral campaign in Nicaragua, she talked to Adriana every day by phone and wrote to her. "It was hard on both of us, but Adriana readjusted well. She was used to my going and coming by then, and she has her whole family around her."

Also, Gioconda returned with a five-week-old Scottie puppy for her daughter. Her son Camilo starts Columbia University in the fall, one daughter is graduating from medical school, and the other has a job working for a design firm. Gioconda has begun writing a memoir.

Amsale, you may remember, was about to open her first dress salon. "It's doing wonderfully," Neil reports, "but it's also a lot more strain than we expected." Their compromise: creating an excellent staff to give the store the personal attention they cannot.

While Amsale's workload has increased, Neil's seems to have eased a bit. For the first time he was able to get away from work during one of Rachel's school vacations to take Rachel and her friend on a ski trip.

Their next project: finding the right after-school activities, an effort, he points out, that takes time, time, time. They aren't worried, though. Neil reflects, "I can remember coming to a bit of a career versus family crisis like this one years ago. But I realized that I was doing fine in what I really cared about. The same is true for Amsale and me now."

Maddy and Patrick have finally found a comfortable routine now that Dierdre is eleven months old, but their work patterns have changed. Patrick is still editing his screenplay, but Maddy's work has picked up considerably. Not only did she score two short features, but she's back full-time scoring television commercials. The real challenge will come, says Maddy, when Patrick's film goes into production. Although he'll probably have to be away for most of the shooting, he's campaigning to do the editing in New York. For his next film, he'll get to choose New York production. Their extended family is still their mainstay. For Christmas, Maddy's parents surprised them with tickets to Paris and took care of the children while they were away.

Quite a bit has changed for Angela and Matt. They were finally able to buy their first home. "It's really tiny," says Angela, showing me its two modest bedrooms. But they are proud homeowners. Angela has three clients in her burgeoning therapy practice, but because "managed care" has made therapy so much less lucrative, she is studying to become a physician's assistant. She will have to be in school eight hours a day, five days a week, she tells me, but Matt supports her decision. He would have liked to go on for his doctorate in religion, but for now he's content to study Spanish five hours a week. Says Angela, "We are constantly nego-tiating and renegotiating. But as long as we organize the child care together, it's *so* smooth."

Mike still does the primary child care while Jennifer works full-time. But there have been some changes. Helen (who is now two and a half) is in preschool four mornings a week but is in no other child-care arrange-ment, so Mike does more. However, he is hard at work on a young adult novel. Jennifer, who says that Helen now often favors Mike, is trying to make room in her life for more family time; she has officially requested to work from home one day a week. They are also thinking seriously about having a second child.

For Elliot and Paul, the parenting balance has shifted. Elliot did most of the child care while Paul was finishing his doctoral thesis in art history.

Now that he's finished and interviewing for jobs, Paul has taken over, giving Elliot four days a week to paint. Paul also spends a lot of time with his sister, who had her baby. "She turns to us a lot," Paul explains, "because she doesn't trust her intuition as much as we did."

Elliot tells me that his art exhibition in Bogota, the TV coverage, and the lectures he gave there were exactly the ego boost he needed to get back to work. But he found that he was just "too connected to Gabe" to work at home, so he rented a studio in Brooklyn. Elliot found out something else in Colombia: it was fine to leave Gabe once in a while. Since then, Paul's mother has stayed with Gabe for a week while Elliot and Paul took a vacation in Mexico. "It was midnight when we got back," Elliot says, "but Gabe got right up when he saw us and spent the next three hours running back and forth from Paul to me. He was so happy. And so were we."

Jim is reaping the pleasures of his fine fathering. Cassie, he says, is not only playing the violin better than he or her teacher ever imagined, but she's doing wonderfully in school. Having spent so much time working alongside her father, she put her knowledge of electricity into a science project measuring the electrical output from microwaves, televisions, and her classmates' heads. It was so successful, says her proud father, that the class applauded her presentation. She's also entering puberty and paying a lot of attention to her looks and his. Not long ago they videotaped Cassie cutting off her dad's ponytail!

Right after we spoke, they were going to pick up one of her "dates" for an afternoon excursion. Jim is also developing some computer techniques with his son Jed, whose new girlfriend just got a job doing photo enhancing for ABC television. The three of them are experimenting with ways to refine her work.

As for Jim, he's enjoying life and work as always, he says. But staying true to his theory that low rent is essential for good parenting, he's looking for another apartment.

Kierra, the single mother whose big problem was money, took a major step toward solving it. She added a third job to the two she has at the New York City high school—teaching a course in African American literature at the College of New Rochelle.

Kathy Meetz tells me that a lot of her energy these days goes toward getting her kids through the teenage years. "I had to come to terms with my daughter's sexuality, for example. I had to accept that it's her body and she can do with it what she wants. So I've become more of an educator than a protector, which is teaching me a lot."

The weekend I interviewed the Reidy family, Sandy was away at a ski resort with five of her oldest girlfriends. When I spoke to her to arrange the interview, she couldn't contain her excitement. "It's the first time I've ever done anything like this!"

Ashley seemed to be having a great time with her dad. The day before they had taken a walk in the woods to look for spots where the deer rub against the tree trunks. Lochlin's life has become more relaxed. Instead of overseeing emergency service for the telephone company, he was promoted to manager of interexchange customer services, an office that processes incoming requests for access from long-distance carriers. "It's totally different from anything I've done, but I really like it," Lochlin says. "And it's a forty-hour week."

Because his office location changed, he and Sandy and Ashley commute together, resulting in more family time. But they also decided to move closer to work to avoid the two and a half hours daily en route. Forced to change Ashley's day care to a center near their offices, Lochlin and Sandy appreciate Country Kids Farm even more. The new day-care center, he tells me, is the best they could find, but not nearly as good. It costs less, but the teachers are younger and less experienced, there's more turnover, and needed repairs are left undone. While Ashley is happy there, they notice that her writing and drawing skills have diminished somewhat. On the other hand, they have forty-five minutes more with her every day, and she sees more of her mother, too.

The only two updates that didn't convey a sense of growth and satisfaction were from Eugenia and Melanie, the two mothers who felt stuck in family lives that did not nourish their independence. Eugenia, who was determined to at least "get a musical instrument" and spend less time in the kitchen, said, "Unfortunately, nothing has changed." Melanie, who is now five months pregnant with her second child, says she still considers the suburb where she lives "a big drag, but Jonathan (her husband) loves it." It helps that she found two woman friends; not coincidentally, as she phrases it, "they both had prior lives."

How is she handling it? "I've *adapted*; I haven't *accepted* my life. If I worked now, I'd still bear the brunt of home and children. I do everything. But I still miss work, that feeling of importance. I wonder what will happen to me when my second child is six and in school. I wonder."

The difference between being stuck and moving toward goals is striking. Where Eugenia and Melanie adapt to lives largely defined by husbands and society, the other parents in this book are inventing their own lives and adapting family routines to them. They all accept trade-offs, giving up some of what they want. But as Neil might put it, they're doing fine in what they really care about.

While these parents all strive to balance work and family, self and children, alone time and couple time, there's a passivity in the way both Eugenia and Melanie are adapting that amounts to giving up on what they want. Kierra and Jim have money pressures similar to Eugenia's, but Kierra added a third job and Jim's looking for a cheaper apartment. Whether any of the solutions turn out to be sufficient doesn't matter. The point is that Kierra and Jim keep trying new things. Angela's work was at a dead end, so she's starting school in an entirely different area. The Reidys had to settle for second-rate day care, but with more family time, more time for Sandy to be with Ashley, and a better job for Lochlin, they all get to move ahead a bit. That is, they sacrifice the expendables to keep the essentials.

These people have much in common. All, including Eugenia and Melanie, are vibrant individualists who love life and want to be the best they can be. Dreams are not what's lacking for Eugenia and Melanie, or potential—just a sense of entitlement, good strategy, and a willingness to hold their own against the sacred mothering ideal. Such small determinants can make all the difference.

CHAPTER 1:

THE MILLENNIAL DILEMMA: OUR CHILDREN OR OUR LIVES?

1   **"We, along with other Western societies":** Margaret Mead, "Some Considerations on the Problem of Mother-Child Separation," *American Journal of Orthopsychiatry* 24, no. 3: 471–73.

2   **"she was having a hard time":** Gina Kolata, "Parents Take Charge, Putting the Gene Hunt onto Fast Track," *New York Times*, July 16, 1996, C7.

3   **The evidence shows that depression:** Faye Crosby, *Juggling: The Unexpected Advantages of Balancing Career and Home for Women and Their Families* (New York: Free Press, 1991), 65.

    A recent British report comparing 100,000 children: Cited in Anne C. Weisberg and Carol A. Buckler, *Everything a Working Mother Needs to Know* (New York: Doubleday, 1995), 85.

    A fourteen-university American study: "Child Development Enhanced by Good Day Care, Study Finds," *New York Times*, April 4, 1997, A24.

    Alison Clarke-Stewart's work on day care: Alison Clarke-Stewart, *Day Care* (Cambridge, Mass.: Harvard University Press, 1982).

5   *Working Mother* **magazine:** *Working Mother* (October 1996): 88.

    "to read them is to be immersed": Susan Chira, "Still Guilty after All These Years: A Bouquet of Advice Books for the Working Mom," *New York Times Book Review*, May 8, 1994, 11.

6   **"unreal, even surreal":** Judith Schwartz, *The Mother Puzzle: A New Generation Reckons with Motherhood* (New York: Simon and Schuster, 1993), 230.

    For example, when Shirley M. Tilghman: Natalie Angier, "Fighting and Studying: Battle of the Sexes with Men and Mice," *New York Times*, June 11, 1996, C1. Also author's phone interview with Angier, July 12, 1996.

    "exhaustion, frustration, working-parent guilt": Joann S. Lubin, "Some Adult Daughters of 'Supermoms' Plan to Take Another Path," *Wall Street Journal*, December 28, 1995, A1.

7   **Among Hispanic high school girls:** Elizabeth Debold, Marie Wilson, and Idelisse Malave, *Mother-Daughter Revolution: From Good Girls to Great Women* (New York: Bantam Books, 1994), 8–9.

    Mexican-born women: Evelyn Nakano Glenn, Grace Chang, and Linda Rennie Forcey, eds., *Mothering: Ideology, Experience, and Agency* (New York: Routledge, 1994), 212.

    "women of color have performed motherwork": Patricia Hill Collins, "Shifting the Center: Race, Class, and Feminist Theorizing about Motherhood," in ibid., 47.

8   **"Hillary's Class":** produced by *Frontline*, WGBH Boston; aired November 15, 1994.

    They may not have read the latest studies: Cited in Pepper Schwartz, "Me Stressed? No, Blessed," *New York Times*, November 17, 1994, C1.

9   **"virtually all the traditional women":** Terri Apter, *Secret Paths: Women in the New Midlife* (New York: Norton, 1995), 83.

    "A mother who stifles her own longings": Jessica Benjamin, *The Bonds of Love: Psychoanalysis, Feminism, and the Problem of Domination* (New York: Pantheon, 1988), 24.

    "if a mother who wants to or needs to work": Linda Carter, phone interview, with the author, May 21, 1996.

CHAPTER 2:

THE DONNA REED MAKEOVER

13   **Never mind:** Betty Friedan, *The Feminist Mystique* (New York: Norton, 1963).

14   **"My folks were typical of their generation":** Nathan McCall, *Makes Me Wanna Holler: A Young Black Man in America* (New York: Random House, 1994), 36.

19   **"These parents read":** Carter phone interview.

20   **Married women do at least twice as much:** Beth Anne Shelto, *Women, Men and Time: Gender Differences in Paid Work, Housework, and Leisure* (New York: Greenwood, 1992).

    By one recent count: Steven A. Holmes, "Is This What Women Want?" *New York Times*, December 15, 1996, 5; Holmes cites a 1993 study by the New York City Family and Work Institute.

    Although 70 percent of American mothers: Bureau of Labor Statistics, March 1995. According to Howard Hayghe of the BLS, this percentage includes women who are receiving unemployment insurance.

21   **"said it was their responsibility":** quoted in Tamar Lewin, "Women Are Becoming Equal Providers: Half of Working Women Bring Home Half the Household Income," *New York Times*, May 11, 1995, A27.

    "for everyone's peace of mind": Weisberg and Buckler, *Everything a Working Mother Needs to Know*, 8.

    "To shake off my case of the blahs": Hal Lancaster, "Managing Your Career: How to Chase Away the Blahs You Get from Working So Hard," *Wall Street Journal*, August 20, 1996, B1.

22   **"ever-present, always-responsive":** Penelope Leach, *Your Baby and Child, From Birth to Age Five*, rev. ed. (New York: Alfred A. Knopf, 1989), 115.

    "makes it impossible for women": Penelope Leach, *Children First: What Our Society Must Do—And Is Not Doing—For Our Children Today* (New York: Alfred A. Knopf, 1994), 39, 41.

    "knowing perfectly well": Gwen Kinkead, "Spock, Brazelton, and Now . . . Penelope Leach," *New York Times Magazine*, April 10, 1994, 34.

23   **"she wanted to be the emotional nucleus":** Elsa Walsh, "The Hell of Having It All," *Vogue* (August 1995): 274.

24   **"Too many seemed overwhelmed":** Ibid., 217.

    "the ideal of the conventional family": Elsa Walsh, *Divided Lives: The Public and Private Struggles of Three Accomplished Women* (New York: Simon and Schuster, 1995), 23, 89.

25   **"The way we institutionalize motherhood":** Jessie Bernard, *The Future of Motherhood* (New York: Dial Press, 1974; New York: Penguin, 1985), 9.

33   **Long-term studies here and in China:** Toni Falbo, *The Single-Child Family* (New York: Guilford Press, 1984); Judith Blake, *Family Size and Achievement* (Berkeley: University of California Press, 1989).

    a single child: Diane Gottlieb, interview with the author, Burlington, Vermont, October 18–19, 1996.

    on average each additional child: Scott Coltrane, *Family Man: Fatherhood, Housework, and Gender Equity* (New York: Oxford University Press, 1996), 162.

CHAPTER 3:

SACRIFICIAL MOTHERHOOD: THE SACRED IDEAL

37   **"second shift":** A term coined by the sociologist Arlie Hochschild; see Arlie Hochschild with Anne Machung, *The Second Shift* (New York: Viking Books, 1989).

38   **Anthropologists point out:** see, for example, T. Weisner and R. Gallimore, "My Brother's Keeper: Child and Sibling Caretaking," *Current Anthropology* 18, (1977): 169–90. Their study concludes that mothers were the exclusive nurturers of children in only 5 out of 186 societies.

      "A young man had fallen in love": I have recently read that a version of this story was popular in Victorian England; see Sara Ruddick, *Maternal Thinking: Towards a Politics of Peace* (Boston: Beacon Press, 1989), 10.

39   **"left little room for a mother":** Shari L. Thurer, *The Myths of Motherhood: How Culture Reinvents the Good Mother* (New York: Penguin Books, 1994), x, 283.

      "If mothers never speak": Jane Smiley, "Can Mothers Think?" in Kurt Brown, ed., *The True Subject: Writers on Life and Craft* (St. Paul: Graywolf Press, 1993), 6.

      As one critic has pointed out: Susan Suleiman, "On Maternal Splitting," *Signs* 14, no. 1 (Autumn 1988): 39.

40   **homicidal baby-sitter:** Mary Gordon, *Men and Angels* (New York: Random House, 1985).

      Not long ago a Michigan judge: "Day Care Costs Mother Custody of Daughter, 3," *New York Times*, July 27, 1994, A2.

      In most cases, fathers win custody: Phyllis Chessler, *Mothers on Trial* (New York: Harcourt Brace Jovanovich, 1991), x.

41   **"we are going to have a nation":** Mary Kay Blakely, *American Mom: Motherhood, Politics, and Humble Pie* (Chapel Hill: Algonquin Books, 1994), 289.

42   **As the birth rate declined:** Nancy Chodorow, *The Reproduction of Mothering: Psychoanalysis and the Sociology of Gender* (Berkeley: University of California Press, 1978), 6.

      An extremely subjective test: Aspects of this critique of attachment theory are developed in Rosika Parker, *Mother Love/Mother Hate: The Power of Maternal Ambivalence* (New York: Basic Books, 1995), 134.

      Despite the fact that attachment theory: Susan Chira, "Study Says Babies in Child Care Keep Secure Bonds to Mother," *New York Times*, April 21, 1996, A1.

43   **"absolutely no research to prove":** Diane Eyer, *Motherguilt: How Our*

Culture Blames Mothers for What's Wrong with Society (New York: Times Books, 1996), x.

"at whatever age": Alison Clarke-Stewart, "The Effects of Infant Day Care Reconsidered," *Early Childhood Research Quarterly* 3, (1988): 293–318.

44   **The real threat:** Lester Thurow, "Why Their World Might Crumble," *New York Times Magazine*, November 19, 1995, 78.

"Rocking the cradle": Bernard, *The Future of Motherhood*, 350.

45   **Although the majority of women are not giving up:** The number of women in the labor force steadily increased from 1990 to 1995, according to Department of Labor statistics. In 1995 percentages rose significantly from 68.4 percent to 69.7 percent.

51   **"we all accept parts":** D. Gottlieb interview.

54   **"If you don't start at the beginning":** Scott Coltrane, *Family Man: Fatherhood, Housework, and Gender Equity* (New York: Oxford University Press, 1996), 60.

the major disagreements a couple will have: Ron Taffel, "Helping Parents and Children Connect," lecture at the 1995 Family Therapy Network Annual Symposium, "Families under Siege," produced by the Resource Link, Norcross, Georgia, 1995.

CHAPTER 4:

REAL MOTHERS ARE GOOD ENOUGH

55   **"the hectic round":** Parker, *Mother Love/Mother Hate*, 72.

"So when I do spend time with my daughter": Andrea Thompson, "The Secret Life of Mothers: Why a Loving Mom Dreads Playtime," *Redbook* (August 1995): 156.

56   **"working mothers and at-home mothers":** Faye J. Crosby, *Juggling: The Unexpected Advantages of Balancing Career and Home for Women and Their Families* (New York: The Free Press, 1991), 122–123.

57   **"Once she attains motherhood":** Thurer, *The Myths of Motherhood*, xvii.

"Your interests and [the baby's] are identical": Leach, *Your Baby and Child*, 8.

"to write about our own experience": Smiley, "Can Mothers Think?" 10.

58   **"the masks of motherhood":** Adrienne Rich, *Of Woman Born: Motherhood as Experience and Institution* (New York: Norton, 1976), 25.

"He falls asleep": Anne LaMott: *Operating Instructions: A Journal of My Son's First Year* (New York: Fawcett Columbine, 1993), 104.

"I just can't get over how much babies cry": Ibid., 114.

59   **One-third of all mothers today:** The sociologist Ann Oakley writes: "One out of five women go through a miserable period of reactive depression; one quarter are severely depressed"; cited in Sheila Kitzinger, *Ourselves as Mothers: The Universal Experience of Motherhood* (Reading, Mass.: Addison-Wesley, 1992), 14. Studies show that working mothers are less symptomatic than stay-at-home mothers; Sandra Scarr, *Mother Care/ Other Care* (New York: Basic Books, 1984), 134–135.

 In one large study: *The Commonwealth Fund Survey of Parents with Young Children,* designed and analyzed by Princeton Survey Research Associates (1996), C-6. More than 2,000 women were studied.

 therapists frequently discuss: D. Gottlieb interview.

60   **"motherhood is governed by frustration":** Parker, *Mother Love/Mother Hate,* 18, 29.

61   **"at-oneness":** Parker writes: "The culture's maternal ideal is the unity of mother and child while the moments that others themselves define as ideal are founded on mutuality"; ibid., 24.

62   **"good motherness":** Ibid., 124, 109.

 "It is in the very anguish": Ibid., 64.

 "allow her to distance": Parker, 64.

 "If we accept": D. Gottlieb interview.

70   **"Early-timed mothers":** Coltrane, *Family Man,* 131.

CHAPTER 5:

THE WORK-MOTHER NEXUS

72   **As documented in a study:** Deborah J. Swiss and Judith P. Walker, *Women and the Work/Family Dilemma: How Today's Professional Women Are Confronting the Maternal Wall* (New York: John Wiley and Sons, 1993).

73   **"blatantly hostile":** Ibid, 220.

 Much of a new mother's anxiety: D. Gottlieb interview.

74   **"virtually all the women":** Weisberg and Buckler, *Everything a Working Mother Needs to Know,* 3.

75   D. Gottlieb interview.

76   **"Like so many women":** Rich, *Of Woman Born,* 23.

77   **"Don't get so involved":** Marilyn Heins and Anne M. Seiden, *Child Care/ Parent Care* (New York: Doubleday, 1987), 23.

 "Far from depriving me of thought": Smiley, "Can Mothers Think?" 15.

78   **"I want to improve myself":** Peter T. Kilborn, "More Women Take Low-Wage Jobs So Their Families Can Get By," *New York Times,* March 3, 1994, A24.

78   **"I'm the one":** quoted in Judith Pierce Rosenberg, ed., *A Question of Balance: Artists and Writers on Motherhood* (Watsonville, Calif.: Papier-Mache Press, 1995), 93.

79   **"women *are* mothers":** Diane Ehrensaft, *Parenting Together: Men and Women Sharing the Care of Their Children* (New York: Free Press, 1978), 96.

80   **"because the child is both a reflection and extension of her":** Ibid., 67.
     "with a pulmonary tube": Blakely, *American Mom*, 141.

82   **mothers are obsessed:** Jessica Benjamin, interview with the author, New York City, June 10, 1996.

83   **"When a working mom gets home":** Robert Frank, "Interesting News on Nurturing," *Working Mother* (August 1996): 74.

CHAPTER 6:
THE CRITICAL MOTHER, THE ABSENT FATHER WITHIN

90   **"wish for a full-time emotional protector":** Colette Dowling, *The Cinderella Complex: Women's Hidden Fear of Independence* (New York: Summit Books, 1981), 5.

91   **This disconnection:** Charles Gottlieb, interview with the author, Burlington, Vermont, October 18–19, 1996.
     "thought her mother had been too available": Walsh, *Divided Lives*, 104.

92   **"Long-buried fears, desire":** Parker, *Mother Love/Mother Hate*, 75.
     since having a baby: Pamela Sicher, interview with the author, Washington Depot, Connecticut, August 30, 1996.

95   **"Men are used to loving":** Samuel Osherson, *Wrestling with Love: How Men Struggle with Intimacy with Women, Children, Parents, and Each Other* (New York: Fawcett Columbine, 1992), 144, 206.
     a man may wish for a stay-at-home wife: Jessica Benjamin interview.

96   **its ironic counterproductivity:** C. Gottlieb interview.

105   **"She lets me have my time with just me and him":** *Commonwealth Fund Survey of Parents with Young Children*, A-3.

106   **"She has no dimmer switch":** Walsh, *Divided Lives*, 112.
     most women still have "pink-collar jobs": Sam Roberts, "Women's Work: What's New, What Isn't," *New York Times*, April 27, 1995, B4.
     One out of ten are victims of domestic violence: Figures from the U.S. Department of Justice, October, 1996.
     because most women see their daughters: Chodorow, *The Reproduction of Mothering*, 109.

107   **"the child can move on":** Jean Baker Miller, "The Development of

Women's Sense of Self," in Judith V. Jordan, Alexandra G. Kaplan, Jean Baker Miller, Irene P. Stiver, and Janet L. Surrey, eds., *Women's Growth in Connection* (New York: Guilford Press, 1991), 17.

"In clinical practice": Janet L. Surrey, "The Relational Self in Women: Clinical Implications," in Janet L. Surrey et al., eds., *Women's Growth in Connection*, 39.

"are liable to overinvest": Chodorow, *The Reproduction of Mothering*, 203.

Again and again in therapy: D. Gottlieb interview.

108   **even if they are spunky kids:** Carol Gilligan, *Making Connections: The Relational Worlds of Adolescent Girls at Emma Willard School* (Cambridge, Mass.: Harvard University Press, 1990).

109   **whenever a baby reached three months:** D. Gottlieb interview.

"there is nothing wrong with leaving an infant": Heins and Seiden, *Child Care/Parent Care*, 104.

couples who find it hard: D. Gottlieb interview.

110   **If they frame a child's night:** Arietta Slade contributed this idea in discussions for Joan K. Peters, "The Mother Triangle," *Family Life* (March–April 1994): 55.

CHAPTER 7:

THE FATHER PROBLEM

112   **"Well, gentlemen":** Kyle Pruett, *The Nurturing Father: Journey Toward the Complete Man* (New York: Warner Books, 1987), 246, 74.

they had higher test scores: Ibid., 76, 210.

113   **In one study of couples videotaped:** Ross D. Parke, *Fathers* (Cambridge, Mass.: Harvard University Press, 1981), 35.

Other observers have noted: R. D. Parke, S. Hymel, T. G. Power, and Br. R. Tinsley, "The Father's Role in the Family System," *Seminars Perinatology* 3 (1979): 25–34.

infants do respond to their father's voice pattern: Observations by the infant psychiatrist Daniel Stern cited in Marshall H. Klaus, John H. Kennel, and Phyllis H. Klaus, *Bonding: Building the Foundations of Secure Attachment and Independence* (Reading, Mass.: Addison-Wesley, 1995), 76.

their fundamental response to infants is the same as women's: Parke, *Fathers*, 48.

For if infants are given the opportunity: T. Berry Brazelton and Michael Yogman's observations of infants are discussed in John Munder

Ross, *What Men Want: Mothers, Fathers, and Manhood* (Cambridge, Mass.: Harvard University Press, 1994), 77.

"play interaction": Benjamin, *The Bonds of Love,* 27.

Never having experienced the discomforts: Pruett, *The Nurturing Father,* 204.

114   **they instill it in daughters:** Ibid., 37.

Even when fathers are initially more awkward: Ibid., 3.

"a strange, foreign, or inanimate body": Ross, *What Men Want,* 51.

in Berry Brazelton's hospital nursery: T. Berry Brazelton, *Working and Caring,* rev. ed. (Reading, Mass.: Addison-Wesley, 1992), 195. Brazelton reports that while working at the Brazelton Neonatal Behavioral Assessment Test laboratory, the nurse Judy Beal showed how fathers become significantly more sensitive to their baby's cries if a professional points out a new baby's behavior to them on the second day of life.

"If you don't start at the beginning": quoted in Coltrane, *Family Man,* 191.

men need the early bonding: C. Gottlieb interview.

115   **"hormone-driven vigilance":** Leach, *Children First,* 43–44.

"intimate and egalitarian pattern": Coltrane, for his discussion of and conclusions about anthropological research, see *Family Man,* 177–198.

116   **"When they are not talking to pollsters":** Nancy R. Gibbs, "Bringing up Father," *Time,* June 28, 1993, 56.

"strangle their nurturing qualities": Kyle Pruett, phone interview with the author, September 25, 1996.

117   **Charles Gottlieb adds that men dichotomize:** C. Gottlieb interview.

Because children blur the boundaries of self: Osherson, *Wrestling with Love,* 213, 12.

"to be charmed by children": Ross, *What Men Want,* 13, 43–44, 4.

"do what [women] do": Ibid., 13, 54.

many of his patients: C. Gottlieb interview.

118   **"they do not have a language for father love":** Osherson, *Wrestling with Love,* 206.

"ultimately, men do have": Benjamin interview.

119   **"fatherhood is the single most creative":** Pruett, *The Nurturing Father,* 281.

122   **"work is easier than relationships":** Osherson, *Wrestling with Love,* 326.

"by fostering, securing, protecting": Pruett, *The Nurturing Father,* 18, 130.

124   **"as productive and content":** Sue Shellenburger, "High Powered Fathers Savor Their Decisions to Scale Back Careers," *Wall Street Journal,* June 12, 1996, B1.

129   **"I found that I always depended on my wife":** Brazelton, *Working and Caring*, 72.

    "All I didn't do was breast-feed": Coltrane, *Family Man*, 61.

130   **the father who has never taken care:** Taffel, "Helping Parents and Children Connect."

    "It is simply patronizing": Ibid.

CHAPTER 8:

FREER MOTHERS, STRONGER MARRIAGES, HAPPIER CHILDREN

131   **I've recently coauthored a book on marriage:** Betty Carter and Joan Peters, *Love, Honor, and Negotiate: Making Your Marriage Work* (New York: Pocket Books, 1995).

133   **"When I call him and say":** "Christina Garcia," in Judith Pierce Rosenberg, ed. *A Question of Balance: Artists and Writers on Motherhood* (Watsonville, California: Papier-Mache Press, 1995), 45.

134   **"These research teams found":** Bernard, *The Future of Motherhood*, 9.

137   **"our lives require that we redefine parental privilege":** Quoted in Peters, "The Mother Triangle," 54.

    "grandmothers, sisters, aunts, or cousins": Patricia Bell-Scott, Beverly Guy-Sheftall, Jacqueline Jones Royster, Janet Sims-Wood, Miriam DeCosta-Willis, and Lucille P. Fultz, *Double Stitch: Black Women Write about Mothers and Daughters* (New York: HarperCollins, 1991), 47.

    "helps to diffuse the emotional intensity": Ibid., 56.

138   **famous report on the problems in the black community:** Daniel Patrick Moynihan, "The Case for National Action: The Negro Family," Office of Policy Planning and Research, Department of Labor, March, 1965.

    "for informal adoptions": Quoted in Pepper Schwartz, "New Bonds: Para-Dads, Para-Moms," *New York Times*, November 9, 1995, C1.

    "para-parenting": Quoted in: ibid.

139   **"in fact, it is probably better for them":** Sandra Scarr, *Mother Care, Other Care*, (New York City: Basic Books, 1984), 4.

    "Do children really need a mother at their disposal?": Kathy Weingarten, *The Mother's Voice: Strengthening Intimacy in Families* (New York: Harcourt Brace, 1994), 100.

140   **"Mutual recognition":** Benjamin, *The Bonds of Love*, 24.

    "one of the things that I came to realize": Quoted in Garcia, *A Question of Balance*, 141.

141   **Nearly half of the grade-schoolers:** Survey of 1,000 grade-schoolers conducted by Ashton Trice, assistant professor of psychology at Mary

Baldwin College, cited in Diane Hales, "I Want to Be Just Like Mom," *Working Mother* (October 1996): 88.

    "I'm sorry": D. Gottlieb interview.

141   **"But Mommy, I want to see what you're doing":** Quoted in Garcia, *A Question of Balance*, 207.

142   **"children are very vulnerable":** Heins and Seiden, *Child Care/Parent Care*, xiv, 188.

148   **"When I dropped my son off":** Benjamin, interview.

149   **We should simply tell her:** Pamela Sicher, interview with the author, New Milford, Connecticut, August 30, 1996.

CHAPTER 9:

EXTENDING FAMILY

150   **Currently grandparents are raising:** Jack Rosenthal, "The Age Boom," *New York Times Magazine*, March 9, 1997, 42.

151   **grandparents can be problematic:** D. Gottlieb interview.

153   **With so many people:** Schwartz, "New Bonds: Para-Dads, Para-Moms," *New York Times*, C1.

154   **Only 3 percent report using baby-sitters:** Jennifer Senior, "In Washington, Au Pairs Are Bipartisan Choice for Childcare," *New York Times*, April 21, 1994, C9.

155   **many parents are willing to pay:** Marilyn Glen, Brookfield, Connecticut, August 12, 1996.

    the woefully inadequate day care: Barbara Hamlin, phone interview, September 9, 1996.

    "if you are going to take a job": Leach, *Your Baby and Child from Birth to Age Five*, 274.

156   **"consistency has been much overrated":** Heins and Seiden, *Parent Care/ Child Care*, 188.

157   **choose a center or a home:** Mary Burnham, interview with author, New Milford, Connecticut, August 16, 1996.

    be wary when a place: Megan Yenter, interview with author, New Milford, Connecticut, August 19, 1996.

158   **live-in baby-sitters:** Ibid., 189.

    "part of the family": Julia Wrigley, *Other People's Children: An Intimate Account of the Dilemma Facing Middle-Class Parents and the Women They Hire to Raise Their Children* (New York: Basic Books, 1995).

161   **"mothers' jealousy":** Quoted in Peters, "The Mother Triangle," 53.

162   **"The right caregiver":** Ibid., 54.

      To help them accept their child's attachment: D. Gottlieb interview.
      "The more love there is": Peters, "The Mother Triangle," 53.

163   **"even when children say 'I don't care' ":** Quoted in Joan K. Peters, "When the Babysitter Leaves," *Family Life* (March–April 1996): 82.

164   **"no matter how operatic a child's grief":** Ibid., 80.

      "as ineffectual as parents might feel": Ibid.

      Parents who did not have enough nurturing themselves: Ibid., 81.

CHAPTER 10:

WHEN THERE IS ONLY ONE: THE SINGLE MOTHER

167   **at one time or another 58 percent of American children:** U.S. Bureau of the Census, Department of Household and Housing Economics Statistics, *1995 Current Population Survey.*

      More than one-quarter of American children: Susan Chira, "Study Confirms Worst Fears on U.S. Children," *New York Times*, April 12, 1994, A1.

      The facts are harsh and startling: U.S. Bureau of the Census, Department of Household and Housing Economics Statistics, *1995 Current Population Survey.*

      less than many men pay: Robert L. Griswold, *Fatherhood in America: A History* (New York: Basic Books, 1993), 232.

      poorer mothers often work: Hillary Rodham Clinton, *It Takes a Village: And Other Lessons Children Teach Us* (New York: Simon and Schuster, 1996), 225.

168   **"Her singleness indicates":** Maya Angelou, *The Heart of a Woman* (New York: Random House, 1981), 37.

173   **"You put the baby to bed":** Quoted in Joan K. Peters, "The Single-Mommy Track," *Cosmopolitan* (October 1994): 128.

174   **"your greatest challenge":** Ibid., 129.

      "abandonment-proof": Ibid., 130.

      "the mother who feels guilty": Ibid., 130.

175   **"story shows how successful":** Sue Shellenbarger, "Single Parent Woes Times Four Didn't Dent Her Career or Family," *Wall Street Journal*, Sept. 18, 1996, B1.

      "The mother who thinks": Quoted in Peters, "The Single-Mommy Track," 130.

176   **"Single mothers don't have to come up with perfect solutions":** Ibid.

      "Know your strengths": Ibid.

CHAPTER 11:

SOLVING THE MOTHER PUZZLE

184   **In August another headline:** Keith Bradsher, *New York Times*, August 14, 1995, A9.

185   **It cuts future budgets:** Peter Passell, "Economic Scene," *New York Times*, August 8, 1996, D2.

   Nor has it allotted the $200 billion: "Children in America's Schools, With Bill Moyers," PBS, aired September 13, 1996.

186   **In a major federal survey:** *Women: The New Providers*, Families and Work Institute (New York: Families and Work Institute and the Whirlpool Foundation, 1995), 11.

187   **Fewer than 5 percent of senior executives:** Hal Lancaster, "Women at Kraft Tell How to Be a Big Cheese While Handling Family," *Wall Street Journal*, April 23, 1996, B1.

   "You did it back then": Natalie Angier (who reported the story for the *New York Times*), phone interview with the author, July 12, 1996.

   Another recent study by the Public Policy Institute: Cited in Jill Smolowe, "The Stalled Revolution," *Time*, May 6, 1996, 63.

   Americans could choose to work: Juliet Schor, *The Overworked American: The Unexpected Decline of Leisure* (New York: Basic Books, 1991), 2.

188   **parents who control how, where, and when:** Sue Shellenbarger, "It's the Type of Job You Have That Affects the Kids, Studies Say," July 31, 1996, B1.

189   **employers lose $2–12 billion:** *Business Week*, September 16, 1996, 74.

   When First Tennessee National Corporation: "Balancing Work and Family: Big Returns for Companies Willing to Give Family Strategies a Chance," *Business Week*, September 16, 1996, 74, 78.

   Among the most effective innovations: Ibid., 76–77.

   When Lotus Development Corporation: Clinton, *It Takes a Village*, 16.

190   **"giving their workers more ease and freedom":** Kerry A. Dolan, "When Money Isn't Enough," *Forbes*, November 11, 1996, 166.

   many of the best and the brightest: Sue Shellenbarger, "New Job Hunters Ask Recruiters, 'Is There a Life after Work?' " *Wall Street Journal*, January 29, 1997, B1.

192   **The four-state study:** Susan Chira, "Care at Child Day Centers Is Rated as Poor," *New York Times*, February 7, 1995, A1.

   Day-care workers are paid: Eyer, *MotherGuilt*, 177.

   "By delegating child care": Wrigley, *Other People's Children*, 133.

195 **Recently President Bill Clinton argued:** Steven A. Holmes, "Public Cost of Teen-Age Pregnancy Is Put at $7 Billion This Year," *New York Times,* June 13, 1996, A1.

197 **"Women can't win":** Benjamin interview.

198 **an article about a Wharton School of Business:** Barbara Presley Noble, "Coming Soon: Get a Life 101?" *New York Times,* February 27, 1994, 41.

200 **One such group, the National Parenting Association:** reported in *Working Mother* (February 1997): 12.

203 **"I have the best job I've ever had":** Robert B. Reich, "My Family Leave Act," *New York Times,* November 8, 1996, A33.

CHAPTER 12:

MOTHERING, GROWTH OF SELF AND SOUL: A PHILOSOPHICAL CONCLUSION

210 **"the honesty and freshness of children":** Mary-Joan Gerson, interview with the author, New York, N.Y., April 9, 1996. The study referred to is "Feminism and the Wish for a Child," *Sex Roles* 11, nos. 5/6 (1984): 389–99.

211 **"If there were no other help":** Sicher interview.

   "The kids motivated me": Quoted in Peters, "The Single-Mommy Track," 130.

216 **"She's not like me":** Quoted in Garcia, *A Question of Balance,* 117.

   "that there are times": Ibid., 120.

217 **"a better life now":** Weingarten, *The Mother's Voice,* 11.

   an incident at the beach: Mary Gordon, "Immaculate Man," *The Rest of Life: Three Novellas* (New York: Contemporary American Fiction Series, 1994).

218 **"Equality of opportunity":** discussed in Peter Passell, "Economic Scene: Hurdles Are Still High for Women Who Want a Career and Family," *New York Times,* September 7, 1995, D2.

219 **"preferable that children feel":** Mary Catherine Bateson, *With a Daughter's Eye: A Memoir of Margaret Mead and Gregory Bateson* (New York: William Morrow, 1984), 38.

   "deep pleasure in mothering": Ibid., 36.

   "That I not be a restless ghost": excerpted in Tillie Olsen, ed., *Mother to Daughter, Daughter to Mother* (Old Westbury, N.Y.: Feminist Press, 1984), 13.